TREE WISDOM

TREE WISDOM

Conceived, written and illustrated by

Jacqueline Memory Paterson

Thorsons
An Imprint of HarperCollins*Publishers*

Thorsons
An Imprint of HarperCollins*Publishers*
77–85 Fulham Palace Road
Hammersmith, London W6 8JB
1160 Battery Street
San Francisco, California 94111–1213

Published by Thorsons 1996

A catalogue record for this book
is available from the British Library

ISBN 978-0-7225-3408-3

For Becky and Jody
and all the children of the world

With thanks to the many friends
who helped make this book possible

LIST OF CONTENTS

Introduction   1

Our Contact with the Trees   7

Introduction to the Trees   13
    Yew   17
    Holly   32
    Pine   47
    Hazel   63
    Blackthorn   78
    Silver Birch   91
    Apple   106
    Hawthorn   123
    Ash   142
    Oak   172
    Elm   198
    Beech   212
    Rowan   225
    Alder   243
    Willow   257
    Elder   276
    Poplars   295
Conclusion   308

Appendices
  I: Arboreal   313
  II: The Effect of Human Activity upon Woodland   325

III: Divination   331
IV: The Ogham Alphabet   335
V: Glossary of Healing Terms   343

Recommended Reading   345

Index   349

INTRODUCTION

That which derives from our native folk tradition springs up like water from the soil, made alive by the good brown earth and fresh with the breath of herb and tree; it springs, it sparkles. It vitalises a man's nature because it puts him in touch with the sun-warmed rain-wet earth – his native earth, that his bare feet trod as a child when his soul was open and he could still feel the unseen.

It blows through his soul like the wind in high places; it drives over him like the waves of the open sea; and his heart leaps to it like the springing leaping flames of the living fire; for by the dust of his fathers he is kin to the elements in his native land, and by the road of his childhood dreams he approaches the Celtic contact.

DION FORTUNE, *ESOTERIC ORDERS AND THEIR WORK*

Many years ago I lived deep in the rich green countryside of north Devon. One hot summer's afternoon friends came to visit, bringing with them news that a local farmer had just cut down six large oak trees, all of which were well over 200 years old. His reasons for the act were poor and my normal reactions to such things suddenly became larger and larger, for while my heart and head knew the wrongness of what had been done, this time my soul reacted, gripping me through an intense physical pain in my gut. It was as though I had connected to the inner spirits of those oaks, feeling their pain and hearing their screams, screams produced from shock and distress as their flesh was ripped apart. I was somehow experiencing their agony! Every day I had strolled beneath those trees and had come to regard them as friends. Now they lay in shock where they had fallen. And yet even after being felled their

1

spirit still lived, for each time I passed their remains there grew a greater conviction within me that I was being empowered to elaborate their story and thereby lessen the distress of others of their kind.

This is how this book came to be born – with my experience of the life of trees as sentient beings. In a flash I had realized a common bond with the things of Nature.

Most people are familiar at times with the bond we share with various animals and many books have been written on the subject. But for all today's fashionable concern with green issues and ecology, very few it seemed had paid any regard to the inner life of trees. Nor had anyone shown just how reliant humanity is upon trees or how the survival of one species of life depends so much upon the survival of others. Great pressure from Nature is now placed upon us, for it needs to be recognized in order that we survive. It pushes us forward to a better awareness in the hopes we may set mistakes right. However, in achieving this, we touch a living energy which is boundless and there begins a fantastic voyage of discovery, as endless in its permutations as Nature itself.

It is impossible to enter the world of trees without entering the world of Nature's magic. When you start to communicate with trees (as I learnt how to do more and more after that first dramatic experience with the oaks) life itself becomes magic, for their spirits echo ages past and tell of life's never-ending mysteries. This process of attunement with Nature I found to be very revealing, for often the trees would seem to know me better than I knew myself!

Being admitted into such a world via the spirits of fallen oaks inevitably led me back into memories, events and emotions of the past. They showed me realms of tree worship and legends of gods and goddesses which escape the limitations of time. Upon this journey (which is both an outer journey into the world and an inner journey through inherited race memory), I began to realize that the energies of trees provided doorways that I could enter mentally and spiritually, doorways of imagination that connected me with the ancient Dreamworld. This world was as real to our Celtic ancestors as it still is today amongst aboriginal people the world over, people to whom ecology is a way of life rather than a neat idea. Within this Dreamworld with its tree guardians I encountered the elemental worlds of faerie, of which so much legend speaks, where gnomes and dragons appear, and many other curious folk normally invisible to the naked eye.

The natural beauty and timelessness of the spirits of trees are illustrated by impressions gathered from tales and legends. Through mysteries found whispered round fires in the still of the night and stories of the travelling peoples, and from words uttered by bards which tell of the heartbeat of the earth and the harmony of the spheres, I began my communication. Like anyone else, I can only tell of what I've felt or seen, accepting that this is my personal view of the archetypal world of trees, and may mean nothing to the man or woman next door. But I hope for the sake of the trees that the words and pictures within this book in some way reflect the Universal, that something in them may catch the eye and jolt the imagination into perceiving the underlying reality. For the more awareness we have of the individual life of trees, the wiser we will be in understanding ourselves and Nature.

If we open ourselves up to Nature, we will receive many teachings, and these are often linked to myth and country lore. As a child I lived for many years within a small bluebell wood teeming with flora and fauna, and when compiling this book I have found myself endeavouring to remember and move back to the innocence of spirit I then possessed, in order to see things clearly. Maybe I have seen again through the eyes of a child, maybe through the eyes of faerie, or maybe merely through the eyes of a woman growing wise. Whatever, I know I've seen a land given grace by the Spirit, where all flows in harmony, pollution is not yet invented, money is of no value and contentment reigns on earth – a state of being we sorely need to recapture. And yet this 'land' is all around us now, barely seen as we toil to create our version of the world, intent on changing Nature's perfection into something less. In our striving, we have forgotten our links with the earth and our conception of the Spirit has likewise become poor.

In this modern world I aim to keep contact and work with the old ways of the land, not because I want to live in the past, but rather because I feel the past can be applied to the present and lessons can be learnt for the future. Looking at the world of today I shudder at the forceful way Nature is treated, for I see living Spirit in all its forms. In ancient world-views which we will discuss shortly, we will find respect accorded for the natural world through concepts which allow humanity to perceive divinity in Nature. In our present ecological state we would do well to regard this, for nothing less will keep us from destroying the very life-forms upon which we depend. The earth is solid beneath us, air and water are around us and within, and fire is the 'spark' of life. We *are* Nature. If we can perceive this through our ancestral world-view and link with our treasurable race memories, then life becomes boundless in its possibilities, for there are no limits in the worlds of memory.

And yet we consistently enclose ourselves in man-made inventions, forsaking the gifts of the natural world, our very lack of acknowledgement risking all, for without trees to process the carbon dioxide of our atmosphere into oxygen we could not breathe upon earth. Nor would we have sufficient rainfall (generated by rain-forests) to drink. And without the produce of the plant world (also given life by such rainfall) we could not eat, for even the animals we feed upon have grown from the eating of vegetable matter. Without trees man could never have kept himself warm by his discovery of fire. In short, without trees, man could not live!

Thus the world of trees has always been an integral and essential part of the world of humans. Since before time was quantified, trees have given us the companionable presence of individual species, copses, forests, woods or groves, from which we have obtained timber, fuel, shelter, protection, food, medicine, magic, mystery, beauty, colour, legends and music. All these have made our lives easier and less barren.

Whilst providing for us and balancing our weather, trees also host an abundance of wildlife which enriches the wonder and usefulness of our natural world. They supply an incredible eco-system upon which we are as dependent as the smallest insect. In return we seem to give trees very little, barely noticing their existence, save perhaps when buds appear on winter twigs, and leaves and fruit fall in the autumn.

How then may we come to know the world of trees? How can we open our conscious minds to their presence to find out why we are here with them on this planet? Many legends and songs tell of the affinity possible between trees and people, and of how we are closely akin to them, following the same cycles throughout our lives' span. For they, like us, stand upright, their 'feet' in (or on) the earth and their 'bodies' and 'heads' in the air. The ancients felt this link intensely, with the added distinction that as trees grew taller and lived to far greater ages than man, they were able to reach that much closer to the abode of the 'Mighty Ones', the realm eventually called 'Heaven'.

I have found from my own early experiences (later confirmed by the classical writers quoted throughout this book) that the spiritual side of trees is very strong, and that they have the ability to blend and work with human spirit. A tree is a memory bank, just like humans and the earth itself. All store by various means data from life as it is lived around them. By working with trees, their memories emerge, in a process somewhat akin to telepathy. These memories tell us of the ways in which Nature and humanity have developed, and of how by understanding both it is possible for us to form our lives to suit the ecology of the earth. They tell us of the ancient Spirit of the land, its times of richness and strength and its times of weakness. They tell us of the old ways of reverence and the meaning of life for our ancestors, their wisdoms and their mistakes. They tell us mostly of ourselves, for they have watched us grow from our infancy; and because we have almost wrecked our mutual home planet, they are now urgent in their telling.

Deep within our inherited collective unconscious mind, way beneath our layers of conditioning, we hold memories of the closeness that once existed between humans and the natural world. The most familiar Western good luck charm is to touch wood, and this is a direct continuation of the actions of our Celtic ancestors, who at times of need went to certain trees and touched and communed with them. These trees were thought to contain or house specific spirits, such as those associated with the elements and gods or goddesses, or the tribe or nation. In order to facilitate the latter, trees were planted upon burial mounds of the dead so the spirit and strength of the deceased could live on within their forms. Through meditation with such trees we are told the special qualities of a tribe could be easily summoned, and by communicating with the spirits of the past through trees, the tribe's collective strength and wisdom were felt to be continuous and united, giving a valuable sense of being part of the Whole.

By communicating with trees as sentient beings our ancestors gained other advantages, for the trees could show an objective viewpoint, allowing people to look, as it were, through another's eyes. Then subjective thoughts and feelings do not colour emotions and wise decisions can be made. Communicating in such ways with the life-forms of the natural world also puts people in touch with their spiritual natures, or 'higher selves'. Thus to ancient peoples, who saw spirit so strongly within trees that certain trees were thought to be an embodiment of a deity or a deceased loved one, touching a tree was perhaps the most fortuitous thing they could do, and in general terms any tree gave spiritual strength and good luck.

Early man was of necessity very much a tribal wanderer, following a seasonal circuit during which he was entirely dependent for survival upon his intimate knowledge of Nature. He knew by experience, or knowledge handed down from his elders, the routes of herding animals and the locations and harvesting times of certain species of plant life. He must also have been aware of (if he did not actually contemplate) the supernatural realms felt to be connected to the natural world. It is difficult for us to realize the extent of the relationship ancient people had with trees or their life-enriching rapport as told in myth and legend. Nevertheless it would ease the strain of modern living if we did. So let us move closer to the trees themselves in order to begin.

OUR CONTACT WITH THE TREES

When you are near trees you are touched by their atmospheres, their emanations, often called 'force fields' or 'auras'. And when you link yourself to a particular tree, you link with all trees of that species and the particular strengths, qualities and ancient knowledge they contain. Thus if you have befriended an oak tree or have spent time regularly near one, you will find any other oak tree approachable. This may sound laughable to those who believe trees are inanimate and insentient things, but I would ask such people to remember their childhood days, for boys and girls commonly have favourite trees. It is a fact that trees breathe, move, feel and reproduce, and that they have, like all other living things, characteristics which can be very individual. These qualities are often visible, being seen firstly through the tree's shape and form and secondly through its guardian entity or spirit, called its 'dryad' or 'wood-nymph'.

Dryads are often seen upon the surface of trees like faces or figures from a fairy tale, and they communicate with humans by imparting sensations or subtle feelings to them. If you are within the aura of a tree (that is, beneath its branches or beside its trunk) and if you still your mind and body so your being becomes receptive, you may feel this communication. But before we discuss this, let us look more closely at the dryads.

In a wood or forest there will be a head dryad, usually found in a large tree near the centre. When there is a large gathering of one species of tree (as for example in a beech wood) the dryad may be in part in all the trees. Specific guardian dryads protect the edges of

7

woods, where they are capable of altering the atmospheres felt by humans. At times, for their own protection, they cause feelings of unease in people, and for good reason, for if a dryad's tree dies naturally it can move easily into a younger tree and continue protecting its domain, but if its tree is unexpectedly harmed or felled by humans, the subsequent realignment of the dryad's protective qualities for the entire wood is difficult and may take a long time to achieve. As this puts all other trees at risk, the guardian dryads have an important role in the preservation of the species.

The shape and character of a dryad is reflected in its chosen species of tree, its texture and form and the feeling it exudes. Dryads also reflect the elemental qualities of earth, air, fire and water. Thus a dryad of an oak tree is wizened and earthy, and yet has such an effect upon the senses that our minds are freed of earthly restraints and we feel elevated, a quality noted by the ancients, who recognized the sky-god energy within the tree.

The atmospheres trees create have great relevance when you approach them for healing and are also relevant to their situation in the environment. Trees growing by running water contain its feeling or movement within them, and those growing in meadows, fields or quiet woodland will reflect the peaceful energies of those places.

On an emotional healing level, trees are excellent counsellors and can be approached easily. Their role of aiding humans is as old as humanity itself and their understanding covers all our conditions. For example, 'underwater' lunar visions which allow you to see the depths of feelings flow via the willow, and many a tearful cry for help has been stilled by the ash, almost as if it understood heartache. The oak gives you strength of vision and 'backbone' for overpowering situations, producing great clarity for judging future events. Hawthorn allows the Spirit to rise, its spines bursting through the dam of built-up emotions and stresses that modern-day living lays upon us. Silver birch replaces lost innocence to the wearied eye, clearing the vision from over-stimulation and the visual bombardment of life, i.e., television and computer screens. It also gives the gift of graceful movement and pliability, showing how the greatest storm or coldest temperatures have least effect. Elder gives us strength of being, a rich comfort and durability. Like lenses in an eye-piece or facets of a jewel, all trees lend their particular 'power' to all aspects of life, and for the caring observer and those who would wish to learn, they can become close companions.

Let us move closer. When you approach a tree and enter its aura, quiet your mind and allow that everyday part of you which takes care of the mundane world to drop from your shoulders like a discarded mantle. You are entering Nature's sacred space, a place where you are refreshed by cleansing energy and surrounded by an atmosphere which opens the doors to the soul. C. E. Smith describes it thus in his book *Trees*:

> And do you remember what secrets the trees told us as we lay under their shady branches on the hot midsummer days, while the leaves danced and flickered against the blue, blue sky? Can you tell what was the charm that held us like a dream in the falling dusk, as we watched their heavy masses grow dark against the silvery twilight sky?

Such feelings or questions receive answers from the trees, which, because they are 'felt', come to you through various degrees of sensation, ranging from the softest feather touch felt upon the surface of your skin to the deepest reverberations within your body. These 'answers' open up to an intense awareness of the miracle that is life, and they allow words, thoughts, pictures, sounds and feelings to arise while you are in a protected place where healing is received. When you become aware of something in such an atmosphere, do not question its validity, and resist the temptation to apply logic, for that conscious ability cancels out the intuitive processes through which our own being guides us from within. It also blocks the senses through which we commune with the natural world.

Rather, watch and listen and *remember*, for while your experience may not seem much to you at the time, sooner or later it *will* have relevance. You will remember and see the experience like a piece of jigsaw puzzle waiting for events to happen to complete a picture or give recognition to an event. Rather like seeing a still-shot from a film, it isn't until you see it within the complete film that you recognize fully what is being portrayed. Sometimes impressions from trees may come as an answer to a question, often one not yet realized, until that certain time when you recognize the question that the answer is for.

If necessary, whilst in communication with the tree, specific areas of healing can be brought to its attention by focusing your mind upon the problem. State your desires mentally, think them or even say them aloud, and remain in a calm state until you feel you have received an answer, or you feel healed or refreshed. If you have any negative states or emotions to clear, allow them to move from you, discard them and the tree will absorb them and transform them back into clear energy. This does not harm the tree in any way.

Then, when your healing or communication is done, with all your being express your thanks to the tree, just as if it were your best friend who had done you the biggest favour. Leave it a gift, a small stone or feather, or tie a bright ribbon in its boughs, and smile, for you have entered the world of the trees which is ever-waiting to show and share the Spirit of Life with you. In these days of ecological concern such sharing is vital, for as we become aware of the world of trees, the trees grow in strength and are better able to aid us in our world, reciprocating in ways of which we are (as yet) only dimly aware.

In this quote from 'Kasyan from the Beautiful Lands' in *Sketches from a Hunter's Album*, Ivan Turgenev describes the delight of communing with Nature whilst under the trees:

> ...I lay down on my back and began admiringly to watch the peaceful play of the entwined leaves against the high, clear sky. It is a remarkably pleasant occupation, to lie on one's back in a forest and look upwards! It seems that you are looking into a bottomless sea, that is stretching out far and wide *below* you, that the trees are not rising from the earth but, as if they were the roots of enormous plants, are descending or falling steeply into those lucid, grassy waves, while the leaves on the trees glimmer like emeralds, or thicken into a gold-tinted, almost jet-black greenery. Somewhere high, high up, at the very end of a delicate branch, a single leaf

stands out motionless against a blue patch of translucent sky, and, beside it, another sways, resembling in its movements the ripplings upon the surface of a fishing reach, as if the movement were of its own making and not caused by the wind. Like magical underwater islands, round white clouds gently float into view and pass by, and then suddenly the whole of this sea, this radiant air, these branches and leaves suffused with sunlight, all of it suddenly begins to stream in the wind, shimmers with fugitive brilliance, and a fresh, tremulous murmuration arises which is like the endless shallow splashing of oncoming ripples. You lie still and go on watching: words cannot express the delight and quiet, and how sweet is the feeling that creeps over your heart. You go on watching, and that deep, clear azure brings a smile to your lips as innocent as the azure itself, as innocent as the clouds passing across it, and as if in company with them there passes through your mind a slow caval-cade of happy recollections, and it seems to you that all the while your gaze is travelling farther and farther away and drawing all of you with it into that calm, shining infinity, making it impossible for you to tear yourself away from those distant heights, from those distant depths...

If we cannot visit trees often we may carry their spirit home with us, for it is possible and permissible to cut small wands from their branches with which to continue meditations and healings. If we do, we should bear in mind the gift being given us and thank the tree, for such a wand will contain the essence of the species, the spirit of its dryad and its specific wisdoms.

Wands are traditionally cut from living trees and are highly prized as healing tools, guardians and friends. Before cutting a wand it is best to visit the tree and its dryad to get to know them, making sure that their energy is conducive to the type of work to be done. Dryads, once they accept you, give freely. They have excellent memories and can show you many things willingly. Out of respect we should ask for our wand, explaining the work to be done by it.

The species of tree from which you cut your wand depends on the affinity you feel towards certain trees or the use to which you will be putting it.

Healing wands can be used in many ways. For direct healing they can be placed on acupressure or chakra points on the body, where they clear and balance energies. If laid on the forehead they aid recall of events during this lifetime and may also at times bring forward memories of past lives, contact with our ancestors, etc. They also show us specific areas within us which need healing, or they offer oracular help or visions connected to questions or problems.

For example, I have a small oak wand which has cup shapes all along its delicate knobbly length. This wand threw itself at my feet as I sat under a favourite oak tree, and after bringing it home I kept moving it about my tables and shelves until it settled into place upon my work table, close to where I do my painting. Since then, whenever inspiration has left me or my energy has drained, the wand has caught my eye and renewed my efforts with its reliability, warmth and strength, its spiritual presence releasing energy blocks within me that keep me from reaching my best. Thus it revitalizes me in a unique way.

So read the words within this book, then enter a grove, park or field and begin to communicate, as did your ancestors, with the trees. And as you do so and realize your empathy with the world of Nature, ancient memories will stir within, and your mind's eye will come to focus upon the Spirit.

INTRODUCTION TO THE TREES

The leaves of the trees are for the healing of the nations.

The above words from Revelations are the prime motivation for this book. The following pages express and illustrate individual species of trees indigenous to Britain and found throughout the world, using the premise that the knowledge they bring of the past makes sense of the present and gives a surer foundation for the future.

Each species of tree is viewed from six angles under the following headings:

BOTANICAL. The physical descriptions of the trees and their botanical illustrations allow them to be recognized throughout the year. By realizing the seasonal mantles of the trees we get closer to them and the rhythms of Nature, and through this we automatically tune in to the earth from which we receive knowledge and healing. The methods by which trees reproduce are also discussed, for they illustrate how life-forms work together to achieve the marvel of continuity in life.

CUSTOM & LEGEND. In recounting the myths, legends and customs associated with trees we touch upon the formation of the land's soul, its roots. Then a reuniting is achieved, for by retracing our native contact with the natural world we find the true foundation upon which to build our individuality. In the words of Lewis Spence, from his book *The Magic*

Arts of Celtic Britain, 'The myth of a people is often the seed of its future greatness, for it frequently projects its destiny in allegory.'

Throughout the legends associated with trees, the characters of gods and goddesses emerge strongly. They are explored to ascertain the specific qualities attributed to these deities, for by also attributing these qualities to species of trees, our ancestors left us clues by which to realize the fullest expression of life. Such clues contain the secret lore of the ancients encoded into symbolic form, the re-enactment of which, given foundation by ancient ritual, became the customs of the people. Seasonal communal celebration reinforced their perception of being an integral part of the Whole.

HEALING. The healings given range from helping the individual to aiding the planet; in reality one is born from the other. Many of the remedies and recipes are taken from ancient herbals, and while they may alleviate certain of today's ailments, it is strongly recommended that a doctor or trained herbalist is consulted for serious conditions. However even the smallest use of herbs has a great effect upon our spirit and this promotes health in body and mind. There are many ways of using herbs, such as adding them to bathing water or to food, teas or wines. They can also be used in leaf or branch form in incenses or 'charm' pouches, or can simply be placed in a bowl near your bed or chair. Quite often meditation with a specific species of tree is recommended for spiritual healing. A glossary (*see pp.343–4*) provides a description of the terms used throughout.

The Bach Flower Remedies also aid our spirit, for they consist of water potentized with the flowers of trees, which have powerful healing properties on a vibrational level. They work primarily on the negative emotional and mental states which manifest as disease if ignored, and are effective on many levels. They are safe to self-diagnose and use, and are easily blended to suit individual needs. One of the greatest blessings these remedies have given us is the Bach Flower Rescue Remedy, for it is most effective for shock and trauma, quickly calming distress on physical, emotional, mental and spiritual levels. In our modern stress-filled world this remedy is a must for any first-aid or survival kit.

MAGIC. In order to perceive the emotive qualities of the trees, it is wise to look at how they were used by people in acts of ritual or sympathetic magic. As many of these acts pertain to healing, we realize that magic is healing as healing is magic, so closely are they intertwined.

The recognition of magic is inherent to indigenous cultures the world over. Magic has many aspects and many levels of reality or understanding. It is the force that makes things happen and is the excitement of creation. It is the spark of life, the surge of the Spirit, the ecstasy of the divine. It is desire and that which is attained at the end of desire. It is the hope which makes you eager to face each new day. It is what has become termed the 'omnipresence of God'.

Magic also pertains to divination and the arts and sciences. It is found in the words of the poet and within the harmony of song, and it inspires the teller of stories. It is theatre, music and dance; beauty, life, death and renewal. It is instinct and intuition and the breath of life, and is thus found within all living things. It is Nature and the heartbeat of the earth, the flow of its waters and the rush of its air. Magic *is* life.

The realms of magic are those of the imagination, and from these realms visions and desires can be consciously brought into being. This is achieved by applying the will (or intent) to 'Universal Laws'. These laws acknowledge the cyclic movements of the celestial bodies and those of the natural world, defining the ebb and flow of universal tides, which can be utilized to great effect.

With regard to trees and magic, it is apparent that the energies of trees have always been used by mankind in many ways. All plants give out an energy which is neutral and this can be used either positively or negatively, according to the will of the user. This explains the diverse ways in which trees have been used, i.e., a plant used for protection from witches or faeries can also be used to attract them.

INSPIRATION. Because inspiration is a product of healing and magic, it often continues points raised on those levels. My experiences and thoughts are shown here, for they illustrate my way of interpreting information from the trees. Other people will have their own thoughts and interpretations and that is as it should be, for our paths are both collective and individual.

Inspiration is also gained from specific contact with the trees, and my words follow trains of thought in order to perceive certain qualities and wisdoms. Showing how the trees speak to me may possibly encourage others to communicate with them.

PHYSICAL USES. This describes the ways in which mankind has used the unique properties of trees to aid his life on the physical level. It shows the good uses to which craftspeople, artists, farmers, builders, etc. have put materials gathered from Nature. Unfortunately it also shows abuses!

ILLUSTRATIONS. The botanical illustrations emphasize the leafing, blossoming and fruiting of the trees in order to express their full glory. In this way a greater identification is achieved and the visual impact opens certain perceptory channels in the beholder, allowing recognition of the part that all things play in the weaving of the pattern of life. Through realizing this within the yearly cycle specific wisdoms can be reached.

The order in which the trees appear in the following chapters corresponds to their seasonal energies and associations as they follow their cycles throughout the year. We begin at the birth of the solar year, midwinter, and follow the seasons through, as each tree in turn becomes imbued with specific energy which it radiates out to the world. At such times trees are magically potent and are thus intimately connected to the wisdoms of our ancient traditions. Their myths and legends provide us with colourful threads of the Spirit with which to weave our future tapestry.

Let us enter the grove...

THE ENGLISH YEW

BOTANICAL

YEW. *Taxus baccata*. Evergreen. POISONOUS.

The yew tree helped form the great primeval conifer forests which dominated the earth long before the advent of broadleaved trees. It lives for
over 1,000 years and it is thought that many living yews pre-date Christ
by many thousands of years. The Fortingall Yew in Perthshire is claimed
to be up to 9,000 years old. Many yews are mentioned in the Domesday
Book of 1086 and one of the oldest weapons found is a crude yew spear
from the Old Stone Age.

The yew gains its capacity for great age from its particular growth of shoots or branches, which root into the ground and grow to form new trunks. These then join the main trunk and become part of it, which gives yews huge fluted girths. It takes 150 years for the main trunk to form and then the yew continues its growth widthways. In old age it continues to grow, even with a completely hollow trunk. This has given yew a reputation for immortality and has made it a symbol of life after death.

Unlike other conifers, the yew produces no cones. It is known to be deadly, for its leaves and fresh seeds contain a poison called Taxin. This is sometimes in moderate strength but is often virulently strong. Humans and animals can die from yew poisoning, though it has been said that cattle can become immune from constant contact.

When the ancient remains of Mildenhall Fen in East Anglia were drained in 1865, the broken stumps of hundreds of yew trees were revealed still standing as they had grown under the peat. Prehistoric vessels of yew are to be seen in the British Museum and a number of place-names reflect the quantity of yew growing in specific areas, such as Mayo, meaning 'yew field', and Youghal, meaning 'yew wood'. Nowadays the yew is much rarer and perhaps the best examples in England are to be found on the Hampshire Downs in Surrey.

The needle leaves, male and female flowers, and fruit of the yew

The yew is common in churchyards and in undisturbed country areas examples are still found of ancient yew avenues. Yew grows well on chalky soil and can reach heights of 80 feet (24 metres) and more, as is evidenced by the many old trees which still grace and guard the land.

BARK
Yew trees become hollow because their red-brown bark is thin and does not give good protection to the heart of the tree. The bark peels off the trees easily, and its long strips or flakes are smooth underneath and coloured in shades of salmony-pink.

LEAVES
The crown of the yew tree is wide and spreading, for it is made up of dense branches and foliage. The yew is evergreen, always retaining a good cover of waxy needle-leaves which are flattened, dark green on top and light green below. The leaves are arranged in two opposite rows in spirals along the twigs and can remain on the tree for eight years before falling. At the end of a yew spray a small cone-like growth of a soft green may appear. This is caused by insects laying eggs in the tree and producing a reaction similar to when galls are formed on oaks (see p.173).

FLOWERS
The yew is one of the first trees to flower in the spring. The male and female flowers are on separate trees, and form in the angles between the narrow leaves and the stem. The flowers may be dormant for several years, especially if not in good light.

The flowering time of the male tree is very noticeable, not so much for the flowers themselves, which are like miniature globes of yellow stamens set in brown scales, but for the quantity of pollen produced in the little sacs beneath them. When the flowers mature in February or March the stamen shields are open, and as the flowers grow on the underside of the branches, pollen is free to fall onto the winds. In good weather the flowers shed pollen and in bad weather they keep the stamen shields in place to keep the pollen dry.

Once taken by the wind the pollen has to reach a female flower-bearing tree, for it is only the female tree which produces fruit. The female flower is the size of a pin-head, with a tip which projects from tiny protective green scales. From this tip comes a mucilage substance. This is most active at the time when grains of pollen from the male tree fill the air.

Because the seed-making process of the yew is dependent upon the wind, i.e. is pretty much a hit or miss affair, it produces extraordinary amounts of pollen, which when released can cover large areas with its yellow dust. On warm spring days the air is filled with its golden shimmer.

FRUIT

Once male pollen grains are caught by the tip of the female flower, it moves back into its ovule and fertilization takes place. The fruit that develops from this is small and green and sits like an egg in an egg-cup. By October the cup has grown to cover the fruit. It is fleshy, red and full of sweet mucilage. The green fruit inside the cup, the ovule, has become a black seed. Now the yew tree relies upon other agents to complete its cycle, for most of its seeds are distributed by birds like the thrush and blackbird, who devour the fruit greedily and emit the seed unharmed upon their flights. It is rare that a yew seed will germinate in its first year, but by its second or third year it will begin to grow in the earth.

CUSTOM & LEGEND

An old folk-tale tells why yews are 'dressed' so darkly. When the yew was a young species, in times when there were few people, it thought that all other trees were more beautiful, for their colourful leaves could flutter in the wind, unlike its stiff needles. The tree pined, thinking that the faeries had deliberately made it unattractive. Yet the faeries wanted to please the yew, and one sunny morning it found its needles had changed to leaves of gold and its heart danced with joy. But robbers came and stripped the tree bare, leaving it confused and sad. The faeries then gave it leaves of purest crystal and the yew loved its sparkle, but a storm of hail fell and the crystals shattered. Then it was given broad leaves and it waved them in the air, only for them to be eaten by goats. At this the yew gave up, for it realized that its original dress was the best, for it was of permanence, of long ages and deep knowledge, and in this the tree found comfort.

There are many tales about yews springing into growth upon the graves of lovers. In Irish legend the graves of Deidre and Naoise were staked with yew branches by the High King Conchobar in order to separate them. Yet the stakes grew into yew trees which wove their branches together above the graves and joined the lovers even in death.

Cornish legend tells of Mark, a king of Cornwall who was wedded to Iseult, a lady of Ireland who did not actually love him. After their wedding as they sailed from Ireland back to Cornwall, unbeknown to anyone Iseult's mother prepared a draught of wine for the wedded pair, in the hopes that a spell would make her daughter fall madly in love with her new husband. Unfortunately the wine was drunk by Iseult and Mark's nephew Tristan, and the two fell passionately in love with each other. The love-spell lasted some three years, during which the lovers took many chances to sleep together. Many times they were discovered and reported to the king, whose love for them both pulled him apart. Likewise his kingdom slowly fell apart because of the situation and the gossip it aroused.

After many partings and tricks of fate the lovers died in each other's arms. Mark gave them a ceremonial funeral, for he had truly loved them both. It is said that Iseult and Tristan were buried either side of the nave in the chapel at Tintagel Castle in Cornwall, above Merlin's Cave, and within a year yew trees had sprouted out of each grave. The king had the trees cut down but they grew again. Three times they grew and three times he cut them down. Eventually, moved by the love he had felt for both his wife and nephew, Mark gave in and allowed the trees to grow unmolested. At their full height the yews reached their branches towards each other across the nave and intertwined so intensely they could nevermore be parted.

In the ancient Irish mythological cycle of the Tuatha de Danaan, the earliest magical race or the gods of ancient Ireland, as portrayed in the *Irish Book of Invasions*, one of the last great warrior queens was Banbha, sister of Fodhla and Eire. She was slain and later became semi-deified as the death aspect of the triple goddess of Ireland. So the yew tree was sacred to her and became known as 'the renown of Banbha'. One such 'renown of Banbha' yew later became known as the Tree of Ross, and was said to represent the death and destruction that was to come again to Ireland, mainly from the imposition of organized Christianity over a bardic and pantheistic culture.

The yew was also regarded as one of the five magical trees of Ireland and a 'firm straight deity', an allusion to the fact that Irish yews are cone-shaped with upward-growing branches, unlike the British yew, whose branches grow horizontally.

Another ancient title for the yew was the 'spell of knowledge and the king's wheel', which refers to the brooch worn by the king which was entailed to his successors. This brooch represented the cycle of existence and reminded the king that death might come at any time. Therefore it emphasized his duty to maintain and pass on a viable realm, with long-lasting virtues which would outlive many monarchs and generations.

Throughout Europe there are similar references to yew being regarded as a symbol of death and regeneration. In Greece and Italy it was sacred to the goddess Hecate. The Romans at one time sacrificed black bulls wreathed with yew branches to her at the midwinter feast of Saturnalia in the hope that she would provide an easier winter and spare the rest of their herds, a dark superstition which Christianity did much good in relieving. Hecate's cult spread as far as Scotland and although she may originally have been a 'fair' goddess, she became better known in her dark aspect of spreading evil bane. In Macbeth her cauldron contained 'slips of yew, sliver'd in the moon's eclipse', and elsewhere Shakespeare makes 'hebenon, the double-fatal yew' the poison which Hamlet's uncle pours into the king's ear.

The yew was revered as a sacred tree, and the custom of the first Christian missionaries to preach under and erect churches near yews was a continuance of the ancient druidic practice of associating the yew with a place of burial adjacent to a place of worship. The main difference between druidic temples and Christian churches is that druids worship in Nature in groves of trees or stone circles, never deeming themselves mighty enough to 'contain' the all-powerful spirit of the gods inside a building. In Christian terms the yew came to symbolize resurrection and it was used in church at Easter and on Palm Sunday. Shoots of yew were put into the shrouds of the dead, for it was believed to protect and restrain their spirits. The Church also thought that the yew protected against evil influences interfering with the shades of the dead.

Other associations between the yew and churchyards were formed when armies met at churches for blessings before battle, for English archers gathered yew branches from the churchyard trees to make their famous long-bows. It is said that many kings ordered the planting of yews in churchyards specifically for this purpose, for the English long-bow was incredibly powerful and fatal to the enemy. Many proverbs arose from the awe the long-bow commanded, such as 'England were but a fling, but for the Eugh [yew] and the grey-goose wing', which refers to the yew long-bow, the arrow of birch and its shaft of goose feathers. 'The war-like Yewgh [yew] by which more than a lance the strong-armed English spirits conquered France' speaks for itself. However yew bows are said to have killed three English kings: William Rufus, King Harold and Richard Coeur de Lion. In the Swiss legends it was possibly a yew bow that fired William Tell's arrow that halved the apple placed on his son's head. Robin Hood is likely to have had the same.

The yew contains the most active of vegetable poisons and because of the reality of its death connotations it is a tree which demands great respect. Because of its sacred associations it was thought unlucky to cut down or damage a yew, and in Ireland only fallen trees were used to make shrines and croziers. However the wind-broken branches of the tree were considered 'sliver'd', and were reckoned dangerous and unlucky to use, for the spirit of the storm remained within them, as is shown by Shakespeare's reference to Hecate's cauldron.

In Scottish tradition it was said that a chieftain could hold up a sprig of yew in his left hand whilst denouncing his enemies to their faces, sure in the knowledge that they would hear nothing derogatory whilst others witnessed what was actually said.

Legend also says that in the thirteenth century Thomas the Rhymer (Thomas of Ercledoune) met with the Queen of Elfland and received from her the gift of prophecy and clothes of elven green. It is believed he still awaits rebirth in a Scottish yew grove guarded by faeries near Inverness (see also Apple, p. 119).

Iona, the sacred isle off the western coast of Scotland, is thought to have originally been called 'Ioha', the Irish/Gaelic name for yew, for its traditions were linked to rebirth and reincarnation long before the coming of St Columba.

The ancestral spelling of yew is 'yeugh', 'ewgh', 'ewe', 'ugh', 'uhe' or simply just 'U'.

HEALING

Warning: It must be stressed that no one should self-administer yew. It is very poisonous and will cause death.

Culpeper states that the yew's poisonous qualities rise by distillation into the most active vegetable poison in the world, which acts upon the nervous system and destroys vital functions, but does not bring on sleep like opium or other poisons. Yew's Latin name, *Taxus*, is derived from the Greek *toxon*, meaning 'bow'. The connection of the tree to poison formed the derivative 'toxin', which was given to poisons in general.

Even to sleep under a yew was once thought to cause death for it produced a sleep from which one would never awake, though the sixteenth-century herbalist Gerard stated that he had slept in the branches of a yew tree and had received no harm. Ancient herbals state that the juice of the yew remedies the bite of a viper, but it should need no Gerard to see that this is not necessarily true.

In homoeopathy a tincture of young yew shoots and berries (not the seed) is used for treating cystitis, headache, neuralgia, dimness of vision, affections of the heart and kidneys, gout and rheumatism.

Recent discoveries about the yew are exciting, for the chemical properties of *Taxus* are believed to contain a formula, Taxol, which is an anti-cancer drug. While tests continue on this, the chemical companies rush to the yews to take the drug from the trees. This they unfortunately do by stripping the bark, thus destroying the trees. Hal Hartzell in his book *The Yew Tree* warns that while protection orders are on American yews they are not on the British or the European yews and that the chemical companies are looking to these giant trees for their next collections. The necessity of such life-saving drugs is paramount, but not to the detriment or death of the species which provides the cure. As *Taxus* can also be obtained from the needle-like leaves of yew trees it is imperative that it is collected in this life-sustaining way, even if the process is slightly more expensive for money-making companies.

MAGIC

IRISH/GAELIC NAME	*Iobo*
OGHAM	╪
RUNIC	Y
RULING PLANET	Saturn
ABILITIES	Guardian to the Door of Rebirth. Rest after the struggle of life. Divination. Dowsing. Bows. To do with the element of Earth.
SEASON	Winter

Yew trees growing in churchyards were thought to protect the spirits of the dead, as already discussed. Because the yew is an evergreen tree of extreme longevity, the ancient custom of mourners putting sprigs of yew into shrouds and graves of the departed showed they believed death was not the end of life, but merely a passing through into the continuance of life to come. It also possibly explains why yew trees grew out of the graves of lovers.

Ghostly 'faces' seen on the trunks of peeling graveside yews were thought to be signs of the rising spirits of the dead freed from earthly restraints. Thus they began their journey to rebirth or reincarnation, which was a major tenet of the old faith. Doubtless with such a sombre reputation revelations of ghosts and hauntings associated with yews grew throughout the centuries. This actually protected the trees, as it was thought extremely unlucky to cut them down. However for more thoughtful souls the graveyard yew represented an ideal place to sit and commune with departed loved ones:

> *What gentle ghost, besprent with April dew,*
> *Hails me so solemnly to yonder yew.*
>
> BEN JONSON

Yew sticks were used by Celts for divination, through reading the signs formed as they were cast onto the ground. The patterns they created produced a more sophisticated version of the patterns associated with tea-leaf reading and were read in the same way. Yew rods were inscribed with the sacred characters of the ogham script, because the yew's resilient nature meant that the rods didn't perish and so the magic imbued by the carved oghams would continue into the future.

In the north of England yew sprigs were used to dowse the whereabouts of lost goods. Yet to druids they gave the power of invisibility for protection, though this may well refer to the impenetrable nature of a 'hide' made out of yew branches. Druids thought the yew could transcend time, and because of its associations with death and rebirth it was regarded as the tree of eternity. This is apparent in the tree's method of self-renewal, as already described, wherein its lower branches root into the ground and become a strengthening outer trunk which encircles the heartwood of the tree. This gives yews perpetual renewal and transformation, the young and old wood being bound up in the one. The yew shows that the source of life continually renews itself, enabling us to transcend old age by a constant renewal and application of our youthfulness. Thus we can transform ourselves.

Death and rebirth are not necessarily physical, in that we do not have to die physically to be reborn. We are able, when viewing the yew symbolically, to experience a symbolic death, a casting away of the outworn physical things and hindering conditions which have encased and limited our spirit and expression. When we do this our being is set free of restriction and we enter a new phase of life. We are symbolically reborn and our Spirit rejoices.

These points were well accepted by our ancestors, who used the cycles of the year to enhance them. As the Celtic year ended (31 October) humans, animals, workplaces and homes were purified to cast off any restrictions which would limit the new year, which began on 1 November. According to ancient druidic practice, sprigs of yew were handed out to people at this time to aid in purifications and communication with departed loved ones. Likewise at the midwinter rites, sprigs of yew were used for purification as people cast off their physically outworn things and burned them on great Yule fires. This freed the Spirit for the new solar year.

The yew is most powerful in midwinter, for it represents the passage of the sun through the darkest time of the year. Along with other evergreens it was revered as a tree of light, its green foliage in the dead of winter emphasizing that life would continue. To enhance this, all evergreens were traditionally dressed with shiny, sparkling objects at Yuletide, to attract the light of the sun back into the year. This tradition was enacted in many countries and still continues with our Christmas trees, even though we've forgotten the ancient reasons behind it.

The yew is also regarded as protectively powerful at Lughnasadh (Lammas) as the harvesting of fruit and crops begins. At this time the sun is near the end of its yearly reign, and in the eyes of the ancients the sun-god now faces the Underworld, below the horizon, which he will traverse until he appears again at the beginning of the new solar year. It is almost as if the yew reminds him of this cycle, ensuring that the life-giving solar forces move through the seasons correctly. Lughnasadh refers to the Feast of Lugh the ancient sky-god, and his associations with the yew and the ogham system are strengthened by the cutting of ogham staves from yew trees at this time.

We can now see that the yew's death connotations work two ways, and that by providing the door to rebirth it allows life to be continuous. Through working with the tree (but *not* imbibing it), direct contact with the past can be revealed and wisdom gained, as well as a renewal of spiritual strength. In this life aspect the yew also represents our children's children's futures as well as our ancestral past. In the druidic initiations and levels of learning it represents the grade of the Ovate, who undergoes symbolic death in order to be reborn into a new level of awareness which transcends the concepts of time and its limitations.

It is known that during public ceremonies druids performed many theatrical effects in order to add emphasis and ensure that certain points did not go unnoticed by the people. One such effect was to instigate great lightning flashes from ceremonial fires, and one of the ways by which they did this was to throw handsfull of plant pollen into the flames. This tradition passed into the theatre, where grains of clubmosses were thrown onto hot shovels for lighting effects. The pollen of different plants produces different results, such as specific colours of flame, gentle sizzlings, flashes or dramatic explosions, and any plant which profusely scattered its pollen could be used. Because yews grew near celebratory places and produced great amounts of pollen, they were well placed to aid the druidic theatrics.

The yew is under the rule of Saturn and because of its connections to bows – and also to arrows which were at times tipped with a poisonous yew concoction – it represents the zodiacal sign of Sagittarius, which takes us through the Winter Solstice.

In the cold regions of the north wind the yew is associated with faerie wildmen and Pictish deities, most of whom are said to have the ability to conjure up a faerie darkness in order to disappear. This may well have reference to the yew's ability to make things invisible for protection.

INSPIRATION

In *The Magic Arts of Celtic Britain*, Lewis Spence tells us that druids in ancient Ireland made their magical wands and staffs from yew, hawthorn and rowan, not out of oak, as did the druids of Gaul. He may well be right; yet whatever wood they are made from, it is known that wands, rods or staffs convey magical or psychic energies, and in the cutting and carving of them, the personal power of the maker embodies the wood with the spirit of the tree, or a chosen elemental form such as a faerie. Thus the implement can become a channel for the energy of a presiding spirit, as well as being able to transfer power or direct energies.

When used positively, a wand or staff is a great healing implement, able to transform illness to health and sadness to joy. In Celtic tales a touch from a wand or a blow from a staff caused great transformations, especially when delivered by a druid, shaman or magician. Many are the examples in Irish literature of the beneficent uses of such implements, such as the power of the gods being transferred to those in need or the mood of a crowd being elevated from the realms of despair to that of creativity. Unfortunately many also are the records of their misuse by power-seeking individuals, especially in regard to their transformational aspects.

For example, in Irish myth the Children of Lir were each given a stroke from a magical wand by their step-mother, at which they were transformed into four swans which flew over Loch Dearg for 300 years until released from the spell by St Caemhoc. Likewise, in the tale of Diarmid and Grainne, a dark magician called Reachtaire struck his son with a magical wand and transformed him into 'a cropped pig, having neither ears nor tail'! In the Irish legend of Finn we are told of his comrade, a man called Illan who had a faerie sweetheart. The faerie, however, was jealous of Illan's earthly wife and struck her with a wand, transforming her into the 'most beautiful wolf-hound ever seen'. This spell was removed only when Illan had promised life-long fidelity to the faerie.

As can be gleaned from these tales, wands in particular were used by women in the casting of spells, doubtless because of their size as compared to a heavy staff. Wands are, however, an exceptional directional implement for the intuitive powers of a woman, forming an extension of their insight with a lightness and swiftness of movement comparable to the needle which sews, the shuttle which weaves or the spindle which spins, and as such, wands and their users are in direct contact with the goddesses of these arts. We have only to wave a wand, or even a small branch from a tree, before ourselves, concentrating on the passes as our hand and the wand move through the air, and we notice that our eyes travel to the tip, to watch and move outwards. Then we feel the hypnotic, weaving, spell-binding power of a wand as it traces its finery between us and the universe. Through wands we can direct our creative energies delicately, as a fine paintbrush paints a subtle picture, and through them we can also weave strong powers to cause great changes.

Magical staffs are more suited to the male physique, though warrior women have always appeared staff in hand beside warrior men. The staff is a mighty wielder of power, strong and straight and able to blast energies apart or draw the gods to earth. Druidic staffs of old were potent tools, for the magical power by which they were embodied (that of the spirit of the tree, the will of the owner and the might of the gods) charged them with exceptional energy, and such was the owner's contact with them that they went to the grave together and beyond. The later staffs of Christian saints embodied the god force but never really contained the raw elemental power of the druidic staff.

A few years ago an Irish druid revealed deeper understandings of the yew tree to me by providing a living example which corroborated a Breton legend I'd heard, namely that the roots of graveside yews reach into the mouths of corpses. To do this he led me deep within a forest to a half-fallen tree and as my eyes followed his pointing finger I looked into the mass of roots at its foot. There, in the eruptions caused by its falling sideways, were revealed many intertwining roots and within them was formed an open-mouthed skull-shape with a large single root entering its mouth. The graphic symbology of this was startling to say the least, touching deep chords and memories within, for the life-sustaining root of the yew within the mouth of death shows life continuous in the resurrecting sense.

The superstitions surrounding the yew tree grew from a fear of death induced by the Christians and their theories of heaven and hell, concepts which the ancients regarded very differently. The deadly use to which man has put the yew tree, as a bow and as a poison, also added to superstition. Yet as a tree of resurrection the yew guards the doorway from this life into the next.

PHYSICAL USES

Yew wood, which is very hard and a golden yellow in colour, has been used for furniture and panelling, as well as for fenceposts, ship-masts and wine barrels. It throws out a great heat when burned, and as it resists the action of water, i.e., it doesn't rot away, it was greatly valued before the general use of iron. The strength of yew wood and its durability was noted by the Anglo-Saxons, who reckoned a post of yew could outlive one of iron.

With age, however, the wood becomes brittle. Because of this at various times throughout history yews with extra pliability were imported into Britain specifically for long-bows with a stronger pull and farther reach. Yew wood was also used for dagger handles.

Yew sticks were cast by the Celts, as already mentioned, to divine the future. Yew rods were used for making written ogham scripts, because when the wood is seasoned and polished it has an extraordinary power of resisting decay. For this reason magical wands of yew are considered especially potent.

The art of topiary, the cutting of the foliage of a tree into metamorphic shapes of birds and animals, is widely practised on yew because of its thick foliage.

Yew was included in the church decorations at Easter as a symbol of the continuity of life.

THE HOLLY

BOTANICAL

HOLLY. *Ilex aquifolium*. Evergreen. POISONOUS (berries).

The holly is an evergreen shrub or small tree which gains heights of 30–40 feet (9–12 metres). It often branches from the top to the bottom of its trunk and needs little sun, for its leaves reflect light like a mirror.

Holly is a native of Britain and central and southern Europe where it once helped form the great primeval forests. It grows slowly and when among trees which are not more rapid in growth, its height may be drawn up to 50 feet (15 metres). It has a preference for growing in oak and beech woods. Holly trees do not like being moved and will exhaust the soil around them.

The holly was once a common tree in woods and hedgerows and on scrubland. A holly sapling is a particularly favourite food of rabbits.

BARK
The bark of a holly tree is fine and delicate. It is an ashen colour with a silvery quality (when not covered with a characteristic green algae).

LEAVES
Holly leaves are tough, leathery and heavily lobed, with each lobe ending in a very sharp spine. At heights above 12 feet (3½ metres) the leaves become less prickly and are often unlobed with just one sharp point at the end, for at this height the tree need not protect itself. The dark green glossy leaves stay on the tree some three to four years and

The leaves, flowers and berry fruit of the holly

as they take a long time to decay when fallen, quite often skeletons of leaves are found on the ground beneath the trees. New shoots and leaves of holly appear in pink, brown and purple tones before they harden into their darker colours. The holly tree produces its best leaves during the summer months.

FLOWERS
The holly blooms in May and most often the male and female flowers are on separate trees. Only the female flower changes into the holly berry and this can only happen if there is a male tree nearby from which pollen can be transferred. Holly flowers are tiny, pale pink on the outside and pure white within. They grow in clusters between the leaf stalk and the twig, and their four petals form an equal-armed 'cross', giving the appearance of little star shapes. The female flower is somewhat larger than the male, for it contains the four-celled ovary which will become fruit.

33

Pollination is encouraged by insects such as wild bees, which are drawn to the flowers by the smell of the honey liquid released from their bases.

FRUIT

As they mature the fruiting berries of the holly grow red. By September the trees glow with them, in striking contrast to their dark green leaves. Inside each shiny berry are four little fruit stones containing seed and after being eaten by birds these are voided during flights. Larks, finches, nightingales and field-fares love to eat holly berries, and by the time they have passed through the birds the seeds have been softened and are ready for germination. Holly seeds are poisonous to all except birds. If a holly crops well one year it will rest the next.

CUSTOM & LEGEND

The evergreen leaves of holly have represented immortality to mystics of all ages. To the druids the holly was especially sacred. When winter descended they advised people to take it into their homes, for then it would shelter the elves and faeries who could at this time join mortals without causing injury to them. However there was a warning attached to this advice, for any holly brought in was to be carefully removed by Imbolc Eve (31 January), as any leaf left in longer supposedly foretold a misfortune.

In later years the Christian interpretation of this ancient custom appointed Twelfth Night for the removal of any green foliage from the home. The following words, written by a man from an old Devonshire village, show just how careful people had to be with clearances:

> Down with the rosemary and so,
> Down with the baies and mistletoe,
> Down with the holly, ivie, all,
> Wherewith ye drest the Christmas hall.
> That so the superstitious find,

Not one least branch there left behind,
For look, how many leaves there be,
Neglected there, maids trust to me,
So many goblins you shall see.

HERRICK

There was another reason for the bringing in of holly, apart from the sheltering of faerie folk, for during winter people were prone to depression and the holly's light-reflecting leaves and colourful berries could lift their spirits. The druids were aware of this, and also that holly protects from evil influences, so they advised people to grow it near their homes. Since early times holly has been regarded as a plant of good omen, for its evergreen qualities make it appear invulnerable to the passage of time as the seasons change. It therefore symbolizes the tenacity of life even when surrounded by death, which it keeps at bay with strong protective powers.

From early days holly has been used in midwinter religious observances. As the indigenous pagan traditions mixed with those of the pagan Romans, gifts of holly were given during the five-day festival of Saturnalia, which celebrated the birth of the sun-god and culminated when the sun moved into the zodiacal sign of Capricorn at the precise astronomical time of the Winter Solstice. The power of these pagan celebrations on or about 22 December and their effect on the people were well recognized by the Church, and so they closely aligned the birth of Christ, on 25 December, to the pagan date. In Christian legend holly sprang up from under Christ's feet as he walked upon earth, and in certain parts of Europe holly is still called 'Christ's thorn', for it was believed that its thorny leaves and bright red berries symbolized Christ's suffering and foretold the Passion.

One of the strongest legendary images we have of holly is that of the holly king. This image, featured in the medieval renaissance of the twelfth century, evolved from an ancient recognition of the spirit of vegetation, traditionally represented as a wild-looking man covered in branches and foliage: the legendary Wildman. In order to understand the full concept of the holly king's character, we can quickly look at his

Wildman roots and at how his character changed over time, especially during periods when the Church decreed that such potent figures contained overt sexual connotations and were therefore evil.

Suppression by the Church forced the blatantly erotic image of the Wildman (and his embodied aspects like the holly-god) into tamed images wherein they lost power. The holly-god became the holly king, and the Wildman evolved into the Green Man, Jack in the Green or May King. These images somewhat parody the fecundating attributes of the Wildman, stylizing him into conformity. However the Green Man image was extremely popular, and carvings of his head, covered in vegetation, with stems and leaves sprouting from his nose and mouth, were incorporated into many buildings, usually in the roof bosses, as a form of protection. Some of these images survive, and when we come across them today we can do well to remember their fertile Wildman origins and touch the echo of the great spiritual realm he expressed, the realm of vegetation.

The holly king was symbolized by a giant man covered in holly branches and leaves, who carried a holly bush as his club. He represents the tenacity of life, the green of Nature carried through the seasons and guarded by his spiky holly-club, his light-reflecting 'mirrored' leaves and his warning fiery-red berries. Within deeper concepts the holly king is twinned with the oak king, and they become dual counterparts of the Nature god in his earth-protecting cycle and role. As such they are the god of darkness and the god of light within the solar year, who guard the transitional points of that year (midwinter and midsummer), when an interchange occurs in the natural world as all life responds to the solar tides of ebb and flow. In this context the holly king reigns over the time of the waning tide (from midsummer to midwinter), when the sun declines in the heavens as the harvest is gathered and the earth withdraws her energy as life moves into its dormant period. The oak king reigns over the waxing tide (from midwinter to midsummer), when the energy of the earth is outpouring into the season of growth and fecundity as the light and warmth of the sun grow. As such, both kings represent the god of Nature who protects, courts and loves the earth-goddess, ensuring fruitfulness of the land.

So powerful was the ancient symbology expressed by these concepts that the Church could not eradicate it from the minds of the people. Even though ritual enactment of pagan concepts was banned, mummers' plays evolved, using festive characters to veil sacred lore. Within these plays it was customary for the oak and holly kings to tussle for the hand of a fair maiden (the goddess). At midsummer the oak king was defeated by the holly king, as at midwinter the oak king overpowered the holly king, expressing the ancient tidal symbology. Mummers also performed plays with resurrection themes: at Beltaine enacting the story of the sky-god who mates with the earth-goddess and is reborn again within the bounty of the earth; and at Lughnasadh (Lammas) enacting the symbolic death of the corn-god and his subsequent resurrection in the growing seed. The medieval legends of King Arthur and the Knights of the Round Table also illustrate this, for in the tales of Gawain and the Green Knight the original concepts of guarding the year and competing for the hand of the goddess are shown.

Pertinent to holly is a tradition concerning Holly Night (Twelfth Night) in which the people of Brough, Westmorland, tied many torches to a huge branch of holly. Once lit, this blazing holly branch was carried by the local strongman, who headed a grand parade of colourful dancing people, as music played and fireworks lit the sky. This custom was performed until recent years and the fact that it continued an ancient tradition in which holly was celebrated some two weeks after the Winter Solstice in some ways reiterates the completion of the tidal changeover, showing the time when the holly-god (as god of darkness) finally let go of his responsibilities.

In Scottish tradition we see the Wildman concept carried through until the calendrical new year, for the traditional 'first-footer', usually a dark-haired man carrying coal and greenery into the home at the chime of the new year's clocks, is believed to be derived from the immortal giant who used the holly-bush as his club.

Tradition says that no branch should be cut from a holly tree, but rather that it should be pulled free in a method considered fit for a sacred tree. It has always been considered unlucky to fell holly or to burn or bury green-skinned holly, yet luck was increased if a small branch kept from the Yule decorations was hung on the outside of the house, where it also protected against lightning.

Holly is especially lucky for men, and if they carry a leaf or berry it is said they quickly become attractive to women.

In the north of Britain prickly holly leaves are called 'he-holly' and the smooth ones 'she-holly'. An old country saying states that if smooth-leaved holly is brought into the house first at Yuletime the wife will rule the household the coming year, if prickly holly enters first the husband will rule.

Pliny tells us of a special power inherent in holly, that if holly wood is thrown in any animal's direction it will compel the animal to obey. This calls to mind tales of holly wands, which have compelling strength.

So sacred was the holly tree to our ancestors that in many areas it was given the alternative name of 'holy tree'. It is also known as the 'hulver bush', 'holme', 'hulm', 'holme chase' and, as already mentioned, 'Christ's thorn'.

HEALING

Most of holly's healing qualities are on the subtle planes, where by its presence or by taking its remedies it helps us transform our 'prickly' bits and improves our reaction to the world.

The Bach Flower Remedies use holly to treat oversensitivity, hatred, anger and aggressive behaviour, especially when there is no response to other treatments or when the patient seems to need many remedies. It is used to control vexations, jealous thoughts, unhappiness, sapping of others' energy, suspicion, violent temperament, thoughts of revenge, envy, imagining others insulting you, irritability, hatred through jealousy, fault-finding with others, being embittered and complaining about others.

LEAVES
An infusion (see Appendix V, p.344) of fresh or dried holly leaves is used to treat catarrhal coughs and bronchitis, pneumonia, influenza, rheumatism

and fevers. In earlier days holly leaves were soaked in vinegar and put on corns for a day and a night in order to cure them. An early remedy for chilblains was to thrash them with a holly branch in order to 'chase the chill out'. The juice of holly leaves, sniffed, was reputed to stop a runny cold.

As a 'guardian' herb holly warns that there may be strong results from our actions which may well wound ourselves or others. It shows the strong need for us to accept full responsibility for our actions, something that most of us don't even think about. To enable wise decisions to be made before a course of action, holly can be used to meditate with or upon, to calm the mind and body of emotions. Then, when our inner being is still, we can unemotionally form true thoughts and make wise decisions about our situation. In this way we are in control of our actions and can thus accept responsibility for them.

BERRIES
Warning: Holly berries purge, but often cause nausea and vomiting. They are poisonous to children.

MAGIC

IRISH/GAELIC	*Tinne*
OGHAM	∄
RUNIC	↑
RULING PLANET	Mars
ABILITIES	Strongest protective herb. Clear wisdom and courage. Dream magic. To do with the element of Fire.
SEASON	Midwinter

On magical levels holly was regarded as an excellent herb of protection, specifically guarding against evil spirits, poisons, short-tempered or angry elementals, and thunder and lightning. The protection against lightning has been verified, for it has been shown that the spikes of holly leaves act like miniature lightning conductors, giving the trees immunity.

Holly leaves are used in traditional ways for dream magic, as performed by countryfolk. In the following divination from the north country a young girl is eager to see her future husband. She gathers nine unprickly she-holly leaves at the midnight hour on a Friday, and then ties them into a three-cornered hankie using nine knots. She places it under her pillow before going to sleep. That night she receives a vision of her future husband in her dreams. Similar procedures can be used for all types of dreams and allegedly holly also gives added strength to make all dreams come true.

To divine and ask for a wish at Yuletide, light tiny pieces of candle and place them on holly leaves floating in a tub of water. Each leaf represents a person. If it remains afloat that person's wish will come true, but if it sinks the wish will lack fulfilment. This form of divination can be very communal and is a good communication booster at celebrations or parties. The theatrical effects caused by the candlelight and reflective water also add to the magical atmosphere and open the visionary senses.

In Custom & Legend we discussed the holly king, and here we can look more closely at his Wildman origins. The initial incentive which prompted people into embodying the Spirit of vegetation into human form was probably an unconscious memory of the early guardian spirits of the land. The earliest myths of Britain tell of a guardian giant called Gogmagog, a club-bearing wildman, hairy and leaf-clad, who epitomized instinctive Nature and the primeval wildness and untamable strength of the forest depths. This primal stereotype encompassed an innate recognition of the life-force of the natural world, in which in the earliest of days the plant world reigned supreme. In later days reverence of the natural world and the recognition of deities connected to its life-cycles became the foundation of the religion we now call druidism.

The earliest druidic rites possibly evolved when certain people enveloped themselves in vegetation, wherein they felt an innate presence of the Great Spirit. This produced ecstatic states in which it was possible to witness and experience the powerful energy which continually replenishes life upon earth. This power filled the druid until he radiated and lit up his dress of leaves from within, making it tremble and rustle and resemble a power-filled 'vegetation-man', the 'wildman'.

While druids of forested lands dressed themselves in vegetation from trees in which they saw powerful expressions of god, so in other lands where animals reigned supreme, people saw powerful expressions of god within them, and thus dressed themselves in animal skins, hides or horns, in order to witness and experience the Spirit. In ancient cultures the world over, aboriginals, shamen, seers, witch-doctors and magicians have gained such contact in similar manner. So powerful were the results of embodiments within vegetation to druids that long arduous retreats in forest depths became a strong initiatory process for them. Possibly Britain became the druidic centre of learning from the strength of its realm of vegetation and the specific wisdoms it could impart to those who opened themselves up to it.

Thus we see that the Wildman expressed the procreative essence of Nature, the Godhead. And from his primal beginnings and through translations of his manifold energy he came to personify specific aspects of the energies of Nature, from which forms like the holly and oak kings evolved, embodiments *par excellence* of the seasonal forces associated with the dark and light periods of the year. As explained in Custom & Legend, such personifications kept the Nature religions alive in the minds of the people, even under the condemning eyes of the Church, and if we today must find our roots, we can do no better than regard the Wildman as expressing our very birth within the natural world.

In the Irish/Gaelic ogham alphabet holly is called *Tinne*, a word believed to have originally meant 'fire'. From this was derived the word 'tinder', which *Chambers Twentieth Century Dictionary* describes as 'dry inflammable matter used for kindling fire from a spark'. This association of holly and fire has been known since ancient days, for charcoal made from holly wood was used by armourers to forge swords and axe-heads. Then the smith was considered a great magician, for with the element of fire he moulded the elements of the earth, creating tools and weapons necessary for survival and protection. In continuation of this, holly is still used today as an incense in the ritual consecration of magical knives.

With such fiery associations, also reflected by its ruling planet Mars and its shining red berries, the holly was presided over by the thunder-gods Tannus, Taranis, Thor, etc. Holly, holm oak and oak have great associations with these gods in their native myths (see also Oak, p.178).

With this wealth of lore surrounding it, holly has always been regarded as a tree with immense positive strength. It is connected to old initiatory rites and mysteries of rebirth and rejuvenation.

INSPIRATION

On a dull winter's day when all colour is muted and vague, how energizing it is to come upon a vibrant holly tree whose dark green glossy leaves intensify the light, reflecting it outwards to make the tree appear enormously radiant. Often the blue of the sky itself is reflected from the holly's leaves and it appears as though a blue aura surrounds the tree. In days when holly was profuse, rather than the scattered bushes we have now, the sight of many holly trees heavily laden with scarlet fruit must have blown the visual senses away with its awesome riot of colour in the bleakness of winter. Thus, in the minds of the people and in Nature itself, holly comes strongly into focus in the midst of winter, when its contrasting red and green colours show vibrant life in a monochrome dormant world.

However, in certain versions of the systems associated with tree lore, the holly has been specifically placed at midsummer. Possibly such a placing was instigated to hide the real tradition, but most likely it arose from someone's mistake in piecing together an old system, a mistake which has been copied by unquestioning minds ever since. Yet Nature herself shows the prime position of holly within the year and we have always reacted to it at midwinter by bringing it into our homes.

'Mistakes' like the above may be passed off as having little relevance, but when you understand the subconscious effect that trees produce in humans, you realize that manipulation of the psychic systems (of which tree lore was the epitome) does have far-reaching effects. In the case in point, concentrating the attention on prickly holly in the middle of summer when everyone is already affected by the sun's 'prickly' heat, could lead to violent thoughts or actions, which even the tree's small white flowers could not lessen, for the mixture of the fiery martial energy of holly and the full force of solar energy is both volatile and dangerous. Given that our magical systems have been open to manipulation for century upon century, the chances that they haven't been used for control, manipulation and dark deeds are slim. Our work this lifetime includes looking into such matters and eradicating misuse. In this our template is the natural world itself, for it is through Nature that the original magical systems arose.

So let us look more closely through our ancestors' eyes at the holly in midwinter, remembering that the concepts of the god and goddess not only symbolize the male and female principles of life, but also their cycles throughout the year as they ebb and flow continuously and affect our life on earth. In the northern hemisphere, at the Winter Solstice, the shortest day, the sun is at its lowest point under the horizon, the point from whence it begins its yearly ascent. According to old traditions the sun-god has travelled through the Underworld since he gave his life to the crops the previous autumn and he is now 'reborn', the sun's appearance from under the horizon symbolizing his birth (from the earth-goddess). So his birth begins the new solar year and thereafter he enters the Land of Youth until he is strong enough to climb up into the heavens, from whence he will rule through his agent the sun. Yet at the moment of the Winter Solstice the sun-god is weak, like any other newborn, and he and the earth-goddess need a strong and protective guardian. What tree is a better guardian than the holly, whose prickly leaves form a barrier few would try to penetrate and whose berries send out a warning red light to those who would attempt to undermine it?

In the last chapter we realized the yew tree as a doorway through which life's energies entered the new solar year; now we can regard the holly as the guardian of life's energies once they have passed through. However after midwinter it is some weeks before the sun begins to shine with any significant warmth, and during this time it is likened to a tentative youngster, making small excursions into the sky and then rapidly scurrying for cover. These few weeks are those of anticipation. It is almost as if the world holds its breath as the bonding of the child and mother is realized. Then, given foundation, the seasons unfold. It is during the bonding period that the holly fulfils its most protective role, as guardian of the precious energies of the year. Then, as these energies gain strength, the guardianship is taken up by other trees. As the holly wanes in power, the power of the pine and hazel trees waxes, and they in turn protect and encourage their charges.

Thus we may perceive the holly tree as guardian of the most precious energies of the year, the energies of life in the midst of death, a perception which may be verified by the timings of the traditional Holly Night, the first-footer, and holly's Wildman origins, as discussed earlier.

One of our best known carols is 'The Holly and the Ivy', which has long been a traditional song of Christmas sung in churches throughout the land. Yet few people realize that it has its roots in paganism, for the holly and the ivy represent the male and female principles of life. These were traditionally celebrated at the four quarters of the year, namely midwinter, the Spring Equinox, midsummer and the Autumn Equinox.

At Yule it was the custom to dress a boy in the foliage of prickly holly and a girl in entwining ivy. Then, to lead the old solar year into the new, the holly-boy and ivy-girl paraded hand in hand throughout the community. This symbolized the god and goddess taking the evergreen quality of Nature through the darkest time of the year, encouraging the sun and the growth of vegetation. In some traditions the holly-boy and ivy-girl take part in competitive games, playing forfeits with the singing of songs.

Looked at another way, the spikiness of holly's leaves and the red of its berries symbolized the rays (the penis) and fiery heat of the sun-god, or the outward-seeking spirit of man, while the entwining habit of ivy represented the embracing female, the tenacious inner-seeking spirit of woman. Ivy also symbolizes the spiralling cycles of the moon, of which there are 12 and a bit to one solar cycle. Through its control upon the waters of earth and the menstrual flow of women and female animals, the moon ensures fertility and continuation in the cycles of all living things.

Thus the holly and the ivy represent the heavenly bodies and their cycles which are reflected upon earth, which in the minds of the people continued to touch the deeper concepts of pre-Christian celebration. 'Of all the trees that are in the wood, the holly bears the crown' reveals not only the importance of the tree, but also of the solar and lunar cycles and their reflection on earth. It also refers to the guardian qualities of holly, wherein it guides the precious energies of life. Royal work indeed!

PHYSICAL USES

Holly wood is ivory white and close-grained, and was prized in earlier days for its ability to take colour through staining, especially blue, green and red. When stained black it was styled the poor man's ebony. It was used extensively to inlay furniture with marquetry. The natural whiteness of the wood allowed it to be used for knife handles that resemble ivory. It was also traditionally valued for safeguarding door sills and handles.

A lot of the old customary uses of holly relied on there being a great number of holly trees around, which tells us how prolific they once were.

Holly wood burns very hot and this quality was used by smiths and weapon-makers. Holly was also used to make wooden spear shafts which gave balance and a good sense of direction. It is said that ancient chariot wheels contained holly wood, and it was used in much the same way in cart and coach wheels in later times, a practice which is continued by traditional craftsmen today.

Holly bark, with its delicate ashen hue, was once used to make bird lime, the terrible substance used by profiteering birdcatchers to trap unwary birds. At one time bird lime was made in great quantity in the north of England for export to the East Indies as an insect destroyer.

Rabbits love to eat holly bark and it can be used as a tonic for rabbits kept in hutches. If you gather it yourself, ensure that only a little bark is taken from each tree, and do *not* ring the tree (by removing bark all the way round) for it will die.

Holly leaves can be placed in the seed-drill in the garden after planting peas, to stop hungry mice.

Collars of holly were once placed around horses' necks to protect them from witches – though I should think that witches might be preferable to such prickly burdens!

Slender branches of holly were used by countrymen for walking sticks and coachman's whips. To make a holly walking stick, select a stout holly branch, cut it in March and peel it at once. Season it for six months (*as described in Ash, page 171*) and then boil linseed oil in a can and apply it with a cloth to polish the stick. A root of holly makes a wonderful handle, but if you gather one, loosen the earth round it gently and cause as little damage to the rest of the tree's roots as possible.

Holly makes brilliant hedges, for its prickles form a good solid barrier. It is slow to grow for its first five years but then grows more rapidly. With its beautiful appearance in all seasons it graces any garden, and can be easily clipped into shape. Birds eat holly berries and deer and sheep eat holly leaves in winter. Young stems of holly were once gathered, dried and used for cattle food, supposedly improving the taste of the milk.

THE PINE

BOTANICAL

SCOT'S PINE. *Pinus sylvestris*. Coniferous. Evergreen.

Conifers hold age records as one of the oldest plant families, for they are direct descendants of the primeval forests which flourished long before broadleaves. The Scot's pine is one of Britain's three native needle-leaved evergreens, along with juniper and yew. The silver fir was introduced from northern Europe in 1603.

Pine is a straight tall tree, reaching heights of 100 feet (30 metres) and girths of 10–15 feet (3–4½ metres), its size dependent on the condition of the soil in which it grows. Pine is easier to grow and transplant than any other cone-tree, growing 20 feet (6 metres) in 40 years. It reaches ages of 600 years. Its strong tap-root helps it withstand high winds, and its beautiful colouring is best seen amongst the heather and bracken of moor and highland. In naturally formed woodland, pine trees grow wide apart and let in light, creating atmospheric glades with magical depths.

Pine is thought to have been prevalent in the Boreal Period of coniferous vegetation when the glacial period ended (Boreas is the name of the north wind). It forms pairs of leaves and this distinguishes it from yew and spruce, which have leaves set singly in spirals on the branch, and from larch which has leaves in groups. The modern day Christmas tree is of the spruce family.

As pine saplings grow, their lower branches fall away to give rise to the characteristic straight trunk which is topped by a glorious crown of branches, needles and cones. If a pine tree is well situated in a bright open space it will begin reproduction after 20 years. If the tree is on damp ground or is hemmed in by others, it will not begin reproduction until it's 40 years old.

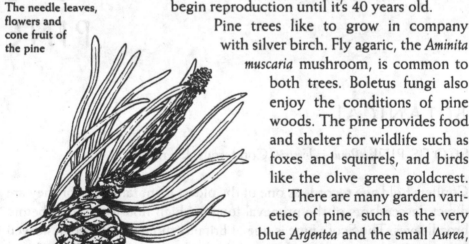

The needle leaves, flowers and cone fruit of the pine

Pine trees like to grow in company with silver birch. Fly agaric, the *Aminita muscaria* mushroom, is common to both trees. Boletus fungi also enjoy the conditions of pine woods. The pine provides food and shelter for wildlife such as foxes and squirrels, and birds like the olive green goldcrest. There are many garden varieties of pine, such as the very blue *Argentea* and the small *Aurea*, which turns a brilliant light gold in late winter. The Weymouth Pine, at Longleat House, Wiltshire, was brought by Viscount Weymouth from the New

England forest in the USA and planted by him in the eighteenth century.
Pine is common in Scotland, the Lake District, Cumberland and parts
of southern England. World-wide it grows from the Arctic Circle to the
Equator, accepting all rugged conditions.

BARK

Pine bark is a beautiful warm coppery-red in colour, particularly at the
top of the tree, where it is thin, smooth and shiny. At the base of the tree
it can become thick, dark and rough.

LEAVES

In the yearly growth of pine each new shoot is in the form of a vertical
'candle'. At the end of each twig grows a large resinous bud wrapped in
thin pinky-brown paper scales covered with whitish resin. In the spring
this bud lengthens and the brown scales peel off one by one to reveal
pairs of leaves, or needles, rising from an axis. Branches grow from buds
set in a circle below this.

Pine needles are stiff, flat on the top and circular below. They vary in
length from two to three and a half inches, and are formed in pairs with
their bases enclosed in a membranous sheath. They have a bluish bloom
which gives the tree a touch of mistiness when seen from a distance. This
coat of blue is formed by a layer of wax which grows over the natural
green foliage. The pine holds these leaves on the tree for three years and
then casts them off, still in pairs and held at the base by a scaly sheath.
New needles are bright green and turn steel blue in a season. That pine
has leaves in the form of needles enables the tree to conserve and limit its
water loss. This means that it is not reliant on moisture held in the soil
and can thus grow in sandy soils.

FLOWERS

In early spring the pine tree produces two kinds of single-sexed flowers.
The male flowers are soft yellow fluffy 'knobs', clustering around the base
of the season's new shoot of growth. Each flower is made up of a number
of stamens set in a spiral and each stamen has two overflowing pollen
sacs. The pollen of pine trees is extremely plentiful. In certain districts it

is called 'sulphur showers', for when released everything in the neighbourhood gets covered in yellow dust. Each grain of pollen has an air sac on each side to help keep it airborne. As soon as all the pollen is released by the male flowers they die away and fall off the tree.

The female flower is a tiny red bud-like object by the tip of the new spring shoot. It is made up of spirally arranged red fleshy scales, each with a sharp point. It is set on a pedestal and looks like a baby cone flanked by brown scales, tilting upwards so that pollen can slip between the scales to the ovules at their base. These ovules emit a mucilaginous substance which catches and draws down the pollen. The scales of the female flowers then thicken at their tips and join together, sealed by resin.

FRUIT

By next spring this little flower-cone is bigger and pendulous and stands some distance away from the tip of that year's newly grown shoot. Towards the end of its second summer, or even the spring after that, the cone scales crack open with the warmth of the air and little brown seeds are revealed. These seeds have a delicate wing, and when loosened by the wind they fall from the cone and are caught on the air. They spin away to their destined places, some quite near the parent tree and others long distances away.

Pine cones open and close as the weather changes from dry to wet, not in advance of the change. They open only when it is dry so the wind-borne seeds have a chance to scatter and not drop wet to the tree's base. In autumn the empty cones fall from the branches, some two and a half years old. Three generations of cone can be found on a pine tree at any given time, sometimes all on a single branch, where new cones, fertilized and sealed cones, and empty cones stand one behind the other.

In the north of Britain and Europe pine cones are known as 'deal-apples'.

CUSTOM & LEGEND

The lore associated with the pine tree is ancient, for the sanctity of trees and vines is far older in the history of man and religion than the veneration of cereals and crops. The old wandering nomadic tribes were hunter-gatherers and took from Nature what was there. The cultivation of grain belongs to a later period in civilization when settlements and agriculture began to develop.

To understand pine more fully we can look at its associations through world legend. In Greece the pine is intrinsically linked to the growing of vines and the production of wine, and so the gods associated with vines are also associated with pine trees. In Egypt, Osiris, the great god of Egyptian magic, was seen as a tree-spirit in his primitive character and was represented ceremonially by the cutting down and hollowing out of a pine tree. Then an image of Osiris was made with the excavated wood from the tree and inserted back into the hollow tree. This was kept for a year to watch over the vines, and was then burned and scattered on the earth in order to fructify it for the next season's crop.

Today there are few pine trees in Egypt, but the above legend tells us that they may have been more widely distributed in antiquity. Osiris originally taught men to train vines on poles and to extract the juice from the grape. His primitive character, felt to be embodied in a pine tree, also pointed to an alternative source of drink should the vines perish, for the resin of the Mediterranean pine itself is to this day a potent drink. Osiris also gave protection to fruit trees, for his mythical body was found by Isis within the conifer-like foliage of a fruiting Erica tree. Because of this his worshippers were forbidden to injure trees that bore fruit – the very origins of preventative ecology.

In Greek legend we are told how the pine became an evergreen. Rhea was the daughter of Uranus and Ge and the wife of Cronus. Under the name of Cybele her worship became wild, enthusiastic and orgiastic, and was closely connected to the frenzied worship of the vine-god Dionysus/Bacchus. She was loved by Atys, a Phrygian shepherd who vowed to be ever faithful to her. But he broke his vow and Cybele in anger changed him into a pine tree. Then, regretting her act, she wept beneath the branches. Zeus, her son, gave her comfort and promised that the pine would never lose its needles, so it would stay green all through the year as a constant companion.

Rhea's priests were the Corybantes, who performed orgiastic dances with drums, cymbals and horns in the forests on the mountains of Phyrgia.

The pine is dedicated to Dionysus/Bacchus and in most representations of these gods a pine cone, phallic symbol of the god's fecundity, tips their thyrsus or wand. The legendary associations between pines and vineyards are very dramatic, for Dionysus gave the first vine plant to Oeneus, but the knowledge of making the first wine from the grapes he gave to Icarius. After Icarius had made wine, he gave some of his trial jarful to a party of shepherds in the Marathonian Woods, beneath Mount Pentelicon. The shepherds drank the draught neat and became so drunk that they saw everything double. Thinking they had either been poisoned or bewitched by Icarius, they killed him and buried him under a pine tree. However his faithful dog Maera saw the act, ran to fetch Erigone, Icarius's daughter, and led her to the grave beneath the pine tree, whereupon it dug up the corpse. On seeing her dead father Erigone in despair hanged herself from the pine, praying to the gods as she did that all the daughters of Athens should do likewise until Icarius's death was avenged.

As Icarius seems to have been the mortal heir to Dionysus's cult of ecstasy, his death greatly disturbed the antique world and although only the gods had heard Erigone's prayer, nevertheless maidens were found hanging from one pine after another. This continued until finally the Delphic Oracle was consulted and it was explained that the only way to end the innocent deaths of the maidens was to find and hang the guilty shepherds, who had fled overseas. This was done and in celebration a vintage festival was instituted which still continues to this day. At this, libations are poured to Icarius and Erigone, and young girls swing from ropes tied to trees, their feet on small platforms of wood. Masks of Dionysus were once also hung on the branches of pine trees in the middle of the vineyards in memory of the hanged maidens and when they turned in the wind they were thought to fructify the vines wherever they faced. This legend was regarded as so important by the ancient Greeks that the image of Icarius's dog Maera was set into the sky to become the lesser Dog Star. Icarius became identified with Boötes and Erigone with the constellation of the Virgin. Similar attributes linking Virgo with ecstasy are to be found in the South Americas, where *mama coca* is said to come from Spica, a first magnitude star in that constellation.

The Greek goddess associated with pine is Pitthea. The god is Pittheus, whose daughter Aethra bore Theseus. Theseus claimed his royalty by moving a huge stone, the Rock of Theseus, in order to reach a sword and sandals, the ancient symbols of royalty. The drawing of the sword from the stone was also part of the Bronze Age coronation ritual performed by such legendary heroes as Odin, Galahad and Arthur. As well as attributing pine with specific royal associations, the ancient Greeks gave crowns of pine to winners in the Isthmian Games.

In Europe druids burned great fires of pine at the Winter Solstice to draw back the sun and this practice became the custom of burning the Yule log. Living glades of pine were also decorated with lights and shiny objects at Yule, which echoes the Icelandic myth described in Rowan (*see p.228*), when the divine light is represented by a tree covered in stars. In later years this tradition became that of the Christmas tree, which is brought into the house rather than being decorated and celebrated outside.

In many traditions pines and firs are associated with birth. Storks have always chosen such trees for their breeding nests and throughout the world legends tell us that storks carry the newborn to its parents. Pine's associations with birth and children does a lot to ease its somewhat dramatic reputation.

The Scot's pine is prolific in Britain. It is unique in that it is the sole northern European pine to have survived the Ice Age. However our great pine forests of yesteryear are but a memory, for man has taken heavily for his needs. The best of those which remain are to be found in Scotland, where the Black Wood of Loch Rannoch is but a remnant of the Great Caledonian Forest which grew out of the Ice Age. The wood is on high moorland and until the eighteenth century was home to wolves. Still within memory are its former animals – wild boar, bears, elks and lynx. The wild-cats still survive. This great wood reputedly covered more than 3,000 acres (1,215 hectares) and it's believed that devastation was forced upon it by the Vikings, who felled the great trees in order to carve dragonhead prows for their longships. It is also thought that the Vikings ate the fly agaric mushroom before roaring into battle. As with all woodland, once the trees are felled the wildlife disappears.

The Gaelic name for pine is *gius* and from this derives place-names like Dalguise and Kingussie. Goose Island, *Lough Derg*, is believed to have originally been the isle of pines, not geese.

Before land clearances the Scot's pine grew wild and abundant in England. James I, the first king of England and Scotland, planted many pine seeds in order to revive this when he took over his new kingdom.

HEALING

Pine has always been recognized as a powerful bronchial disinfectant. The Ebers papyrus of Egypt show that in early times the doctors of the Pharoahs prescribed from the pine tree, using pitch and turpentine resin to treat pneumonia and lung problems. It is very effective when used as an inhalant to ease respirational problems, for it specifically soothes irritations of the mucous membranes.

Pine also has uses as an antiseptic, an expectorant, a stimulant and a tonic, and it aids in the treatment of bladder and kidney problems. It has also been used as a treatment for gout and as a preparation to cure skin diseases.

BUDS
The buds can be made into a decoction (*see Appendix V, p.343*) and used in drinks and inhalants to ease bronchial infections, cystitis and rheumatic ailments. They are picked in spring before they open and are dried in the shade. A syrup made from pine buds is an excellent bronchial tonic.

CONES & NEEDLES

Pine cones and needles are used in decoction, and are added to bathing water to ease breathlessness, rheumatics and skin diseases. They are picked when green and fresh. Pine needles boiled in vinegar were once reputed to relieve toothache when packed around the tooth or when the liquid was swilled around the mouth. They were also used to heal 'green' wounds.

The Bach Flower Remedies recommend pine to treat despondency and despair, and for ridding yourself of feelings of self-condemnation, guilt, extreme sensitivity, self-blame and over-conscientiousness.

On emotional levels pine gives us the quality of 'not dwelling upon mistakes made' and it helps us to persevere with humility, which is known in some traditions as the 'way of the warrior'. All our discontent with ourselves can be overcome by working with, meditating upon or using treatments of pine, for it gives us the ability to work with what we are and not feel a lack of confidence.

MAGIC

IRISH/GAELIC NAME	*Ailim*
OGHAM	+
RUNIC	∧
RULING PLANET	Mars
ABILITIES	Foresight. Long sight. Purification. Births. Incense. To do with the element of Air.
SEASONS	Winter, Spring

The resin of the pine tree, collected from cuts in its trunk which ooze the gummy substance, can be used as an incense gum which when burnt clears a place of negative energies. It can also be used as a 'counter-magic' incense, for it repels evil or spells cast against us by returning them to source.

To purify and cleanse living spaces during the winter months, when people can feel trapped within their homes by the weather, pine needles can be burned and carried around the house or room so that the smoke permeates the place. Any specific areas of negativity, say, a room where you've had a row or where things go continually wrong, can be cleared by burning pine needles or by scattering them on the floor. Pine needles can also be added to the burning of the resin gum of the tree, as explained above.

To clear ourselves of negativity, our dark moods, grumpiness, black clouds, self-blame, guilt, etc., pine needles or oil of pine can be added to our bathing water. As we soak, we can then concentrate on allowing negativity to float out of us into the water. Each dark thought, each ache or tension, each pain or discontent can be mentally pushed to the surface of our body and can be seen to flow out from us into the water, and thus, when the plug is pulled, down the drain. This is the principle behind magical cleansing baths. Once cleansed we gain the chance to fill ourselves with positive thoughts, visions and actions. In this way we can turn ourselves into positive beings. The universe will then respond to us in positive ways, for in the world of magic like attracts like.

Pine cones were once regarded as 'tree eggs' and as they grow in a sunwise-turning spiral, i.e., to the right, they form good magical conducers. This is why they were traditionally used to tip the god's thyrsus in fertility rites. The fact that they are also phallic in appearance, especially when tipping a wand, gave added impetus to the fertility of the rite. Such wands are still used in Wiccan rites today. Pine cones were often carried to increase a person's fertility and were also believed to give old people more vigour. Through such use, the energy of pine's ruling planet, Mars, is transformed into activity and sexual transformation, rather than into martial dominance and war-like activities.

The winter months have always been regarded as powerful times for evergreens. Pine's influence is found throughout this time, but it is at its most powerful after the Winter Solstice, when the solar energies begin to grow and spring and the season of birth seem just around the corner. Then the pine seems to guide the first creative energies of the new solar year to where the process of life on earth awaits ignition. It stands sentinel as the energies of the year move forward to the birthing season of spring, when Nature's clock starts ticking again. And as it does, so other signs of life appear in the hedgerows, like the delicate snowdrops and hazel catkins.

As spring moves into early summer, the pines shed clouds of pollen-dust into the air, often creating thick floating hazes on sunny days. In ancient days this dust was collected by druids for magical and theatrical purposes, as was yew pollen (*see p.28*).

Pine pollen was also used in money spells, for its yellow colour was believed to attract gold. Sawdust of pine wood can be used as a base for any incenses used in money rituals.

Pine branches and sprays have always been used for protection, for when placed at doors and windows they were thought to keep out evil. When placed above a sick person's bed, pine branches aid their recovery.

In hot vine-growing climates the pine was honoured at the harvest festivals when the sun was waning. At this time of year the ripe cones and seeds that fall from pine trees give the onlooker assurance that all cycles are continuous.

Pine is represented by the ogham *Ailim* and its powerful position in the year, as winter moves towards spring, allows us to utilize our fore-sight and set ourselves on the right course of action for achievement in the coming year. The quality of foresight associated with pine is empha-sized by the great height of the tree and the fact that if you climbed a pine you would see great distances in every direction.

The deities associated with pine trees are Osiris, Cybele, Dionysus/ Bacchus, Erigone, Icarius, Pitthea and Pittheus.

Pine is used for healing, fertility, exorcism, protection, purification and money spells.

INSPIRATION

In order to set the scene and touch the inspirational qualities of pine, we can use the words of two major bards of Britain. William Wordsworth said of pines:

My thoughts become bright like yon edging of pines
On the steep's lofty verge, how it blackened the air!
But touched from behind by the sun, it now shines,
With threads that seem part of His own silver hair.

William Shakespeare, describing the curious and beautiful effect as the sun rises behind distant ridges of pine, turning them to silver, then into a 'burning fringe before the sun', put it more succinctly:

When from under this terrestrial ball,
He fires the proud tops of the pines.

A natural pine wood is a place of intoxication, as heavy resin-scented air creates a magical stillness, evoking visions of prehistoric beasts stalking midst ancient red boles and steely blue needles. The dense shade created by pine canopies keeps undergrowth sparse, but the soil underfoot is rich with fallen cones and needles, and often scattered with red-capped mushrooms which add splashes of brilliant colour. Squirrels and birds such as the cross-bill make their homes in pine woods and their presence is shown by the abundant litter of dislocated cones beneath the trees, dropped from branches far above after the seeds have been eaten from them.

A natural pine wood grows to Nature's plan, forming where the wind and birds have carried the seeds. It is very different from a man-made plantation, and this is felt in the atmosphere of the place, the way the light expresses itself and the feelings given off by the trees. The reactions of the needles and cones to the chemicals of the soil are also important, for they are reflected in the health and number of animals, insects, birds and flowers that are native to that area. Pines planted in areas not conducive to such chemical reactions do little to aid the flora and fauna. Many plantations of pine are dark eerie places, devoid of life. Trees are planted in neat sterile rows, unnaturally planted and not in their place of natural seeding, not in their place of power!

Every living thing without exception has its place of power. Such a place is where you personally touch and feel a positive energy, a place where you are clear and strong and feel vibrantly alive. Being there allows your energies to balance and your senses to find healthy expression. The imaginatively provoking books of Carlos Castaneda describe how the Native American shamen recognize and sympathetically utilize places of power in the natural world. Such places, invariably found near large stones, rocks, streams, springs or trees, are critically necessary to the healthy functioning of life in the natural world. They are in fact only recognized by humans through an intense understanding of that world.

Thus, in a plantation of pine forced to grow on the wrong spot, it is possible to hear and feel the misery of the trees. We can sense their loneliness and apathy, and their seeming ability to know that they are being used as products of man's needs, merely fulfilling his money-chain. We cannot wonder at the gloom of such places. Yet to step into a natural pine wood is to step into a place of magic, still dark and maybe eerie in places, but containing mystery as opposed to apathy. It contains a positive energy, and its smell is of life and health, for it is founded upon natural positioning, upon the place which provides for the healthy functioning of all forms of life necessary to that locale.

The richness of pine's colouring and its proud poise set it apart from any other tree, and it is always expressive, no matter how grey the day. The bark is a rich earthy red, giving the tree a glow of warmth, and it flakes off the tree like butterfly wings in hues of salmon pink and green. Pine needles are also provocative and to handle a resinous spray of pine intoxicates the senses. When you do so, look within the needles and find the small unripe cones which are formed in a clockwise spiral pattern, following the earth's movement round the sun. See the delicacy and miracle of the small jade-coloured seeds, which hold within them the genus that may become a pine tree some 100 feet (30 metres) or more in height. Atop the giant trunks the canopies of blue-green needles reach into the sky, giving the trees the appearance from a distance of gnarled craggy beings, for, like the oak, the pine has a courageous quality which suits its wild surroundings. The pine is at its most majestic standing proud against the lochs and glens of the Highlands.

In 1987 terrible storms raged over Britain, causing chaos to people and trees alike. In the first of these storms the tops of all the trees were ripped off and they ended up looking like they'd received very brusque haircuts. Though dramatic, this seemed fairly easy to recover from. However a few months later a gigantic storm arose, and any tree not of full strength, any tree with a weakness, as well as many healthy ones, fell in the face of the wildest elemental disturbance for many, many years. Countless trees were ripped from the earth or had limbs torn away, and the screams of their breaking branches and trunks joined that of the wind, adding to a nightmare of devastation.

Many people's lives were changed by that storm, for it rained havoc, and the loss of so many trees brought home to a lot of people just how precious are those that remain. Walking in Nature after that was a sad affair, midst the fallen, lying, roots exposed, like stricken sentinels, and even though pine trees set good long tap-roots they suffered quite badly in the storm. I'll recount an experience with some fallen pines, for part of me still feels unease at its memory.

Rambling with friends through a forest one afternoon, we came across what seemed like hundreds of pine trees which had been hit by the storm, their exposed root-balls scrawling from giant eruptions of earth which had given way during their devastating demise. The atmosphere above and around these trees was awful, and even though many months had passed since they'd fallen to the storm, their state of shock still filled the air. The whole thing looked like a massacre, as chasms and eruptions of earth exposed dead tree roots. Still-rooted trees that had snapped off in the winds reared their broken trunks, cutting the air with painfully jagged and splintered tops. All I could think of was an elephants' grave-yard, where large bodies are left to rot and disarticulate, their bones and broken tusks screaming to the sky.

Needless to say, we could not enter this area of devastation, but on returning home later that moonless night the blackness of the forest was disorientating and suddenly, unknowingly, we found ourselves within the mass of fallen trees. To my left someone stumbled into a crater, another person to my right walked into a fallen tree trunk and I found myself scrambling up what, to my horror, I realized was the huge root-ball of a fallen pine. Given that no one could see a thing, the only safe way to earth was to slide down through the roots, but on doing this in the utter darkness my nerve was sorely tested, for through my thin dress the pine roots seemed to grab and slither and hold. And yet the greatest unease of that moment came from the screeching echoes and vivid memories that those roots still contained, for they gripped me with the terror of their uprooting. The devastated, shrieking energy we had so carefully bypassed earlier that day now came full force through those roots. 'This,' they said, 'is the other side of the story, just as necessary to tell as the one that sparkles with light. This is the culmination of a chain of events that must be seen, for trees suffer now but next in line are humans. We are your closest allies and we die and suffer from your ignorance of our world, your world. Do not let our deaths be in vain. Show man the devastation he has created from the world. Do not allow ignorance to flourish. For when we are gone you will have nothing. You will not survive.'

These words may sound over-dramatic, but of all the trees native to our land the pine is the oldest species, having flourished here well before the Great Ice Age. Having watched man from his infancy and having seen him pollute and violate the earth with mistake upon mistake, so that global warming, holes in the ozone layer, deforestation, etc., etc. create natural disasters such as the storm described, I do not doubt the pine's message. Without global ecology there may soon be no more planet.

PHYSICAL USES

Many products are collected from pine. Its resin was once used for sealing-wax and to improve violin bows by adding resonance to their sound. It was used to coat the insides of beer casks and was known as 'brewer's pitch'. It also forms the 'pitch' used medicinally by veterinarians, who use oil or tar of pine as an antiseptic. Pine resin has always been used as pitch to seal boats and is reckoned to give them magical protection. In the Mediterranean the resin of the sabina pine gives distinctive flavour to the popular retsina wines.

Pine trees have good trunks which produce quick-growing wood.

When sawn, pine timber is yellowish in colour and is fairly soft and slightly resinous. In the past it was mainly used for pit props and rough building work, and in more modern times for railway sleepers and telegraph poles.

The best pine building timbers are imported from Europe and Russia and are named red or yellow deal. The wood from the north is much harder and of much more value than the softwood from the south, which is mainly used for rough timber and firewood.

Commercially grown pine trees are ready for felling between 70 to 100 years, but are best if left longer. Pine is best, like all trees, if allowed to live.

THE
HAZEL

BOTANICAL

HAZEL. *Corylus avellana*. Deciduous.

While hazel is usually a large shrub, it can grow to the size of a small tree. On the Duke of Northumberland's estate at Syon House, Middlesex, a hazel is recorded to have grown 60 feet (18 metres) high, but their average height is 12–20 feet (3½–6 metres). Hazel is plentiful in copses, oak woods and hedgerows.

The hazel is common throughout most of Britain, Europe, America, Africa, Turkey and western Asia. It thrives in damp places near ponds or streams, though it fruits better if the land has drainage. It has various species to its family.

BARK
The bark of the hazel is smooth and light brown in colour. It is speckled with lighter brown lenticels, the pores of the tree, where the cells of the bark are drawn apart to let air pass to the inner tissue, allowing the tree to breathe. Hazel has always been extensively coppiced by man (*see pp.327–8*), for its smooth reddish-brown stems have great toughness and elasticity, qualities which have many uses.

LEAVES
Hazel leaves open in early spring. They are a beautiful lime green in colour, grow singly on the branches and are a pointed oval, slightly heart-shaped and asymmetrical. They are toothed at the edges and vary in length from 2 to 4 inches

The leaves, flower catkins and nut fruit of the hazel

(5 to 10 cm). They turn from their summer colour of mid-green to greeny-browns and pinks in the autumn. They stay on the tree longer than most species, quite often well into December, by which time they have turned yellow.

FLOWERS
The hazel brings us a whisper of coming spring, often as early as January. Then its male catkins leave behind their stiff winter brownness as they grow and fill with pollen, becoming like tassels of gold which hang vividly against the dark bareness of the winter branches. These male catkins, called 'lamb's tails' by country folk, shed their pollen to

the wind long before the first appearance of leaf and flower on the land, save perhaps the snowdrop.

The female flowers are small, like stalkless buds. They stand upright with red styles which look like small crimson brushes. These threadlike styles catch the pollen shed from the male catkins and carry it to the seeds, which are hidden inside scaly covered bracts. As spring advances the crimson styles disappear and the seeds inside the bracts begin to grow, forming into hard green nuts which turn brown by autumn.

Once the hazel's pollination is complete, the male catkins fade, their work done. Now other trees and plants begin to come alive, their swelling buds visibly unfurling into flower and leaf to bring colour to the land.

FRUIT

The hazelnuts are ripe by September and can be eaten straight from the tree. The shape of the leafy frills around them distinguishes the hazel species. These frills are formed from the small scales at the base of each ovary, which develop into the ragged-looking leafy wrappings which hold the nuts. The Latin name *Corylus* was given to the tree because this leafy wrapping resembled a style of helmet called *Korys*. The tree became known as 'the helmeted one'.

Hazelnuts provide food for many small animals such as squirrels and dormice. Common birds around hazel trees at nutting time are nuthatches. These birds take nuts to convenient crevices, like deeply fissured oak bark, wedge them in and proceed to hammer away at them with their beaks until the shells crack and they reach the kernels. The woods in autumn are full of the sounds of such activity.

If any hazelnuts fall to the ground and are left to germinate, when winter has passed the shell splits and out of the tip comes the first root. The stem follows, and the root and stem form into a straight line, joined to the nut and sustenance by two thick white fibres. When the root has established itself within the earth, the stem rises and a young hazel sapling is born. Hazelnuts keep for thousands of years in petrified form and many (hard and black as jet) are found in ancient bogland.

CUSTOM & LEGEND

The hazel was anciently regarded as the Celtic tree of knowledge and its nuts were believed to be the ultimate receptacles of wisdom. Thus it is intrinsically woven into the very fabric and foundation of the Celtic culture and nation.

The most prolific legends concerning hazel come from Ireland and we look to that Emerald Isle for the greatest understanding of the tree. In Keating's *History of Ireland* we are told of a king named Mac Coll, meaning 'Son of Hazel', who was one of the three earliest rulers in Ireland. Mac Coll was one of the last of the kings of the Tuatha de Danaan. The hazel tree from which he took his name and power was specifically associated with wisdom. In the *Triads of Ireland* it is recorded that Coll (hazel) and Quert (apple) were the only two sacred trees whose wanton felling carried the death penalty. In the *Dinnshenchas*, an early topographical treatise of Ireland, the hazel and apple are associated with oak, for the Great Tree of Mugna is recorded as containing within itself the virtues of apple, hazel and oak.

Man's ancient use of the combinations of different trees, mixing their energies and qualities in order to obtain specific results, is shown in many excavations, especially those of burial mounds. From such a mound in Tresse, Brittany, charcoal of willow, hazel and oak was recovered in quantities enough to suggest that they had constituted the funerary pyre. One possible theory of their use is that they brought the qualities of enchantment, wisdom and royalty (respectively) to the funerary proceedings. In which case the Great Tree of Mugna may well have represented beauty, wisdom and strength.

Also recorded in the Irish treatise is a description of Connla's Well: 'a beautiful fountain, over which nine hazels of poetic art produced flowers and fruit [beauty and wisdom] simultaneously'. And we are told that as the nuts dropped from the trees into the water, so the salmon which lived in the well ate them, and whatever number of nuts the salmon swallowed, that many bright spots appeared on its body.

Other druidic legends concerning Connla's Well describe it as being under the sea and the source of the River Shannon, and tell us of the salmon of wisdom. This father of all salmon, when first going to the sea, was drawn to the magical well and his journeyings thence instilled in all future salmon their migratory genes. On reaching the well the salmon was given the great gift of wisdom by the well's guardians, for each of the nine hazel trees dropped a sacred hazelnut into the water. On swallowing these nuts the salmon became the recipient of all knowledge.

The sacred hazelnut was so highly esteemed that it was called the food of the gods. That people desired to eat it, together with its mythical recipient the sacred salmon, is also apparent from old lore. Druidic legend tells of Fionn, a pupil of a chief druid who lived on the River Boyne. The druid master intended to eat the salmon of knowledge which he had caught in a deep pool, for its flesh, it was said, 'would make him conscious of everything that was happening in Ireland'. Young Fionn was told to cook the salmon for his master, but not to taste it. Yet while he cooked the fish a blister appeared on its side and Fionn used his thumb to burst it. Having burnt his thumb, he automatically put it into his mouth for relief. Thus it was Fionn who received the salmon's gift of farsight, 'seeing all that was happening in the High Courts of Tara'. This story has a Welsh equivalent in the legend of Cerridwen and Gwion.

In Scottish legend there was a pair of mystical fishes which were regarded as the presiding spirits of a similar sacred well and its hazel tree guardians. These fish were holy and to kill or eat them was a grievous crime punishable by the gods themselves.

The atmosphere around a hazel tree is easily recognizable, for it is quick-moving and mercurial, like silvery fish. In south-west Britain country people say that 'silver snakes' surround the hazel's roots, which illustrates the swiftness of its energies. To understand this energy better we can look at the associations of hazel and the god Mercury, for the hazelnut was especially sacred to him and is still held to be under the influence of the planet Mercury.

Mercury, or Mercurius, is often given the same attributes as the Greek god Hermes, and they both have three extra articles which aid their speed, namely a travelling hat, a staff and a pair of sandals. The hat has a broad rim, which is often replaced by wings, and the sandals, which carry the god across land or sea with the rapidity of the wind, also provide wings at his ankles. The staff is sometimes depicted with two ribbons attached to it, which show the speed of travel as they flow through the air. Often these ribbons form into snakes intertwining along the staff, becoming the caduceus symbol of the healing arts used by healers and physicians to this day. Mercurius and Hermes were heralds of the gods, and they gave the qualities of eloquence, heraldry, inventiveness and cunning to the lives of men. They taught the arts of cultivation and flying, and were regarded as gods of the roads who offered protection to travellers.

Thus the spirit of the hazel is strongly aligned to speed through the air as well as through water, and in its legendary links with the sacred salmon we see possibly the birth of both these elemental associations, for salmon swim exceedingly fast in water and then leave the waters in mighty leaps, appearing to fly through the air.

The shoots and twigs of hazel have the power to show where water is and have been used throughout time for dowsing. Cornish people still use hazel to dowse for mineral veins as well as for water, though they stress that they do not have success without help from the piskies (Cornish faeries). Before the seventeenth century hazel rods were used to discover the whereabouts of thieves, murderers and treasure, and in France they were used for beating the bounds, i.e., boundaries of a community, so they did not fall into neglect.

In Wales supple hazel twigs were woven into 'wishing-caps' which granted the desire of the wearer. Hazel hats were also used by sailors when they had to weather hard storms at sea, for it was believed that they gained magical protection from them. Pilgrims' staffs were made from hazel and so attached did the owners become to them that they were buried alongside them after death.

In ancient days hazel was plentiful in Scotland, for the name Caledonia comes from *Cal Dun*, which means 'Hill of Hazel'. Also possibly born in that land was the Hallowe'en love divination of naming two hazelnuts with the names of lovers and placing them in the hot embers of a fire. If the nuts burn quietly side by side the lovers are faithful, but if one nut moves away the pairing is viewed as ill-matched, for one of the lovers is faithless. Aengus, the Celtic god of love, carried a hazel wand.

In Anglo-Saxon England swineherds used 'haesel' rods to control their animals, and it is thought that the name passed from the rod to the tree and it became known as hazel, rather than Cal or Coll. Haslemere in Surrey is a very evocative place-name, linking both *hasle*, 'hazel', and *mere*, 'a pool' or 'the sea'. This implies a connection between hazel and the creatures of the deep sea, which emphasizes the druidic associations of hazel and the salmon. No doubt Haslemere was named for its inspirational atmosphere, for many well known artists and poets have chosen to live and work there. The area also has strong associations with musical families and great recitals were played on antique instruments – very much the creative hazel energy, fully captured in an ancient place-name.

HEALING

As the tree of immortality hazel was especially revered, and because its nuts were believed to contain all wisdom they were in themselves talismans for a healthy life. Hazel was esteemed as a plant of great virtue, said to have the power to cure fevers, diarrhoea and excessive menstrual flow. But despite all this, specific healing uses of the hazel are few.

An old country charm to prevent toothache was to carry a double hazelnut in the pocket, and a cross fashioned from hazel wood and laid on a snake-bite was an ancient remedy to draw out the poison.

The kernels of the hazelnut, mixed with mead or honeyed water, are good for coughs which will not clear. Mixed with pepper in decoction they clear the head.

The greatest healing provided by hazel is found within its atmosphere. Being near hazel trees or meditating upon a piece of hazel brings the spirit alive and allows us to quickly cast off the old and move on to the new. Hazel's atmosphere exudes exhilaration and inspiration.

MAGIC

IRISH/GAELIC	Coll
OGHAM	▤
RUNIC	⟨
RULING PLANET	Mercury (nuts); Sun (plant)
ABILITIES	Intuition. Divination. Dowsing. Wands. Individuality. The power to find that which is hidden. To do with the element of Air.
SEASONS	Spring (Imbolc); Autumn

Hazel has always been regarded as magical for its presence inspires our intuitional senses. It was called the 'poet's tree', for in the minds of the ancients it had great associations with faerie lore and supposedly allowed entrance into such realms. Presumably this was achieved by sitting under a hazel tree at a propitious spot and going into trance. We can glean the correct atmosphere for this from a seventeenth-century recipe, which reputedly gives the power to see faeries by anointing the body and/or ingesting the following concoction:

First pick wild thyme from the side of a hill where the fairies still live. Take a pint [½ litre] of sallet oyle [salad oil] and mix it with rose and marigold water, the flowers of which should be picked in the east. Shake or stir the oyle until it becomes white and then put it into a glass vial, adding buds of hollyhocks, flowers of marigold, the flowers from the wild thyme and the buds of young hazels. Then add the grasse of a fairy throne [a suitable grass tussock], and allow them to dissolve for three days in the sun.

This mixture is then stored and used when needed.

Shakespeare also associates hazels with faerie lore when he portrays the Queen of the Faeries riding in her chariot, for:

> Her chariot is an empty hazelnut,
> Made by the joiner squirrel, or old grub,
> Time out of mind the fairies' coach-makers.

Druids carried rods made from hazel, for when in contact with the mecurial energy of the tree, poetic and magical inspiration was gained. Hazel rods were also used to divine suitable places for magical workings, and when a chief druid raised such a rod during vital ceremonies and debates, all chatter and unnecessary argument ceased and continuity was achieved. It is quite possible that hazel rods were also used as 'talking-sticks', the holder of the stick being the only person allowed to speak during communal meetings.

Under certain conditions druids used hazel to invoke invisibility. In the Book of St Albans we are told that it is possible to become invisible 'as if we had eaten fern-seed' by 'carrying a hazel rod a fathom and a half [2 metres] long, and by inserting a green hazel twig into it in a particular manner'. As with all these old recipes, altered states of consciousness induced by psychotropic substances in Nature often prompted the senses to attain the desired result.

The strong chieftain qualities of the hazel were recognized in ancient days and the severest penalties were laid upon those who harmed hazel trees. An old method of cutting a hazel wand is to find a tree which has not yet borne fruit and, with a single stroke of a magical sickle, cut a branch at sunrise on a day ruled by Mercury, i.e., a Wednesday. This method also unfortunately states that the sickle is made 'magical' by using a formula containing magpies' blood! However, hazel walking sticks need no blood to make them magical, and they are cut and prepared in the same way as ash (see p.170).

The hazel is powerful in early spring when its energy and sap are surging outward, and in autumn, when its energy is contained within its harvest of magical nuts. Such timings should be noted when cutting wands or staffs, for the sun rules the plant and Mercury rules its fruit. Traditionally hazel twigs and forks for divining should be cut on Midsummer's Eve in order for them to be at their most powerful, although other times of the year will suffice. A good divining rod is said to 'squeal like a pig' when held in water, and its energy completely dominates that of the dowser. In other words it 'kicks back'.

Hazel can be used at all times for protection. Its ruling planets, the sun and Mercury, make it a brilliant healing plant and if hazelnuts are used the healing will be extra rapid. Hazel has great affinity with water, but its ruling element is air, through which the greatest movement and speed can be achieved. The air surrounding hazel trees is always magical.

The deities associated with hazel are Mercury, Hermes, Thor, Mac Coll and Aengus. The hazel is very much a 'masculine' tree.

Hazel is used for luck, fertility, protection and wishes.

INSPIRATION

As shown by its legends and by its preference for growing in damp places, hazel is strongly associated with the qualities of water. These include its fast-flowing energies, such as in rivers or streams, its tidal energies, as of the sea, and its reflective, visionary energies, found on ponds, pools, wells, etc. Thus on many levels hazel has great association with the moon, controller of the tides on earth.

The epitome of hazel energy, the movement and the emotion and the visuals, is in the magical salmon, the 'flying-fish' which leaps from the water in pure exhilaration, like flashing quicksilver. Ancient druids observed Nature closely and such association was exemplified in their teachings and legends. As the salmon acquired mystical knowledge through eating hazelnuts, the salmon and hazel energies became woven together into an exceptionally strong magical formula which was strengthened every time the legends and teachings were told. To the British and Irish Celts the sacred salmon was known as *Eo Feasa* and it was sought anxiously, for to partake of its flesh, as already mentioned, was to acquire universal wisdom and be close to the gods.

However there was more to the druidic understanding of the salmon than this, for it was seen to reflect humanity in its cycles and gave great examples of the perfection of druidic values. The salmon is known to wander the seas upon its ancestral journeys for two years after its birth, and then to retrace its path back upriver to its birthplace in order to spawn and reproduce. In returning to its origins it takes no easy course, for it must swim back against the tides and flow of the waters. At times, to gain obstacles such as weirs or waterfalls, it leaves the water completely and jumps through the air almost as if it were flying. At other times it crawls through the mud of dried-up streams or rivers until it reaches its destination, its birthplace, the spawning-pool anciently known as the sacred Pool of Rebirth.

Modern research has followed the salmon's journey, explaining factually what was seen in ancient days. Through this it has been discovered that in every stream or river there is a small channel of water which flows contra to the main flow, a sort of tunnel which goes in the opposite direction. The salmon is clever enough to find this channel and uses it to advantage when it retraces its route. However, for many reasons, the ancient druids saw the salmon's expertise as a magical feat and the fact that it set itself apart from the masses by moving upstream when all else flowed the other way was deemed the reason why it was given the great gift of wisdom. This point had deep relevance for the druids, for they saw it as being symbolic of specific individuals who are set apart from the mass, those who are touched by the Spirit and must follow its calling. To such people moving from the collective human 'family' is no easy task, for within the mass is found security and protection, a point which was realized far more in ancient times when the land was beset with dangers. A certain strength is needed to overcome such trials and this is comparable to the strength of the salmon, for like the salmon we too can travel the paths of our ancestors to reach the fertile waters of our own 'sacred pool'.

We have already looked at the hazel when its catkins bring life to the wintry hedgerows and now we can look at its other powerful time, when its harvest of nuts ripen on the trees. Autumn is the nutting season when branches bend under the weight of the tree's bounty. It is a time of fruition, when crops ripen and feeding creatures gather and store in preparation for the coming cold season. At this time the salmon is also ripe, having returned from the oceans to its native pool. Throughout the summer it made its homeward journey in order to spawn and during its journey it did not eat, but rather drew its energy inwards into its eggs, with which to ensure a future for the species. This is brilliantly described in a book on the life of a salmon written by Henry Williamson. *Salar the*

Salmon is highly recommended, for it is truly evocative, showing the beauty and reality of the natural world and its creatures, and how such things change through the forcefulness of man.

In druidic legend the salmon and hazel meet in autumn when their seeds (the salmon's eggs and the hazel's nuts) are ready for germination and growth as individuals. This timing was emphasized in the recounting of legends and teachings, for it reiterated the continual replenishing of life through birth. When told in the autumn of the year such legends empowered people for winter survival, for they opened certain percep-tory doorways through which knowledge was assimilated, allowing for the growth of creative energy throughout the winter months and creative manifestation by springtime.

However, in order that the inner secrets of the magical systems were never touched by the profane, druidic teachings also tell us how the hazel could transform itself for defence, for if necessary it became gnarled and leafless, dripping poisonous milk. As such it was known as the 'dripping hazel' and was home to vultures and ravens. In this context, on a druidic initiatory level, those who attempted to enter the highest magical realms, if they had not truth within their hearts would face such a guardian, which no doubt fed upon the bones of profanity!

Now we leave the waters to look at the associations of hazel and the element of air. As well as being ruled by the sun, hazel is also under the planetary influence of Mercury. This is extremely obvious to those who perceive its fast-moving, quicksilver energy. In most representations of the god Mercury, he has a hazel wand which is sometimes entwined with serpents. This wand symbolizes the qualities of divination, communication and healing. As messenger of the gods, Mercury's winged shoes or hat emphasize his fleetness and today such quick-moving associations can provide great impetus when hazel is used for healing or magical purposes. Yet to some this extra 'push' may be too much to handle and if you're not prepared to have your eyes opened quickly, steer clear of using hazel, for the answers to big emotive questions can become very dramatic. Use instead a slower, earthier tree such as apple or oak.

The capacity some trees have to move you, emotionally, psychically and mentally, can be very strong. To cope with this is not easy, for the 'leaps and bounds' that are sometimes triggered off in us by Nature can propel us into worlds we do not understand. However it is possible to learn how to adapt to and use this by understanding the principles involved, in this case those of flight.

Birds have the capacity to leave the earth, to fly around in the air and return to earth again, an experience man has yearned for throughout time. They conduct much of their life around trees and many magical traditions revere them as carriers of the Spirit. The dove, hawk and eagle are especially seen in this way. Aboriginals the world over have read omens from the flight of birds and from their singing or nesting in specific trees, and this, alongside a host of other evidence, leads us into contemplations of magical associations and practices.

In Ancient Egypt, magicians, shamen or priests were reputed to be able to join spirits with (or transform into) hawks in order to traverse the magical realms. How they were able to achieve this we can glean in part from the Egyptian *Book of the Dead*, where there is a conducive meditation to such a practice:

I have risen, I have risen like the mighty hawk [of gold] that cometh forth from his egg; I fly and I alight like the hawk which hath a back four cubits wide, and the wings of which are like unto the mother of emerald of the south...

CHAPTER LXXVII

While such meditations or prayers concentrate on preparing the soul for the inevitable death of the body and ultimate rebirth into a new body, similar meditations can be used in a magical sense to aid the living. In taking on the concept of flying like a bird, which we do mentally by 'becoming' the bird, and feeling and moving as is described in the meditation, we can, as it were, escape the confines of normal perception. We begin to see through the bird's eyes and move with the aid of its wings, and so we are able to rise above our situation, atop the noise and confusion. By repeated meditations we gain strength in this and learn to adapt to being moved in leaps and bounds as described earlier. Through learning how to soar and fly we gain many advantages, especially with regard to our relationship with the natural world, for as we become aware of things on other levels we become less earth-bound and more able to relate to the universal.

While the practice of flying may seem strange, it is in fact a normal capacity of us all which usually occurs in sleep when our conscious body rests. Unfortunately when we awake we mostly forget our dreams, especially the details. However in a conscious mediative practice as described above, we employ our subconscious mind to go flying while our conscious mind is alert but held at bay, and we remember all the details and can utilize them in our everyday affairs. Seeing to every little detail enables us to perfect our creations.

PHYSICAL USES

Hazel provides small timber useful for the countryman. Beaters for pheasant rousing, bean-poles, twigs for peas, clothes-props, thatcher's 'springels' (which hold the thatch in place), wattles and hedge-stakes are but a few of the uses to which it has been put.

The hazel's spreading roots allow man to reap great rewards by coppicing the tree (see pp.327–8). The long straight shoots that coppiced hazels send up from the ground are pliable and difficult to break. They are used in various ways, for basket-making, hoops and hurdles, fishing rods and walking sticks.

The Romans used supple hazel twigs for tying vines to stakes. In the Middle Ages hazel was burned for charcoal. Roger Bacon mixed hazel charcoal with saltpetre and sulphur to make gunpowder.

Since early days coracle boats have allowed man to travel the marshes and rivers and have helped greatly in his survival. Traditionally coracles are made from a hazel frame tied with withies, covered with cow-hide and sealed with the resin of pine. These one-man boats are believed to have originated in Wales, but recent information on Far East traditions has revealed that they have been used there and that possibly their usage predates the Welsh. Coracles are also made from willow (*for their construc-tion, see Willow, p.274*).

Another ancient tradition which has become very much a part of life in Britain today is the construction of shelters called 'benders'. These are like upturned coracles which sit on the ground. They are made from long hazel poles which are bent and tied in place upon a circular base-frame to form an igloo shape, with a tunnel-shaped doorway made of smaller poles. This frame is then covered. In the past, furs, skins, hides, leaves, branches, reeds or thatch would have been used; today rain-proof tarpaulins make the structure warm and dry. Where permanent housing is unavailable, unaffordable or simply not desired, benders are literal life-savers, giving good shelter from the weather. They can be permanently constructed with windows, stoves, separate rooms, etc., and become warm burrows beneath the hedgerows.

Hazel rods are still used for dowsing for water. The diviner carries a hazel rod across the land, and on reaching a spot where water lies or flows beneath the surface of the earth, it moves dramatically. Hazel was also used for dowsing mineral ores and it has been said that its liking for certain minerals draws it to them.

Hazel has always helped man look after his livestock. A horse which had overeaten could be aided by binding its legs and feet to hazel rods, and by whispering certain words into its right ear. The words were known only to members of the gypsy fraternity and the ancient plough-men's guild. Tying hazel twigs onto a horse's harness was a traditional way of protecting horses from enchantment by fairies. In Ireland cattle were traditionally driven between huge fires at the Beltaine and midsum-mer celebrations, and their backs were singed with burning hazel wands to protect them from mischievous faeries or ill-luck. At lambing time hazel catkins were placed around the kitchen fireplace to aid the births and as they resemble lamb's tails, as already mentioned, this act could be viewed as one of sympathetic magic.

THE BLACKTHORN

BOTANICAL

BLACKTHORN. *Prunus spinosa*. Deciduous.

The blackthorn is typically a crooked little tree or shrub, with many thorny angular branches and black or dark brown knobbly twigs. It blossoms in early spring, just preceding hawthorn's leafing and flowering, and its sudden blaze of perfect white flowers brings a glorious light to our hedgerows long before any new leaves have appeared.

Blackthorn grows densely in hedgerows, woods and thickets throughout Britain, most often in the company of the gentler hawthorn. It is rarely found in the north of Scotland. It is thickly invested with strong thorns which are long sharp spines. These form in place of twigs and can give painful stabs and scratches which usually turn septic.

BARK
Blackthorn bark is extremely dark in colour. It is very tough and grows rugged and stone-like upon old trees.

FLOWERS
In blossoming so early, even before its own leaves are out, blackthorn defies the still-cold northern winds that continue to grip the land in winter. Its small flowers are five-petalled, star-shaped and abundant. Small white buds like little white balls intersperse giant clusters of newly opened blossom. Blackthorn blossom has a potently erotic musky scent which lures insects and begins their year of nectar-hunting, ensuring that pollination of the flowers is achieved to provide an abundant production of seed.

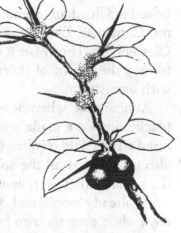

LEAVES
The leaves of the blackthorn are neat small oval shapes of a dark matt-green colour. They are abundant on the tree and seem to mass even more strongly when blackthorn is a regularly trimmed hedge-plant.

The blackthorn is deciduous and sheds its yellowed leaves by winter. Then the massed shape of its knobbly branches is revealed.

The leaves, thorns, flowers and sloe fruit of the blackthorn

FRUIT
Blackthorn fruit are called sloes. They develop from the flower and transform from a green hard state to soft plum-shaped purply-black fruit with a silvery-blue bloom. They are more or less inedible because of their dry

acrid taste and are mainly used as a 'bitter' in drinks. By September the hedgerows are filled with them, and they add to the autumn colours of hedgerow and field. The cultivated plum, greengage and damson are closely related to blackthorn, possibly even derived from it.

CUSTOM & LEGEND

By tradition blackthorn was regarded as a sister of the hawthorn. The customs attached to fertility celebrations used the qualities of both plants to great effect, particularly the erotic ones with which fertility was evoked. When blackthorn was used in the Mayday celebrations, it topped the maypole entwined in a hawthorn garland and was called the 'Mother of Woods'. As sister trees blackthorn and hawthorn are also linked in Christian legend, for blackthorn was said to bloom at midnight on Christmas Eve, as did the miraculous hawthorn known as the Glastonbury Thorn (see p.128). Both plants were also believed to have formed the crown of thorns, a belief which did much to overlay them with superstition.

At new year, when people gathered together to celebrate, crowns of blackthorn were made and ritually burned as firecharms, so their scattered ashes could fertilize the fields. Blackthorn crowns or garlands were also used to wassail the apple trees and when mistletoe was woven into the garlands they were hung up to bring luck in the coming year.

As already mentioned, blackthorn blossoms in the earliest pre-spring days when even its own branches are bare of leaves. At such times the cold wintry winds are still strong and it became the custom to call these cold days 'a blackthorn winter'. In some parts of Britain this period was called 'a blackthorn hatch', for it usually followed a milder one in which the blackthorn had burst into flower. The blackthorn hatch was a well established phenomenon.

In Ireland blackthorn wood was used to make traditional shillelaghs (clubs or cudgels) and Irish folk-tales speak of giants who carried similar clubs. In one of these tales, however, we are told that heroes were given aid from the blackthorn in order to escape giants, for if they threw a twig of magical blackthorn between themselves and a chasing giant, it would quickly take root and become an entire wood of blackthorn trees, with spines and tangled branches forming an impenetrable shield through which the giant could not pass.

Unfortunately blackthorn also has a grim reputation which was exaggerated over the centuries by superstition, for its thorns were linked to the nefarious practices of people who took chances to seize power by harming others. The thorns are incredibly strong, sharp and long, which makes them ideal for piercing or jabbing flesh. As already explained, a scratch often leaves wounds that turn septic, and if, as legend tells us, such thorns were also tipped with poison, we can well imagine the death-blow they dealt. On certain levels this parallels the 'sting' of the Egyptian asp, which was also used in the removing of opposition to the changing and building of empires. When the blackthorn was used thus it was called the 'pin of slumber'.

Even more unfortunate were the superstition and paranoia of the witch panic throughout Britain and Europe, for it was claimed that certain people were guilty of using blackthorn wands with fixed thorns on their ends and carved blackthorn sticks called 'black rods' which caused miscarriages and harm to others. Added to this, rumour asserted that the devil himself pricked his initiates on the fingers with thorns and many 'witches' were searched for the 'devil's mark'. This eventually became the label of any mark found on the body of any suspected person, and was deemed enough evidence for a death sentence. Such were the associations thought to exist between witches and blackthorn, it was reputedly one of the woods used to burn witches on the pyres. Such usage was meant to deliver a final insult to the victim.

The black witch legends moved from the realms of superstition into folklore and faerie tales. There are many versions of the *Sleeping Beauty* tale, in which a beautiful maiden is set up by a jealous witch to prick her finger and fall into a sleep so deep that she is thought to be dead. While the beauty sleeps the centuries away so the country around her becomes dormant and an impenetrable thorny thicket forms a barrier to the outer world. The whole country is held under the witch's spell, until a handsome prince cuts his way through the barrier of thorns and brings Beauty and her realm back to life with a kiss. The thorn in this tale pricks the finger and also forms the barrier, impenetrable to everything except love. As such it demonstrates how the power of love can remove all obstacles.

Witches apart, many kinds of people used blackthorn negatively, for old legends tell of blackthorn spines being placed under the saddles of horses in order to make them unseat their riders when the spine went into the horses' flesh. In ages when the horse was the main means of transport this was an easy and deadly way for people to get rid of their enemies or rivals, and its use was open to anyone with a grudge.

Because of all the secrecy attached to such actions, blackthorn became known as the 'increaser and keeper of dark secrets'. While we may acknowledge this, we will hopefully realize in the following pages that blackthorn also has a positive quality which cleanses and prepares us for personal progress and development.

HEALING

The fruit of the blackthorn is very astringent, and for this reason in the seventeenth and eighteenth centuries thick brews of unripe sloes were used to treat 'fluxes in the belly', and as strong purgatives. Thankfully nowadays with cleaner conditions and methods of refrigeration we have little need to evacuate the stomach so dramatically, and a much safer and comfortable cleansing purge can be obtained from drinking a light infusion of a small handful of blackthorn flowers, made like weak tea.

On a spiritual and emotional healing level, blackthorn flowers exalt the spirit and help us open up to Nature's vital energies. In purifications and cleansings the thorns represent our negative attitudes which rend and tear at us and our lives, and which we need to cast off if we want to be happy and creative. By using blackthorn in meditation, or even by just having it around, we can begin such a process.

There are two powerful times when blackthorn specifically aids us in such cleansings, and these are Imbolc (1 February) and Samhain (31 October). In Magic we will look at blackthorn's pre-spring blossoming *(see p.85)*. Here we can look at the fruiting blackthorn, which leads us back into the darkness as winter descends at Samhain and the solar year wanes. Then blackthorn has a specific strength which can help, for as winter forces us into our homes we have to adapt to new circumstances and are made to face our inner realities. In order to understand why this is so, we can look at the changing energies of the natural world at this time and the effects they have upon us.

As already explained, like the trees themselves, people are moved by the rhythms of the earth, its tides of ebb and flow caused by the cycles of the sun and moon. While the moon magnetically controls the waters, the sun controls the seasons. With the withdrawal of the sun's light, warmth and energy, like Nature itself, we automatically draw our energies inwards in order to sustain life.

But unlike Nature, people cannot go into complete dormancy, for we are still pulled by the world, our families, work, etc. And yet even while we perform our daily tasks through the winter months, the inevitability of the earth's cycles forces the focus of our senses and attention inwards where we must enter our unconscious world. According to *Chambers Twentieth Century Dictionary*, the 'unconscious' refers to 'the deepest, inaccessible levels of the psyche, in which are found, in dynamic state, our repressed impulses and memories'. Hence facing our inner world is not always easy, for invariably we come face to face with our negative selves, which are often surrounded by unquiet emotions, memories of painful experiences, outworn conditioning, etc. Most often these refer to complicated unfinished business we have pushed aside in an attempt to forget or lose. Often they touch our deepest fears and weaknesses, for the unconscious world is full of such shadows. Yet now they must be faced and dealt with.

Most times we can cope with this turbulent sea of emotions and memories, yet sometimes the task is so daunting that fear or deep depression sets in. When things get this bad, blackthorn in meditation helps us face our negativity. It also helps us to burst through any dammed-up emotions, rather like lancing an emotional abscess so that the area can drain and heal. Today many people realize that our true evolution as humans is found by such a process, in which we heal our negative selves and become positive beings, rather than through technological advances. As a species we have pushed outwards beyond our limits in our race for speed, control and power, and now is the time when we should balance this by once more regarding our inner beings and their expression.

The wintry blackthorn specifically helps with the deep psychic levels of this process, guiding us to our positivity so we can come to terms with what we are, and thus function strongly and clearly in the world. When we are drawn to blackthorn we are being shown by the Spirit that it's time we underwent such a process to better fulfil our lives. A word of caution should be brought in here, though, for such is the purgative nature of the blackthorn and its winter fruit that its action can be harsh and unrelenting as it pushes us closer to karmic issues. For those who need a gentler process, the spring blackthorn with its massed white blossoms provides a lighter cleansing, as is shown in Magic.

MAGIC

IRISH/GAELIC	*Straif*
OGHAM	𝍖
RUNIC	ᚻ
RULING PLANETS	Saturn (plant); Mars (fruit)
ABILITIES	Cleansing. Karmic issues. Lack of choice but with hope rising from the depths. To do with the element of Fire.
SEASONS	Spring (Imbolc); Late Autumn (Samhain)

Under the seventh-century Irish Brehon Law blackthorn was classed as a shrub tree, small and yet powerfully potent. As it grows alongside the beautiful hawthorn in hedgerows, like sisters they reflect the dark and light seasons of the year. In being such representatives they also provide

us with revelations, healing and strengthening guidelines for our development. Their presence helps the human spirit undergo the correct
seasonal changes, which move from light to dark, summer to winter, to
summer again.

With its beautiful mass of white blossom in earliest spring, blackthorn
shows the irrepressible force of Nature from which we can gain so much
strength. Its blossoming within the still wintry landscape stirs our spirit
and its spines give us the ability to rend our wintry cocoon, allowing us
to step forward into the awakening year, as does the goddess whose
beauty is reflected upon the face of each delicate flower. We then begin
to open up to the seasonal energies like the flowers and leaves upon the
land, as the growing warmth and light of the sun fill every living thing
with vital energy.

This energy peaks into full-frontal fertility by Mayday and, as already
mentioned, to express this blackthorn blossoms were traditionally woven
into the hawthorn crowns which topped the phallic maypoles.
Blackthorn wishing-wands were also used at this time for divination and
obtaining desires. The heady fusion of Nature's fertile energies is
expressed by the erotic perfume of spring flowers and on this, the traditional wedding day, hedgerow flowers adorned the bridal couples and
were used to decorate the chambers in which they made love.

While the Imbolc blackthorn helps us burst through our wintry state
and the Mayday blackthorn enhances our communal sexual spirit in the
full throes of spring, the Samhain blackthorn, as discussed in Healing (see
p.83), guides individuals through the darkening weeks to the Winter
Solstice. Here we can compare the human passage with that of the mythical sun-god, for like him we too enter the Underworld, in terms of our
unconscious realms, as the sun completes its cycle. We also face the same
initiatory process, that is, overcoming our negative selves in order to
facilitate rebirth, which is comparable to the sun-god being reborn into
the solar cycle.

If we take this comparison further we realize there is help for us in this
process, for in the myths of the sun-god we are told he received aid from
the trees – a talismanic branch from a specific species of tree enabling
him to escape his Underworld confines. There are many trees which

help in this process, and each species is concerned with specific areas of mind and body. As already explained, blackthorn helps us burst through and cleanse our blockages caused by negativity. This gains us a clearer entrance into our inner worlds and the ability to survive the facing thereof.

Let us look at blackthorn's thorny legends, for its use in affecting people by the pricking of their fingers leads us into areas of 'finger magic'. In centuries past when heating was rare and the body was heavily clothed for warmth, only the fingers and face of a person were accessible, and this was used to advantage in both positive and negative ways. On the positive side, finger magic was a powerful tool which could be used to good healing effect, rather like the laying on of hands, and the fact that it was part of the druidic lore of trees made it even more potent and far-reaching.

Blackthorn is a very protective tree, able to form impassable barriers, yet piercing such barriers when necessary. It is ruled over by Saturn and Mars, hence its ability to move deep energy blockages within us. In this it is very thorough and very strong, and because it primarily deals with karmic issues we often have little choice as to when it turns its influence upon us. Sometimes the cleansings it brings are severe, and at those times gentler tree energies can be introduced, such as apple, which provides comfortable healing to the areas we have cleared, and silver birch, which gives us graceful pliability to adapt to our new state.

However, no matter how amenable we are in life, it seems we often find ourselves confronting people who regard us as their enemy, and sometimes such people won't let go and throw nothing but negativity our way. To rid yourself of such a person, here is an ancient spell which uses the thorns of blackthorn.

Create a rough image of the ill-wishing person by simply carving a candle into a rough body shape. Do this in such a way that the wick is uncut and the candle will still light and burn evenly. Name this body shape as the person, carving the name upon it if you wish. Then take three blackthorn thorns, and push one into the image's forehead, one into its heart area, and one into the abdomen. When the thorns are placed, light the candle-body, and as the flame meets each thorn repeat the following words:

> Evil return to the one who sent thee,
> For me and mine are now set free.
> No hurt nor harm can enter here,
> For my life and way are now made clear.

Allow the candle to burn down completely, concentrating on your release from the person and seeing the ill-wishing return to source.

In performing this spell correct intent must be held, for we do not wish to practise with thoughts of hatred, etc., i.e., in the same way as the person from whom we are being released, but only to be freed from them. The correct intent in this case is justice, not revenge.

INSPIRATION

Blackthorn has had a great deal of superstition woven around it and when researching specific species of trees to which this has happened, remembering that trees are sentient beings, I have often wondered just what they themselves felt as they were shrouded by negative reputations.

If we look through pagan eyes we see trees revered as an integral part of life and religion. The main suppressor of the pagan religions was the Church, which deemed that the divine should only be regarded through their God and that all else was sin. Such dogma severely affected native people who regularly communed with the natural world, for they saw the divine expressed there. Yet this natural reverence was outlawed as fear and control were exerted over people's lives. The full expression of this culminated in a severe persecution of indigenous races, in which countless people were scapegoated under such labels as 'witch' or 'heretic', and were put to death in order to put the 'fear of God' into the rest of society. Blackthorn was condemned as a 'witch's tool' and was purposefully used as a wood of the pyres to burn countless innocent people to death. How can that not register on the spirit of a tree?

Religions apart, trees have always been the people's confidantes. They have always been spoken to, touched, hugged, leant against, dreamed or cried under. Like us, they have unique characters and their long life-spans ensure they know generation upon generation of people. When severe changes occurred and communities were forbidden recourse to Nature, what did the trees feel as people were forced to shun them? Did they not miss our company or our spirit? Did they not shudder at man's mistakes or wonder at his interpretation of a god denying the natural world? Did they not then view the negativity which became the ecological and spiritual disaster we now face?

Perhaps such questions may never be fully answered but they should be thought about deeply nevertheless, for if we do not learn from our mistakes and quickly realize the necessity of communication with the natural world, we may never repair the damage we have done and we will not survive.

The strongest messages come from blackthorn spines and to explain this I'll recount an experience of a few years ago at the time of the Autumn Equinox. When out on an incredibly stormy day gathering fruits for the celebration that night, the skies literally opened and sheets of rain instantly soaked me to the skin. Hurriedly gathering fruiting hawthorn from the hedgerow, I reached deep into the hedge to pick some blackthorn sloes, but on withdrawing my hand from the tangled branches I was stunned to see it completely covered in blood. Such was my wet state that a small amount of blood spilt by an unfelt scratch from a thorn had spread across the entire surface of my skin. But before my mind had time to reason this out, suddenly the rain washed my hand clean, transforming it in an instant from red to white. So strong was the visible impression I got from this that it was some minutes before I could collect myself and return home.

Many months later, when compiling notes for this book, many similar experiences with other trees were remembered, and their symbolic messages provided guidelines and proved invaluable to gaining a fuller comprehension of the trees and their messages for humanity.

So what can my experience with the blackthorn reveal? Well, first that it's incredibly thorny, an attribute which, as we have seen throughout this chapter, allowed people to impress their will and negativity onto others. So there has to be a lesson there for us. Secondly, blackthorn spines draw lots of blood, which graphically shows the harm we can inflict upon ourselves and others. Possibly it also shows that we think very little about the value of life and that it is only when blood is spilt that we remember it. We do take things for granted.

Going deeper, there is usually pain when blood is spilt and blackthorn reminds us that there are many levels of pain as well as the physical. There are many ways through which we hurt each other. In the context of personal relationships, blackthorn tells us of respect, of not crossing lines beyond which we will inflict pain. This point is especially important as we learn of the other's pain thresholds, the places where we touch old wounds, weaknesses, etc. How often do we forget respect and stab at our loved ones in anger or frustration, how often do we throw trust to the winds to make a point or revel in our power over another's weaknesses? If we are honest, we are all capable of it, especially when we ourselves are in pain.

Yet blackthorn is not all about pain, for our ancestors used its blossom in fertility rites, where its erotic perfume helped evoke love. And in my experience, the element of water with which the rain had encompassed all symbolized the realms of the emotions whose perfection is love. Thus the true message given by the blackthorn is that by understanding and calming our emotions, and by being aware of the capacity of our negativity, we can ease our own suffering and eventually the suffering of the world. Thus we can come to love the mystery that is life.

PHYSICAL USES

The wood of the blackthorn is very tough. It was used to make the teeth of rakes, as well as for cudgels and sticks used for fighting at fairs. When made into a walking stick and highly polished, it reveals a dark rich shine.

Blackthorn is useful to the farmer, for it is a good hedge plant, its spines protecting the young foliage of the hedge from browsing animals, as well as forming a strong barrier.

Sloes give the strongest natural red dye, which has always been used by country people. As sloes are very astringent they were added to drinks as 'bitters' and were used in jam-making. Sloe juice was used as a marking ink.

Sloe gin, which is very potent, is possibly the best known use for sloes:

To make sloe gin, use 2 lbs (900 g) (8 cups) of sloes to 3½ pints (1 litre) of gin. Pick the sloes in autumn when they've developed their blue bloom. Remove the stalks, prick them with a needle or fork, and place them in a large bowl or jug with the gin. To this add ¾ lb (350 g) (1½ cups) brown sugar, ¼ lb (115 g) (½ cup) white, and stir.

Put into a demi-john, cork and leave in a cool room for three months, inverting and shaking it up every other day.

When it is time, strain the gin through thick (double) muslin until the liquid is clear. This may take several goes as the sloes should not be squeezed.

Pour into bottles, cork and leave for one year before drinking!

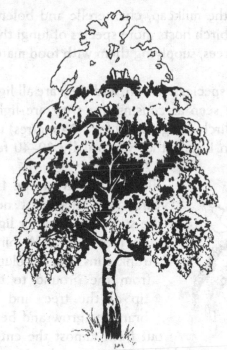

THE
SILVER BIRCH

BOTANICAL

SILVER BIRCH. *Betula alba (Pendula)*. Deciduous.

Besides being one of the daintiest trees the silver birch is the hardiest of all broadleaves, a native of Iceland, Greenland, Britain and most of the northern hemisphere. It is easily recognized by the tracery of its delicate twigs and branches. It is an extremely feminine tree and has distinctive silvery-white bark with grey-green fissures.

The earth beneath a birch tree is lush and welcoming to flowers, and the tree's affinity with water encourages the growth of many forms of fungi, like the scarlet fly agaric, the milkcap, chanterelle and boletus. With the exception of beech, the birch hosts more species of fungi than any other tree. The fungi aid the trees, supplying them with food material.

World-wide there are about 60 species of birch, and they are all light and graceful. Birch and alder are seen as cousins, for they are light-weight trees of the forest's edge. Birch can grow 80 feet (24 metres) tall in the right conditions, though in Britain they are usually 30–40 feet (9–12 metres).

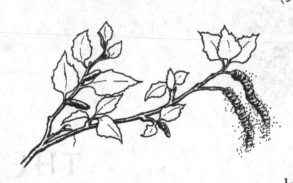

Birches can live to be 100 years old. They root near the surface and prefer light and moist soils. A birch trunk runs like a column from the ground to the tip of the tree, and its branches grow and bend out from almost the entire length of its trunk. As you look at a silver birch tree you see a slight trunk, slighter branches and even slighter twigs, until you reach twigs almost threadlike. 'Birchen twigs break no ribs' is a saying born from their suppleness.

The leaves, male and female catkins and seeding catkins of the silver birch

'Burelles' of twigs may appear high in the crown of some trees, looking like old birds' nests. These are called 'witch's knots' in Scotland and are made by insects which lay their eggs in the tree. The defence mechanism of the tree then overproduces in that area and 'glues' the excessive twig growth together.

Birch is common in woods and heaths in the east and south of Britain and it makes a healing, graceful companion in the garden. It takes 25 years for the silver birch to begin to fruit, and with old age its bark loses its silvery whiteness and the branches of the crown hang lower. Cattle and deer don't like the taste of birch and leave it in peace.

BARK

The silvery-white bark is thin and paper-like and peels off the trunk to reveal an inner bark of russet brown. Though transparent and fragile-looking, the thin outermost layers are in fact incredibly strong and tough. Birch bark does not rot, and trees have been found in peat bogs with petrified interiors and perfect bark. If a birch tree is blown down and left, all the inner wood decays, but the bark remains intact in a hollow tube.

With age the trunk bases of silver birches become rough, dark and deeply etched with fissures. The dark transverse markings on the tree's trunk are lenticels, spaces where air is let into the living tissues beneath the bark.

From the silver birch's tall graceful trunk rise many long supple branches of a reddish-brown colour. These branches are warty and whip-like, bending upon the slightest movement of air. They have a mass of thin supple twigs growing from them, and are very delicate. Any new twigs are quite soft and do not toughen until late in the year.

LEAVES

At the beginning of spring the birch opens its leaf-buds to reveal leaves which are ace of spades shape, small and very pointed, with double-toothed edges. They are a delicate light green colour, touched with yellow and tinged with a pink underside which can show through to their upper leaf. These new leaves cover the birch with a green mist, and because of their slender stalks they move on the gentlest of winds. A motionless silver birch is a rarity.

By autumn the leaves turn a beautiful golden yellow and the grass below the trees becomes carpeted with their rich colour as they fall from the branches.

FLOWERS

Birch has both male and female flowers on the same tree. The female flowers are small erect catkins. They await the touch of pollen from the male catkins, which wake from their wintry dormant state just prior to the appearance of leaves on the tree. Long and pendulous with pollen, the male catkins need insects and wind to help pollinate the female flowers, which then become swollen with the bulk of seed.

FRUIT

By July the seeds have become light brown and hang, still clustered in a catkin shape, waiting for the wind to make them airborne. A single female catkin contains hundreds of the tiny two-winged seeds, each one capable of becoming a new birch tree.

In autumn, when all the seeds are finally taken from the tree by the wind, the young male catkins for next year appear on the tip of each new shoot. They turn from green to purply-brown and remain in this wintry state until the following spring.

CUSTOM & LEGEND

The silver birch is known as the 'Lady of the Woods'. It is womanly, constant and friendly, a tree of enchantment. When seen by moonlight it presents its most outstanding feature, a gleaming silvery bark, which legends throughout Europe describe as the hallmark of faerie. This white bark also gleams attractively in the sun and shows the lightness of the tree's spirit, the ethereal beauty of the innocent dancing quality of the female in Nature, with delicate branches and leaves to match.

As birch is one of the first trees to leaf in spring it is known as the tree of inception. It is also seen as a tree of purification, cleansing the old to make way for the new. At the ancient Beltaine festivities birch twigs were used to light the oak fires and traditionally the Mayday love-making was enjoyed in a birch wood or forest.

Birch is dedicated to the Norse goddess Frigga, goddess of married love and the sky and clouds, who became Odin's wife. Frigga had 11 handmaidens who aided her in caring for humanity, and she span golden threads and the rainbows of spring. It was believed that her seven mortal sons founded the seven Saxon kingdoms of England.

The birch is well known in the cold regions of Europe where many

legends are formed around it. Ancient Finnish folklore is set into traditional ballads, and amongst these is found the bardic epic called the
Kalevala. Traditionally such potent epics were performed by story-tellers,
whose voices rose above the atmospheric chanting of other singers.
Originally such songs were never written down, but in the seventeenth
and eighteenth centuries certain works were printed and published. The
first German translation of the *Kalevala* formed part of the base of
Longfellow's 'Hiawatha', and the English translation by Elias Lonnrot is
entitled *Kalevala: The land of heroes*. In the saga, the hero Väinämöinen has
a journey full of magical adventures as he moves through the ages of man
on a long quest for a sacred talisman called the Sampo.

In Runo XLIV Väinämöinen loses his *kantele* (harp) in a lake, and,
unable to find it, makes a new one from a weeping birch which could
find no joy in life. In doing so he enabled the birch tree to bring great joy
to the world with its music, telling it:

> *Soon shalt thou with joy be weeping,*
> *Shortly shalt thou sing for pleasure...*

Then:

> *...the aged Väinämöinen*
> *Carved into a harp the birch tree,*
> *On a summer day he carved it,*
> *To a kantele he shaped it.*

Once the harp-frame was constructed, Väinämöinen formed its pegs and
screws from acorns with golden kernels, upon which cuckoos sat and
sang in five beautiful tones. To obtain the strings he persuaded a maiden
(the goddess) to give him of her hair.

> *Now the harp at last was finished,*
> *And the aged Väinämöinen*
> *Thus upon his harp was playing...*
> *Then rang out the wood so speckled,*

Sang the sapling green full loudly,
Loudly called the golden cuckoo,
And rejoiced the hair of maiden.

All of Nature – men, women, children, animals, birds, insects, plants and trees – rejoiced and were entranced by the melody as Väinämöinen played his birchen *kantele*. Thus the birch found new expression in beautifying the world.

This legend from northern Europe parallels the ancient Gaelic creation myth, in which Dagda, the god of Nature, played creation into being upon a harp, for its music encouraged the seasons to wax and wane and the cycle of life to begin.

In Irish legend the lovers Diarmid, King of All Ireland, and the goddess Grainne made their home in shelters of birch twigs as they fled from their pursuer, Finn Mac Coll. The lovers are said to have also slept each night beside a fresh dolmen. They journeyed throughout the west of Ireland, stopping at Cork, Kerry, Limerick and Tipperary, and their numerous bed-places are still recognized by people in those areas. Their flight lasted a year and a day before Finn Mac Coll eventually took the shape of a boar, killed Diarmid and claimed Grainne.

An old Welsh custom was for a man to give a birch garland to the woman he loved and she gave a similar one back if she felt the same affection.

In many parts of Britain and Europe birch was anciently used as a living maypole at Beltaine. Conversely, in Scandinavian legend the birch was regarded as the tree around which the last battle for worldly existence would be fought.

Being a white tree, the silver birch was seen to have the ability to ward off evil or negative spirits. Traditionally birch rods were used to drive out the spirit of the old year and for beating the bounds of a parish. They were also used in the none too kind practice of beating spirits and demons out of lunatics. The Romans carried birch rods when they installed their consuls, no doubt to beat back the crowds in an early use of caning.

Birch is also associated with the spirits of the dead and mourners, for the tree was seen to be in sympathy by its pendulous habit of 'weeping':

Weeps the birch of silver bark with long dishevelled hair.

ANON

The birch is believed by some to grow at the Gates of Paradise. It is primarily a tree of sun and sky. When used for the first ogham inscription in Ireland the birch became associated with the sun-god Lugh, for this first inscription warned him that his wife was being taken away to the land of faerie.

The name 'birch' is thought derived from the Sanskrit word *bhurga*, which means 'a tree whose bark is used to write upon'. The second King of Rome, Numa Pompilius, successor to Romulus, is said to have written books on birch bark c.700 BC, which legend says are still buried along with their author. In all probability, because of the indestructible quality of birch bark, these books would still be in good repair if found. So far this has not occurred.

Various origins of the word *beith*, *bith* or *beth*, variations of the Gaelic name for birch, are given as meaning 'existence', 'enduring', 'world' and 'shining one'.

HEALING

Water collected from the birch tree is called 'birch blood' as well as 'birch water'. In some parts of Europe country people still lay in a supply in the spring before the trees leaf. To do this they bore a small hole in the tree's trunk, into which they insert a straw. The rising sap of the tree then trickles out of this straw and can be caught in a jar or dish. This operation is done for a couple of days only so as not to exhaust the tree. The collected water is then preserved by adding four to six cloves and a little cinnamon, and although it does not last as long as that prepared by sterilization, it does, however, maintain all its properties. A sweet fizzy wine can be made from birch water and it is also used medicinally to prevent stones in the kidneys or bladder. It is invaluable for treating rheumatic diseases or for use as a cleansing mouthwash. It cures skin of spots, fades freckles, and is used to clear scurf and heal acne.

BARK
Birch bark is diuretic, antiseptic and a tonic, and it contains an anaesthetic which causes nerve-endings to lose sensation, making us less aware of pain. If applied externally, putting the wet fresh internal side of the bark against the skin, muscle pain can be relieved.

Gypsies use birch bark for treating eczema and a decoction of bark treats intermittent fevers. The bark should be collected in late spring and early summer, taking care not to ring around the tree, for it will die.

LEAVES
The young leaves are used for treating cystitis and other infections of the urinary system, removing excess water and 'flushing' the body. A decoction of birch leaves made into a tea greatly increases the output of urine from the body. It also dissolves kidney-stones and gives great relief from rheumatism and gout.

Rheumatic and arthritic pains are eased if a warm bed is filled with birch leaves, for they induce a heavy sweat and bring the patient relief.

When we are under stress we can lessen tension by relating to the silver birch, for the pliability of its branches and the strength of its trunk show how we may stand tall midst the winds of change. It is very easy to lessen pain when surrounded by this spring-like tree of youthful femininity and gaiety.

If you cannot get to the woods often, take some leaves and twigs home with you when you do. Arrange them with flowers or on your worktable, so that each time stress appears you can look at, or touch, the birch. Then, via your imagination, take yourself back to the woods where you picked it in order to heal. The knowledge that you are capable of healing yourself through Nature gives a positivity which also wards off pain. We can then choose to find pleasure in our existence.

Looking at the birch tree or remembering its refreshing grace clears the head of stuffy thoughts and replaces them with the gladness of Nature. The silver birch is a supreme healer.

MAGIC

IRISH/GAELIC	*Beith*
OGHAM	├
RUNIC	↓
RULING PLANET	Venus
ABILITIES	Healing. New starts and beginnings. Mysteries of the young goddess. To do with the elements of Air and Water.
SEASONS	Spring; Autumn

As the tree of inception the silver birch is radiant in spring, for it reflects the growing light of the sun which encourages Nature to blossom. Thus it can be included in all rituals of light and life. As its ruling planet is Venus, it invokes the qualities of love and beauty into all workings.

The resinous quality of the birch tree's bark gives off a pure clear fragrance after rain has fallen. If strips of birch bark are burned, they give a clear blue flame and scent the air, so it is an excellent wood for any small magical fires. It also aids concentration and uplifts the spirit.

Because birch casts off malignancy and allows a fresh start, it was often used at Samhain, the start of the Celtic year, when purification was believed to be essential. The dried leaves of birch were also used to 'charm' a baby's cot, giving the child inside strength to cast off any weakness and gain the best start in life.

According to legend, all respect should be shown to the birch tree, for if this Lady of the Woods finds you maligning trees, anger rises in her whip-like branches. Always ask if you need something from the trees, especially if you want to take the bark. Birch bark makes exceptionally potent magical parchment. If you can wait, find a tree that has been struck by lightning to obtain your needs, for then the tree is deemed usable by the gods.

Traditional broomsticks are made from birch twigs, which are tied around a stout ash or hazel handle with strips of osier (withy branches of willow). Besides being an excellent broom, birch twigs also brush away evil spirits from the immediate area.

On magical levels there are many variations of broomstick, each containing different associations and qualities by virtue of the various woods used to construct them. If the handle of the birch broom is of ash wood it is traditionally believed to protect the user against drowning, by virtue of the fact that ash wood floats well in water. If the handle is of hazel, the broomstick can be used in the visionary sense, as a divinatory tool. If of apple, it would be excellent to use in works of love and fruition. Small pieces of wood from specific trees can also be inserted between the handle and the brush, giving a secret 'edge' for obtaining specific results. The use of osier to tie the twigs of the brush to the handle dedicates the broomstick to the witch's moon-goddess. An older tradition of using branches of broom in the brush makes them extra magical, but for the greatest flying possibilities birch twigs are most airborne of all, ever moving upon the air as they are upon the tree.

It is the astral body of the witch which rides the night sky. The phallic associations of broomsticks come from the fact that prolonged sexual ecstasy is a strong way of leaving the body or 'flying', which is why there were orgies in many ancient rites. However an orgy isn't necessary for sexual ecstasy, for the love between two people brings such, and if we are to be alchemically correct, the people should be male and female. Dion Fortune has written much about the state of our beings during sexual congress, explaining that at orgasm the soul reaches out onto the astral plane, a journey which can be prolonged, and which ultimately, on magical levels, allows us to work in other dimensions.

Witch tradition decrees that if a couple 'jump the broomstick' together at a special hand-fasting ceremony, they are married for a year and a day, after which time they can remarry or go their separate ways. In witch ways, before casting a magic circle the broomstick is used to sweep the space clear of negative influences. It is also used to sweep the night sky to ensure a clean contact with the heavens during circle working. Then we can truly live up to the old adage 'as above, so below'.

The deities associated with silver birch are mostly love- and fertility-goddesses. In northern Europe, where the birch is profuse, Frigga represented married love, and Freya was the Norse goddess of love and fecundity. The birch is also associated with the 'northern lights', the aurora borealis, which were anciently regarded as the 'crown of the north wind', the corona borealis. The goddess Arianrhod, who is in charge of 'the Silver Wheel of the Heavens', was believed to have her throne (*caer*) within the corona borealis. Arianrhod was invoked through the birch tree for her aid in births and initiations. The Greek version of Arianrhod is Ariadne, whose orgiastic celebrations were a somewhat heightened version of the Mayday love-making enjoyed in birch woods.

Closer to home, Eostre, the Anglo-Saxon goddess of spring, was evoked and celebrated around and through the birch tree between the Spring Equinox and Beltaine. All goddesses of spring and flowers are invoked at this time. In the Welsh tradition Blodeuwedd would be especially esteemed.

Blodeuwedd was created by the magician Gwydion as a wife for Llew Law Gyffes, the son of Arianrhod the star-goddess. The flowers used to create her were blossoms of oak, broom and meadowsweet, along with six other flowers from specific plants and trees. Because she was made from nine different blossoms Blodeuwedd is also regarded as a moon-goddess, nine being a number attributed to the moon. This night-time association is strengthened by legend, for Blodeuwedd betrays Llew Llaw Gyffes who then turns her into a night owl.

The silver birch is used in all works of love, protection and purification, for it contains the caring qualities of the feminine. Its main ruling element is air, upon which it is never still, although it has a natural affinity with water.

INSPIRATION

The silver birch is the most faerie-like of all our trees, for it is light and airy with foliage and branches which dance upon the breeze. As, according to Culpeper, it is ruled over by Venus (both planet and goddess), graceful qualities permeate all birch woods, giving a youthful feeling and a refreshing innocence like the promise of springtime. Such an atmosphere allows us to relax from the pressures of the workaday world and helps us become reinvigorated.

I never tire of watching birch trees, for they remind me of childhood days spent running through woods, wherein they grew tall and airy midst fallen old boles of more solid earthy trees. In childhood you do not question feelings and contacts with Nature, it just is, and you experience all its aliveness with a joyful innocence. It is later, with hindsight, that you realize more fully the magic you touched and accepted and lived.

Thinking back to those days I see glades of dappled green full of ferns and flowers, where young deer, rabbits and squirrels roam freely, and wood pigeons 'chant' continuously through the day, as do owls by night. To a child it is easy to find special places in the natural world, places where the imagination is acted out and games are invented within make-believe. Fallen trees become tables, chairs or whatever, and natural niches or arbours become rooms, castles, ships, carts, trucks and so on. All the while during play the creatures of the woodland are conversed with and such communication is accepted as the most normal thing in the world.

Many years later, living with the pressures of the adult world, I often cast my mind back to those woodland glades, for they are like fresh springs of healing water which clear and refresh the soul. I know I have touched real treasure and in that I am lucky. Any wish for the future contains the hope that more children may experience the joys of Nature in a world so unlike that of yesterday.

Sweet bird of the meadow, soft be thy nest,
Thy mother will wake thee at morn from thy rest;
She has made a soft nest, little redbreast, for thee,
Of the leaves of the birch, and the moss of the tree.

LEYDON

The strength of most of this book and the energy needed to endlessly work with words and recapture visions come in no small part from silver birches, for as well as childhood memories, I had for some years the added impetus of a glade of silver birches growing less than 30 feet (9 metres) from my work tables. At times when my energy flagged or when inspiration left, the birches restored me. At times, when my emotional world engulfed me in a sea of tears, they taught me pliancy and suppleness in the midst of struggle, and how to bend to the winds of change.

It is not surprising that in all ancient tongues the name for birch derives from a root meaning 'bright' or 'shining'. This stems partly from the reflectiveness of its white trunk, but is in fact more descriptive of the inner light that the tree radiates out from itself, which at times lights it up like a beacon. The Lady of the Woods is a constant vision of beauty:

No beauty she does miss
When all her robes are on,
But beauty's self she is
When all her robes are gone.

ANON, 1602

The fertility associations of the birch are reflected in the courting of the god and goddess. The Gaelic name for birch, *beith*, also means 'inception' or 'beginning', and while this alludes to the beginning of the light season, it is also descriptive of the courtship of the earth and sun which grows and culminates throughout the solar year. The goddess was acknowledged at Imbolc, the first spring festival of the year, when she led the young sun-god forward and introduced him to the world. At the Spring Equinox she makes her full entry into the year, appearing once more as a seductive maiden. Her mother/guardian mantle is cast aside to reveal her graceful beauty. She is the apotheosis of daintiness and charm, as is the silver birch. On seeing her in this wonderful season of flowers and perfume, the heart of the youthful sun-god is captured, and as the sun grows in the heavens, so his love grows. He courts her as the sun courts the earth with its warmth. This was celebrated at Beltaine, as already mentioned, with love-making (between couples who in themselves personified the god and goddess of Nature) in graceful birch woods.

In Egyptian, Mayan and Aztec cultures the hare greeted the dawn of the year, the season of spring. To the Celts it was a potent fertility symbol and totem animal with great protective taboos surrounding it, and was thought to bestow degrees of shape-shifting ability. To carry a hare's foot brought good luck, and if barren people carried its genitals it was believed they would become fertile. To eat a hare supposedly gave your body sexual attractiveness for nine days, and from my own experience, allows you to be fleet of foot within your dreams.

The hare was thought to have the power to lead people into the lands of faerie and witches were believed to be able to change into hares. Such were the pagan customs attached to the hare, especially with regard to fertility, that the Church could not entirely dismiss its importance, and the tradition eventually arose of giving chocolate hares as presents at Easter. Nowadays these have become chocolate rabbits.

PHYSICAL USES

While the birch graces our land with its daintiness we must not forget its hardiness, for birch trees flourish on ground where snow lies all year round and survive where much larger trees fall.

Birchwood is heavy, and in the past was mostly used for bobbins, barrel-making, hoops for casks, clogs and various small items like toys. The shafts of arrows were made of birch branches and birch twigs were used for brooms.

Birch is grown in northern Europe to produce plywood for furniture-making and in northern countries birch bark is used for roofing, baskets, cord, woven shoes, nets, plates, torches (when rolled up), parchment and paper. The oil from the bark is used for tanning Russian leather, giving it a unique smell. Birch bark is water-resistant because it contains large quantities of resin. In Norway, for weatherproof roofing a layer of earth is placed over a bark-laid base. In Lapland the bark is also used for cloaks and leggings. It burns well when everything else is wet and this is more or less the only way to destroy it.

Birch bark is like paper and from time immemorial it has been used to write upon. In the north, after the bark has been stripped off a birch tree, the wood is used for the Yule log.

Native North Americans use birch bark in the making of canoes. A birch bark canoe is ribbed with cedar and bound with larch roots, and its seams are made watertight with pine resin.

In Sweden and Lapland birch sap replaces sugar, and in Scandinavia farmers use the leafing time of the birch to gauge the sowing of their wheat. For our use today, here is a recipe for birch wine:

To every gallon (4½ litres) of birch water (*see p.97 on how to collect*) add a quart (1 litre) of honey and stir. Boil for 1 hour and add a few cloves and a little lemon peel. Remove any scum that forms. Let the mixture go cold, and add 3 to 4 spoons of good ale which contains yeast. Put into a fermenting bottle. When fermented, bottle and store.

This wine is a brisk and spirituous drink given especial virtue by the birch water. A less poky wine can be made from birch leaves, using an everyday recipe.

THE
APPLE TREE

BOTANICAL

APPLE. *Pyrus malus* or *communis*. Deciduous.

The wild crab-apple is Britain's only indigenous apple tree. It is small and beautiful, a delightful tree, especially when in flower or fruit.

In ancient days there were some 22 varieties of apple world-wide according to Pliny, but it was not until the eighteenth century that hybrids appeared in Britain from Europe, in particular from France. Different species were then grafted onto wild trees to produce the greater fruit-yielding trees known as *Malus domestica*. There are now thought to be about 2,000 species of apple world-wide.

Cider-apples are probably the closest species to the original crab-apples, though wild crab trees can still be found in hedgerows, scrub and woodland. It is not easy to recognize a genuine crab-apple tree, for seeds of orchard apples revert to ancestral type if sown in the wild. The main differences are that the wild crab is much smaller than the ordinary crab or domestic apple, its branches hang lower and its apples, which grow in bunches, are much smaller and tarter to the taste.

The crab-apple belongs to the rose family, along with hawthorn, wild pear and blackthorn, and like these it also has thorns which develop from spurs on its branches. Old apple trees are the commonest trees to host mistletoe and as such were sacred in druidic lore.

BARK
The trunks of old crab-apple trees become very aged and gnarled-looking. The trees often lean at crazy angles, as they try to hide themselves amongst other trees in hedgerows and the fringes of woods. The winter twigs of the crab-apple are long, slender and whippy, and often form a tangled mass in the crowns of old trees.

LEAVES
In early spring the leaf-buds are small, with purplish bud-scales fringed with white hairs. They open into leaves which are almost heart-shaped, mid-green and somewhat glossy.

FLOWERS
When the crab-apple's flower-buds open in April and May, they reveal small flowers tinged with deep pink which smell very similar to the flowers of honeysuckle. When in flower the apple tree is most beautiful and during the day

The leaves, flowers and fruit of the crab-apple

its blossom attracts a great number of bees with the honey scent of its rich nectar. At night-time the flowers exude a perfume attractive to night insects, and this ensures a complete 24-hour pollination of the flowers. As with cultivated apples, cross pollination is also necessary for a good crop of crab-apples.

FRUIT

After pollination the apple's flowers give way to the development of the fruit, which by autumn have become bunches of delicate little crab-apples, ripened to yellow and red and measuring about an inch (2½ cm) across. They are broader than they are long, with deep depressions at either end of the core, and they hang on long stalks. Any tree with short stalks and larger fruit, hanging singly or in pairs rather than bunches, is not an original crab-apple.

The very sour fruit of the crab-apple is called a pome, which is very close to *pomme*, the French for apple. Some crab trees hold fruit on their branches throughout winter and are a marvellous sight on grey days.

CUSTOM & LEGEND

The apple is very important in Celtic legend, yet in order to fully understand its importance we should look first at its world associations, beginning with the legends of Greece.

Aphrodite (Venus in Roman myth) was the supreme goddess of love and beauty. She was the daughter of Zeus and Dione, ancient deities of oak cults. Aphrodite's symbol was the apple, and she possessed the power to grant beauty and invincible charms to others, for whoever wore her magic girdle immediately became an object of love and desire. The rose, myrtle and poppy were also sacred to her, and her messenger birds were the sparrow, dove, swan and swallow. Her son was called Eros (Cupid), which refers to sexual passion, and Aphrodite appears to have been originally identical with Ishtar and Astarte and the Hebrew Ashtoreth. She was portrayed by artists and poets as born from the sea, rising naked from the foam upon a giant shell. When upon land it was said that grass and flowers sprang from the earth beneath her feet.

According to legend Aphrodite aided the love of Paris and the beautiful Helen of Troy. This came about because Paris was asked by Hermes (in the name of Zeus) to stop the many arguments that raged between three great goddesses as to who was most beautiful. Hermes gave Paris an apple and, to end all argument, told him to award it to the most beautiful goddess, who would thereafter bear the title. Aphrodite, Hera and Athene used their beauty and all manner of briberies to charm Paris, and Aphrodite finally won, for she promised him an introduction to the love of Helen of Sparta. However, the two chagrined goddesses then plotted to overthrow Troy, Helen's home, and so she became known as Helen of Troy whose beauty started the Trojan Wars. Paris and Helen set up many shrines in recognition of Aphrodite, and the apple became known as the source of beauty, love and wisdom. When cut in two transversely, an apple shows Aphrodite's five-pointed star in the shape of its pips.

Within the Greek myths the apple orchards of Paradise were known as the Garden of the Hesperides. In this garden there grew an especially sacred apple tree whose fruit conferred immortality. It was tended and guarded by nine fair maidens, the Hesperides themselves, who were representatives of the goddess of love. These maidens symbolically joined hands around the sacred tree and became its outer protection, along with a serpent which coiled around its roots. They sang songs about the red, yellow and green of the sunset and likened them to the colours of fully laden apple trees. As the sun set below the horizon, it appeared to them as a crimson apple sinking into the western ocean. When the sun had gone from view, Hesperus (Venus), the 'star' sacred to Aphrodite, goddess of love, rose in the sky.

In the Greek myths of Heracles (Hercules) we find the origins of the sacred apple tree which grew in this famous garden. It had been Gaia's (Mother Earth's) wedding gift to Hera when she married Zeus. Hera had planted the tree in the divine garden on the slopes of Mount Atlas and entrusted its guarding to Atlas's daughters, the original Hesperides. But then she found out that they were pilfering the apples and she set the serpent called Ladon to curl around the roots of the tree to guard it even more closely.

Heracles' eleventh labour was to fetch fruit from this specific tree. He learnt the position of Hera's garden from an old river-god called Nereus, who also advised him that he should not pick the apples from the tree himself, but rather that he should trick the wily Atlas into getting them for him. Atlas by then had been given the great burden of carrying the celestial globe upon his back and through Heracles' request saw a way of being freed from his task. He agreed to get the apples, but only if Heracles shot Ladon the serpent and took over the weight of the globe for him. Heracles did this. Atlas, finding great relief from his burden, cunningly obtained three apples from the tree with the help of his daughters the Hesperides, and then, liking his freedom, returned to Heracles to tell him that he could continue to have the glory of carrying the celestial globe, while he, Atlas, took the apples to Eurystheus, the god who had set the labour.

However, Heracles had been warned by Nereus not to trust Atlas and had already devised his answer, saying that he agreed, but as the weight of the globe was so heavy, could Atlas hold it a moment while Heracles put a pad on his head? Unthinking, Atlas laid the apples on the ground and complied, resuming the burden of the globe. Then Heracles triumphantly picked up the apples and to Atlas's astonishment left with them.

The theft of the apples from the divine garden caused great consternation in the heavens. Eventually Heracles gave the apples to the goddess Athene and she returned them to the Hesperides, sternly reminding them that it was unlawful for Hera's property to pass from their hands. Hera herself was so upset by all the events, especially the death of Ladon, that she set his image amongst the stars as the constellation of the Serpent and then sent Heracles mad.

The above legend of Heracles describes the sort of ancient tests that a candidate for kingship would receive: to overcome a serpent or dangerous dragon and take his treasure. Such tests or labours are found in ancient myths the world over. The most famous in Britain, which was known throughout the world as a place of initiation and learning, was linked to Llew (Lugh), who asked the Sons of Tuirenn to acquire for him the apples which 'grow in the Garden of Light over an ocean'. The myths of King Arthur and his Knights also tell of strange tests.

In Western legend the apple orchards of Paradise were known as 'the Isles of the Blessed' and they housed the Tree of Knowledge upon which three sacred apples grew. The boughs of this sacred tree pointed to the north, indicating the region traversed by the sun from spring through summer to autumn, and also pointed south, to the region of the dominion of winter, when the sun is beneath the horizon, the traditional place of the Underworld. The serpent which guarded the tree and its sacred apples was seen as the goddess Cerridwen, guarding the knowledge of the seasons.

In druidic lore the essence of the sacred apples was recognized as three drops of liquid which escaped Cerridwen's cauldron, drops which druid tradition taught had originally descended to the cauldron from heaven. Symbolically, from these three drops rose three streams corresponding to the three pillars of the druidic Tree of Life, which represented male and female and their united expression. They also corresponded to the druid's most holiest of symbols, the Three Rays of Light, the first ray of which pertains to vision, the second to letters or symbols, and the third to the understanding of the other two. From these rays (called the 'Awen') was born all art. The Three Rays are expressed vocally by intonation as the 'IAO', the Western mantra by which to intone or express the Creator (see also Rowan, p.234). The three sacred drops of the essence of the three sacred apples also represent the juices or inspirations from which all carnal beings derive their life-giving force. Thus the symbolic apple of the druids held a most sacred character, the more so as apple trees are the preferred host trees of the especially sacred mistletoe.

It is very noticeable how the Biblical legend of the Garden of Eden runs parallel to earlier tales of a sacred garden with a special tree bearing fruit, and it becomes very obvious how the monotheists changed the legends to suit their purpose. In their eyes the serpent became representative of all evil, woman became the tempter and the apple became the symbolic fruit of the downfall of man from grace. From the ancient recognition of the apple as a sacred fruit capable of transporting mortals to the land of the gods, as well as providing them with an earthly life of love and joy, came the deliberate misinterpretation in which the 'poisoned' apple represented seduction, wickedness and false knowledge. Such a concept entered the realms of folk and faerie tales, and eventually emerged personified in stories like *Snow White*, in which a wicked witch uses a poisoned apple to fulfil her jealousies.

Yet in myths and ancient legends the world over the apple is symbolic of the giving of love and of the goddesses of love. The Welsh goddess of apples is called Olwen or Arwen, the British goddess was Gwen and in Qabalistic tradition, the Grove of Paradise and the Tree of Life itself were presided over by the female-godhead called Shekinah. The Greek goddess Nemesis, who handed out divine justice *(see p.146)*, also presided over such a sacred grove. She carried an apple branch in one hand which she gave as a gift to heroes and in her other hand she held the symbolic 'wheel of the seasons' or an ash wand.

In Irish legend there was a magical Silver Bough cut from a mystical apple tree and upon this bough hung nine apples which played incessant music which lulled people into a deep trance-like sleep. In his *Mysteries of Celtic Britain* Lewis Spence tells us that the Silver Bough was, in effect, a link with the unseen world, 'a talisman by the aid of which certain mortals with whom the gods desired to establish communion and fellowship, were enabled to make entrance into the overseas paradise of these divinities while still alive'.

In Celtic times apples were considered food of the gods, and by tradition apple trees have been wassailed over the centuries by druids and country people to ensure good crops. Wassailing is a seasonal ceremony in which blessings and prayers are said to the trees. To encourage them to fruition a toast is drunk to the spirit which inhabits them, songs and poems are performed, and generous libations of cider are poured onto their roots:

> *Here's to thee, old apple tree!*
> *Whence thou may'st bud, and when thou may'st blow,*
> *Hats full! Caps full!*

Bushel – bushel bags full!
And my pockets full too! Hoorah!

TRADITIONAL DRUIDIC RHYME

At the Winter Solstice and Twelfth Night, all those present at wassailings called back the sun to aid the growth of blossom and fruit upon the trees. In the autumn the trees were thanked for their harvest. Other wassailing times are discussed shortly.

According to Norse myth, apples were given to the gods by humans in order that the gods might help them and keep old age at bay, and in old Saxon manuscripts there are numerous mentions of apples and cider. Apple wood is still seen as an emblem of security and a symbol of poetic immortality. Because it is a universal symbol of plenty, felling an apple tree has always been said to bring bad luck and in earlier days it brought the death penalty. To burn an apple tree is considered sacrilege indeed.

Country names of the apple tree include 'tree of love', 'the Silver Bough' and 'the fruit of the gods'.

HEALING

How many of us realize that we are remembering deep spiritual healing and ancient traditional customs when we give thought or voice to the adage 'An apple a day, keeps the doctor at bay'? The mere presence of apples heals our spirit, and the trust our ancestors placed upon them for their health of mind and body was later proved when it was realized what they contained.

Apples are filled with strong therapeutic agents: sugars, amino-acids, vitamins, malic and tartaric acids, pectin and numerous mineral salts. They can be prescribed for infections of the intestine, constipation, mental and physical overstrain, fatigue, hypertension, rheumatism, gout, anaemia, bronchial diseases, urine retention, hepatic insufficiency, demineralization, gastric and kidney conditions, hoarseness, coughs

113

and excess cholesterol in the blood. They are best eaten first thing in the morning and last thing at night, when they encourage sleep. Grated raw apple can be eaten slowly when you wake in the morning to prevent morning sickness in pregnancy, as I've found many times to my own relief.

Raw apple can be made into a poultice (see Appendix V, p.344) for inflamed eyes, badly healing wounds and aches and pains. A compress of the pulp or the juice restores skin tissue and warts can be cured by rubbing them with two halves of an apple which are then buried. As the apple decays the warts disappear. With the above list of healing properties we can see just how precious the apple was to our ancestors in a world without modern medicine. Nowadays, luckily, the fruit of the apple tree is with us in all seasons.

The Bach Flower Remedies use crab-apple for curing self-dislike, despondency, obsessions, over-anxiousness, getting stuck over details, house-proudness, fussiness and as an internal cleanser.

The apple is ideal for bringing about a communion of male and female, for meditation within an apple orchard, or even with an apple or a bunch of blossom, helps us find certain qualities of love and trust. These qualities not only relate to our feelings towards others, but also to our feelings towards ourselves. In our dealings with the world, most often we unconsciously project our fears, uncertainties and lack of self-love onto others. When we do, we start a ball rolling, as it were, for the way we project ourselves determines the ways in which we are accepted or rejected by others. Apples help us find harmony within ourselves, through which we may discover harmony with the world.

MAGIC

IRISH/GAELIC	*Quert*
OGHAM	ᚊ
RUNIC	K
RULING PLANET	Venus
ABILITIES	Healing. Love. Poetic inspiration. Works of destiny. Foundation. To do with the element of Water.
SEASONS	All

The apple has always been regarded as the possessor of amazing healing and magical qualities. It is a symbol of beauty and fruitfulness. Apples have been used for love, immortality and healing spells, and were capable, legend tells us, of healing severely wounded men in battles past.

Early blossoming apple trees reveal great beauty which was likened to the beauty of the goddess of flowers. Apple blossom raises the spirit of love and fertility in any celebration.

In the magical realms, as there was a springtime flower-goddess created from nine types of flowers, so there was an autumn fruit-god created from nine kinds of fruit. The flower-goddess and the fruit-god guarded the seasons and ensured good harvests in the world of Nature.

Fruit trees were always blessed at each turn of the seasons. On Twelfth Night this was done to ensure a Maytime blossoming of the trees, in order to miss the early blossom-killing frosts. Traditional customs defended apple trees against bad weather and pieces of coral were hung in the trees' branches to give extra protection, along with the wassailing.

A traditional time of planting apple trees was May-eve. Small pieces of coal were placed beneath their roots and a good libation of cider 'watered' them in.

At midsummer, as apple trees are the most common bearers of the sacred mistletoe, they were paid homage by the druids, and the giver of the mistletoe was revered as the goddess of the apple orchard. At this time of year the fusion of Nature's energies was likened to a marriage between the sun and the earth, and within an apple orchard is found the 'marriage-couch' wherein the god and goddess conjoin, their fertility guided by the love expressed by the apple tree's planetary ruler, Venus.

Lammas is the beginning of harvesting-time. It heralds long hot days and hard work, companionship and beautiful sunsets, when the land is rich in colour like an apple. The legends of the Garden of the Hesperides reflect the colour and atmosphere of this season (see p. 109). As harvests of all fruit and grains takes place, refreshment for the workers is provided by last year's apple harvest made into cider. Traditionally, when collecting the harvest from fruit trees, the last apple is left on the tree for the wise old 'Apple-tree Man', the 'Fruit-man' who ensures good future harvests. The Apple-tree Man is the personification of the spirit of the apple tree, and anciently he was duly respected and paid homage to.

Apples are specifically used at the Samhain festivities to ensure that the correct atmosphere of trust and friendship ensues. Samhain is the time when the light half of the year moves into the dark, and the eating of apples at this time also helps us make the corresponding internal changes, lining us up spiritually and magically. This is also the time when the veils between this and the Otherworld are at their thinnest and we can commune with departed friends. The presence and use of apples ensures that only good spirits prevail during this.

Many apple games, such as 'bobbing' for apples floating in cauldrons of water, enliven celebrations at this time. The atmosphere is also enhanced by apple juice flowing from the ritual cup. As the apple is known as both the food of the gods and the food of the dead, and as the apple bough was believed to be the talisman which enabled gods and heroes to rise from the Underworld, altars are piled high with them at Samhain. It is known to the Wicca as the feast of apples (see also Willow, p. 271).

Roasted apples were an essential ingredient of the wassailing bowl, the large drinking cup our ancestors passed amongst the people when toasting fruit trees. Within the bowl was found hot spiced cider with bits of apple and toast floating in it. Each person who drank from the bowl took part of an apple, wishing good luck to the company as they ate it. An old recipe for this drink is given below (see p. 122). Originally the recipe was secret, for it was a sacred drink of the druids who called it La

Mas Ushal. It was brewed specifically at the end of October in preparation for rituals on the first day of November, the druidic 'day of the apple'
and the beginning of the new Celtic year.

Apples are sacred to the love-goddesses, and any rituals or gatherings
of people are enhanced by their presence or use. Many love spells and
charms are worked with apples. A girl who was unable to choose
between lovers traditionally took two apple pips, named each for a lover
and then stuck one on each cheek of her face. She then said: 'Pippin,
pippin, I stick thee there, thou that is true thou may'st declare.' The pip
that remained on her cheek foretold the faithful lover.

In love divinations the pips of cut apples were counted. If they were of
an even number, marriage was foretold, if an uneven number, the querant
would remain unmarried for some time. If a pip were cut, any forthcom-
ing relationship would be stormy; if two were cut, the marriage would
not last long, for the love would fade away. A simple act of love magic is
to share an apple with a friend, for it is guaranteed to aid companionship.

Apple blossoms are added to all love spells, used either in the incense,
love-mixtures, ritual cups or embrocations, or just simply scattered
around the ritual area.

Apples are also an essential part of garden magic. Apple wood can be
carved into talismans or amulets to attract love and longevity. It is excellent to carve into a magical wand or an image for specific healing or love
spells.

The deities and heroes associated with apples are Aphrodite, Venus,
Helen, Hera, Astarte, Ashtoreth, Ishtar, Cerridwen, Athene, Nemesis,
Eurystheus, Olwen, Gwen, Arwen, Shekinah, Heracles, Atlas, Dionysus,
Zeus, Paris, Cupid.

INSPIRATION

An apple orchard in full bloom is a magical place filled with golden haze.
As white and pink blossoms shed pollen to the air, insects drone from
flower to flower, becoming drunk on sweet nectar. It is said that all

Neolithic and Bronze Age paradises were called orchards. 'Paradise', a Persian word, literally means 'orchard' or 'stand of trees'. To the Persians trees were especially sacred.

The apple was one of the seven chieftain trees of Britain, and as such potently pagan. In Europe the juice of the apple was used in the druidic sacrament, much as the grape was used in sacrament to Dionysus/Bacchus in other lands. Yet as already seen, many sacred trees were decried by the Church. In the words of an old druidic wassailing song we see the threat to the powerful associations between trees and people:

> Sweet apple tree, learning, a tree that is fair,
> Thy crop is not small, the fruit that is on thee.
> And I am anxious about thee,
> Lest the woodmen, hewers of trees,
> May bury thy roots and corrupt thy fruit,
> That thou mayest no more bear one apple!

ANON

In looking closely at these words, while bearing in mind our cultural history, we may regard the 'hewers of trees' as those who derided indigenous Nature religions. 'Bury thy roots' could refer to overlaying the deepest traditions of the land with dogma, and 'corrupt thy fruit' could reference the introduction of propaganda and superstition which purposefully sullied the pagan concept of the natural world. This interpretation may seem exaggerated or petty, but it is a sad fact that in researches for this book, countless examples of such manipulation have surfaced, all designed for one purpose: to keep people away from the wisdom and power engendered by Nature, for that very power puts people in touch with their roots and thus in charge of their lives, making a mockery out of those who would seek to control. When looking at the politics of today, it could be said that little has changed!

Many Celtic tales were woven around apple trees and their wondrous fruit, and tradition tells us of a wonderful apple orchard which held the secrets of the earth and the understanding of the movements of the planets. This orchard was revealed to Merlin by his master the Great

Bard Hierophant Gwendolleu, 'before Merddyn became aged', and it consisted of 'seven score and seven delicious apple trees of equal age, height, length and size, which spring from the bosom of Mercy', producing 'sweet apples for those who can digest them'. Legend tells us that this orchard grew apart from any others and that it was guarded by two 'dusky' birds, each wearing a 'yoke of gold'. It was supposedly borne from place to place by Merlin. From this we can deduce it was possibly descriptive of one of Merlin's magical 'working places' upon the astral plane, within the realms of his powerful imagination.

This whole concept is still viable within our powerful imaginations, for in a healing and personal development capacity we can intentionally 'construct' such an orchard within our own minds; and we can construct it upon and fill it with specific qualities, so it becomes our personal place of power. Such a place is built up slowly within the imagination, until a clear visual and sensual impression of it is obtained when the eyes are closed in meditation, when in our mind's eye we can see ourselves walking into it. It becomes a foundation, haven and security, a place of work and a place of rest and healing, a place of your particular values and strengths. It can be with you always. No matter where you go or what you have to go through, you have only to 'call it up'.

Merlin also speaks of the Queen of Faerie who gave out apples to confer the gifts of prophecy. In thirteenth-century Scotland, Thomas of Ercledoune is alleged to have met with her and to have visited her country. He was given the gift of prophecy, but was warned to eat 'neither apples nor pears whilst in her land lest he should never return to his own folk'. Legend says that the people of the Sidhe, i.e., the faeries, are themselves waiting to be reborn and that they await this in a dim paradise beneath the earth. Irish legend tells us that the *sidhe* (or raths) were hollow hills or round barrow fortresses and the name became attached to the faerie races which dwelt within them. All mortals who enter their realms must neither eat nor drink whilst there, no matter how pressing the invitation to do so, for to eat the food of the dead trapped them in that realm. Thomas of Ercledoune was named Thomas the Rhymer after his gift of prophecy and is reputed to have remained seven years among the Sidhe (*see also Yew, p.23*).

In the Glastonbury area of western Britain, with its many apple orchards and pagan air, you cannot fail to acknowledge the collective power of apple trees, for within such orchards mysteries come alive. We are told that Glastonbury has been surrounded by magical orchards since time immemorial, and such is the atmosphere they create that one can easily imagine they once numbered as many as those attributed to Merlin, and that he could possibly have lain them on the ground in this magical place. Even though many orchards have been felled in recent years to make way for car parks and supermarkets, the magic still lives on in the souls and hearts of the people, for the 'astral orchards' of our traditional past still exert their power in these Islands of the West.

PHYSICAL USES

The fruit of the apple tree is the part most used, though apple wood is beautifully grained when carved into small objects, and is ideal to carve into a love-gift. The apple is a rich source of health-giving food and drink for humans, and is excellent for healing both the mind and body. The taste for eating apples is one of our earliest and most natural of inclinations, and the fruit is delicious both cooked and uncooked. In days past all meals and banquets had an apple course. Apples also provide abundant sustenance for animals and insects. They have always been used as a symbol of harvest and form an integral part of the traditions of the land, being a strong link between Nature and the country people.

An apple stuck with cloves was most likely the original pomander, used in the home to keep a freshness in the air, and in clothes and linen cupboards to keep things smelling sweet. Lightning was said never to split an apple-tree trunk, for it was protected by the great quality of love it contained. Because of this people were advised to plant apple trees near their homes, both as a protection against lightning and to generate love in the household.

Cider apples, a step in the development between wild apples and dessert apples, were the traditional mainstay of most farming communities, for the cider produced on farms refreshed farm workers and was a health-giving commodity. Great pride was taken, and still is in some country communities, in the qualities of cider produced, which were distinctive to each farm.

Here is a traditional way of making cider:

At the autumn harvest of apples, great heaps of them are piled on the strawstrewn floor of the pound house, a building covered with thatch which houses the pounder, press and vats. The pounder is then filled by tipping apples in at the top, and a handle is turned which crushes the apples between two teethed rollers.

The pulp and juice are then put into the press, which is huge and tray-like, with a lip from which the liquid flows during pressing. The supports and any wooden parts of the press are traditionally made of oak, for it is impervious to damage by the acidy liquid. The pulp of the apples (placed into the press between layers of straw to a height of 3 feet (1 metre) or more) is called the 'cheese'.

Once it is in place, the screw of the press is turned to compress it, until clear apple juice runs freely into a vat placed under the lip of the press. The juice is then poured into casks and left to mature for some four months before drinking.

Cider-making has become very commercial, but the best varieties of this country drink are still to be found upon farms which continue to produce their own.

Before the introduction of pesticides, apple trees were rid of insects and bugs by lighting bonfires to the windward side of the trees. As the smoke reached the grubs on the trees, they curled up and fell to the ground, where they were swept up and burnt. In this way consideration was shown to the land, for no suffering was given to the forms of life surrounding the pests. This is more ecologically sound than today's overuse and abuse of chemicals.

The sour fruit of the crab-apple are used in jellies, along with other fruit. Their juice makes an excellent substitute vinegar. Here is a recipe for spiced crab-apples which can be served with cold meat dishes:

Wash and halve the apples, taking out any bad bits but leaving the skin and cores. To 1½ lbs (600 g) (6 cups) of apples, heat½ pint (¼ litre) of cider vinegar and 1½ lbs (600 g) (3 cups) of sugar in a pan until the sugar is dissolved, then add the apples and half a level teaspoon of both ground cloves and ground ginger, and 1 level teaspoon of cinnamon.

Simmer gently until the apples are tender but unbroken, then take them out with a spoon and put them into clean warm jars. The syrup is then boiled until it is reduced to about half its volume and when cool is poured over the apples in the jars, which are then sealed.

After 2 to 3 months the syrup will have been absorbed into the apples, and their skins and cores will have become soft and spicy.

This is an excellent old English side dish for that special occasion!

At Yule festivities a wassailing bowl with roast apples gives any party good cheer. Crab-apples are an ancient ingredient, and they are collected in late autumn and are put aside, individually wrapped in newspaper, in a cold shed. Here is a recipe for a wassailing bowl drink:

Before making the drink, wash the crab-apples and give each a shallow cut around their middles, through their skins. Then place them on a buttered tray in a moderate oven for about 20 minutes, until they split around their middles to reveal the soft apple inside.

To make the drink, take 2 pints (1 litre) of brown ale or Old English ale (or cider for a lighter version) and pour into a large pan. Add 3 tablespoons of brown sugar or 2 of honey and a large teaspoon of cinnamon, ½ teaspoon of ginger and ¼ teaspoon of cloves, and heat almost to the boil. Take off the heat, drop in the crab-apples and allow to stand so they absorb some of the liquid. Allow one apple for each glass.

To boost this spicy drink, whiskey or brandy can be added, and anciently small squares of toast like croutons were set to float in the liquid.

On cold days the hot spicy drink from the wassailing bowl provided a warm glow of inebriation to all present at the outdoor seasonal festivities, a glow with which all toasted the fruit trees, wishing them health and good future harvests. Such fruition can also be called for when we toast trees or our friends at Yuletide or Christmas.

THE HAWTHORN TREE

BOTANICAL

HAWTHORN. *Crataegus oxyacantha*. Deciduous.

The hawthorn is a small tree of the rose family. It can grow up to 30 feet (9 metres) high but is usually smaller and is more often than not broader than high. Given encouragement by man, it is very much a hedge-tree. 'Haw' is believed to mean 'hedge'. Hawthorn is more a village tree than a forest tree, for it seems to prefer to grow close to people. It provides food and shelter for many birds and small mammals, as well as some 50 species of insect life, and is very important to the wildlife of hedgerows.

Hawthorn is most often companion to blackthorn in the hedgerows, but the two are easily distinguishable, especially in spring, for blackthorn blossoms before leafing, and hawthorn blossoms along with its newly opened leaves. It grows quickly and sends out many side shoots and branches which make a sturdy impenetrable barrier to livestock, even though cattle and horses love to eat its leaves.

Unlike blackthorn, which sends out suckers, hawthorn does not have a large root system and is therefore not greedy with the soil's nutrients. This encourages many forms of plant life to grow in its vicinity.

Pollen counts have shown that hawthorn was widespread in Britain before 6,000 BC, and remains of hawthorn have been found in megalithic tombs. Hawthorn used to be a proud blossomer by the month of May, until the calendar changed by 12 days. It is also known as 'whitethorn' or simply 'the May'.

The leaves, thorns, flowers and fruit of the hawthorn

There are about 1,000 species of hawthorn world-wide. In Britain there are two main species: the English and common hawthorn. Hawthorns can live for over 400 years and have the capacity to flower twice a year, though this depends upon weather conditions. They are common throughout Europe, though not in northern Scotland.

BARK

The trunk of a hawthorn tree becomes gnarled with age and its bark is thick with scored furrows. The whole tree often appears to be very old, especially in winter when its dark grey trunk looks like twisted old rope.

As a wild-looking 'orchard-shaped' tree it is dense with intertwining branches and fiercely armed with short sharp thorns or spines. When in a hedgerow hawthorn sends out many more spines, almost as if it accepted its work of being a barrier, while as a tree it is less thorny and much more knobbly in appearance. Hawthorn spines are really stunted shoots.

LEAVES
In April the hawthorn's leaf-buds open and little bundles of pale green leaves appear on every branch. The leaves are deeply divided into toothed lobes. They become shiny green on top and grey-green below, and are abundant on the branches.

The English hawthorn does not have much colour to its autumn leaves, for its main colour is given to its blossoms. The common hawthorn's leaves, however, take on beautiful colours of reds, oranges and yellows.

FLOWERS
Interspersed with the newly opened leaves are masses of flower-buds, looking like tiny white balls. When these open they reveal flowers with five snow-white petals set around slender stamens with bright pink heads. With its mass of blossom and leaves, each branch becomes weighted down and the rich evocative scent of the flowers permeates the air. Hawthorn blossoms contain both male and female parts and are fertilized by insects crawling over them.

The English variety of hawthorn has blossoms of pink or red, or white tipped with pink, which have a haunting smell, the perfume of early summer.

Common hawthorn grows big, and its mass of pure white flowers can cover and hide the tree.

FRUIT
On the back of each hawthorn flower are five green sepals, looking like the rays of a star. Below this the stalk looks slightly swollen, for it contains the seed which by summer will have grown into a small green

berry. As we move into autumn they have grown and ripened, and are a shiny dark red. They hang in long-stalked bunches awaiting the attention of birds, which love to eat them. They then propagate the seeds upon their flights.

The English hawthorn has two or three seeds to each berry fruit. The common hawthorn's fruit contains a single seed.

CUSTOM & LEGEND

No tree is more deeply enshrined in the traditions of the English countryside and the affections of the people. Chaucer, Milton, Swinburne and poets throughout the centuries have sung the hawthorn's blossoming praises.

In pagan terms hawthorn is a prime symbol of fertility. It was always the traditional tree used at marriages, for it reflects the union of the forces of Nature. Hawthorn blossoms have a potently erotic perfume which has been likened to the aroma of the sexual secretions of females and was thought to enrich fertility. In Celtic times most marriages took place at Beltaine, the beginning of summer when hawthorn is a mass of blossoms and new leaves.

In ancient times there were many hawthorn cults ruled over by goddesses to whom the tree was sacred. In Britain one of the earliest hawthorn-goddesses was Olwen, daughter of Yspaddaden Pencawr, a wild man called Giant Hawthorn. Olwen was known as 'She of the White Track', for it was observed that white flowering trefoils sprang up wherever she set her foot upon the earth. In our present day it can be observed that hawthorn's blossoming in the hedgerows also appears to form white tracks through the fields.

In the tales of the *Mabinogion*, Culhwych, nephew to King Arthur, fell in love with Olwen when under a spell from his step-mother, a queen who was angry that he refused to marry her daughter. The step-mother's actions were also prompted by Culhwych's father Cilydd, for he had killed her husband, King Doged, and had thus claimed his lands as well as his wife and daughter. By delivering the spell upon Culhwych so he should wed none other than Olwen, the queen gave him the hardest of tasks, for Olwen's father Yspaddaden was frightening to behold and impossible to confront. Culhwych had forcefully to demand assistance from Arthur and his knights. However, when he did confront Yspaddaden, he was set 39 impossible tasks to perform before he could claim Olwen's hand.

Legendary ritual tasks were set upon candidates for important marriages the world over and were similar to those set upon a candidate for kingship. In his tasks Culhwych had to find the Thirteen Treasures of Britain. He was helped by Arthur to overthrow Yspaddaden's mighty power and married the beautiful Olwen.

Another of the spring-goddesses associated with hawthorn is Blodeuwedd, who, as already mentioned, was magically created from flowers as a consort for Llew Llaw-Gywffes, a Celtic sun-god. As a spring-goddess Blodeuwedd was conjured up from nine kinds of spring flowers. She traditionally represented the light part of the year which gave balance to the autumn, when the autumn-god was made from nine kinds of fruit. It is Blodeuwedd who the May Queen represents when she is dressed in blossoms at the Mayday festivities. The May King (also known as the Green Man or Jack in the May), who courts the May Queen at the celebrations, also wears hawthorn blossom in his leafy costume. As a symbol of fertility he represents summer, the fields and woodland.

It is perhaps through the hawthorn that we see the greatest tussle between pagan Nature worship and the strictures of the Christian Church. For the hawthorn stands supreme in the month of May, where it represents human nature, sexuality, reproduction and fertility. This is expressed by Chaucer:

> *Mark the fair blooming of the Hawthorn Tree,*
> *Who, finely clothed in a robe of white,*
> *Fills full the wanton eye with May's delight.*

These words capture the pagan atmosphere of the season of May, expressing its fullest mood. Yet in what became the dogmatic rituals of the Church, in March, April and May chastity was the goal. Lent is the 40 days fasting before Easter, symbolic of Christ's fasting in the wilderness; and the first day of Lent is at the end of March, around the time of the Spring Equinox, which is on or about 21 March. Easter itself, which commemorates the death and resurrection of Christ, is held in April, timing itself from the Spring Equinox by being the first Sunday after the first full moon of that date. The descent of the Holy Ghost, Whitsun, is on 15 May. As we can see, between Easter and Whitsun lies Mayday, the pagan day of revelry and sexual merriment, where people are moved to express the creative spirit felt to emanate from the world of Nature!

Festivals were also held from 28 April to 1 May in honour of the Roman flower-goddess Flora and they reeled from extravagant merriment and lasciviousness. No doubt this added to the Church's concern over excessive Maytime festivities.

The most famous Christian legend concerning hawthorn is that of the Glastonbury Thorn. This sixteenth-century story tells us that as Christianity entered Britain the Celtic spirit was moved by the spirituality it expressed and that this was emphasized when Joseph of Arimathea came to Glastonbury. On Wearyall Hill he rested, leaning upon his staff, which during the night rooted into the ground and became a blossoming hawthorn tree. This was taken as a sign that the new religion of Christ was to be founded at Glastonbury, and Joseph and his 12 disciples built the first Christian chapel there.

Joseph's staff became known as the Glastonbury Thorn, which ever after blossomed on Christmas Day in honour of the divine birth of Christ. The original tree was said to be still living in Puritan days and is believed to have had a double trunk. It is recorded that a soldier of Cromwell went to cut the tree down and a splinter from it blinded him. In the reign of James I, large sums of money were paid for cuttings from the tree and to this day a blossoming twig from the Glastonbury Thorn is annually sent to the Queen at Christmas.

There is a Judaeo-Christian legend about a species of hawthorn (*Crataegus pyracantha*) which was the tree through which Moses spoke to God on Mount Horeb. Christian legend also tells us that an eastern species of hawthorn, known as the Albiespyne, formed the crown of thorns used in the Crucifixion, and that because hawthorn had touched the Lord's brow it was sanctified. However in later times as the Nature religions were being suppressed, it was decreed that the pagan use of hawthorn was blasphemous and under the power of the devil.

Therefore alien concepts were enforced upon the people's intuitive associations with the hawthorn tree and the powerful season of spring. In all previous civilizations and cultures, and in the natural world itself, May was a month of joyous celebration, when by a reiteration of the life-force, all living things exalted at having come through the dark times of winter. The Church's misrepresentation denied the use of hawthorn as the people's contact with the changing seasons and led to artificial super-stition and a control of the population by fear, for their feelings of being part of the intrinsic pattern of Nature were now considered sinful. This severed the closeness people had with the land, cutting off their 'roots'. Even today this continues, for children are often told more in school about ancient foreign legend than they ever are about the indigenous beliefs and practices of their own lands. The strength of a nation is built upon the knowledge of its roots. Surely it is time that such knowledge is made accessible, for it will ignite the true spirit of learning.

Back to hawthorn legend. The Italian goddess of hawthorn was Cardea, who presided over childbirth and protected infants. She was propitiated at weddings with hawthorn torches. Cardea's symbol was the hinge of the door of the year and her consort was the powerful god Janus, who opened the year of seasons and presided over the beginning of everything. Cardea was also worshipped as a calendar-goddess under the names Post-vorta and Ante-vorta, and was known as 'She who looks prophetically forward to the new king's reign' and 'She who mourns the old'.

In European myth hawthorns are connected to miraculous concep-tions. In Greek myth Hera conceived Ares and his twin-sister Eris when she touched hawthorn blossoms. However Ares (called Mars by the Romans) was an Olympian god of war, and his sister Eris provoked many quarrels and became symbolic of the type of strife usually associated with blackthorn (see pp. 80-2).

In Britain Henry VII claimed hawthorn as the badge of the House of

Tudor, because at the Battle of Bosworth Field the crown of England was stolen from Richard III and hidden in a hawthorn bush. It was found by Lord Stanley, who placed it upon Henry's head and thus made him king. From this comes the old proverb 'Cleve to thy crown, though it hangs on a bush.'

Many hawthorn customs are associated with the month of May, and in Cornwall the Helston Furry, or Floral Dance, survives as a Mayday celebration. Dancing takes place to songs like the following:

> *For we are up as soon as any day-o,*
> *And for to fetch the summer home,*
> *The summer and the May-o,*
> *For summer now has come.*

At Padstow in Cornwall a bucking hobby-horse is still paraded through the streets, with obvious phallic connotations. In continuance of tradition, if any woman gets drawn in under the horse's 'skirt' she will easily conceive thereafter.

The following words of Rudyard Kipling refer to the continuity of the seasonal fertility celebrations associated with hawthorn and also to its later opposition:

> *O do not tell the priest of our Art,*
> *For he would call it a sin,*
> *For we'll be out in the woods all night,*
> *A-conjuring summer in.*
>
> 'A TREE SONG' FROM *PUCK OF POOK'S HILL*

Only a few of the hawthorn legends have been told here yet it is easy to see why it was regarded as a sacred tree and why great misfortune was deemed to come to those who destroyed one.

HEALING

Hawthorn radiates qualities of growth and health. People have always approached it for healing, especially those trees that grow near wells and springs.

Modern science shows that hawthorn contains chemical components which are sedative, anti-spasmodic and diuretic, and this makes the plant a remarkable natural regulator of arterial blood pressure. Known as 'valerian of the heart', hawthorn is most valuable as a heart stimulant, especially if the treatment is to be lengthy, for it possesses a great lack of toxicity and does not accumulate in the body. It therefore brings a sense of tone and health to the heart, making the patient feel more alive and vital.

Hawthorn is also used with digitalis to treat heart diseases, though it must be stressed that qualified advice should be sought from a herbalist or doctor if such conditions are suspected or being treated.

With its excellent sedative effects hawthorn also helps people who suffer from palpitations, angina pectoris, the menopause and any disturbance of the blood circulation.

The homoeopathic name for hawthorn is oxyacantha. The spiritual healing associated with it is discussed in Magic (see pp. 132–6).

FLOWERS

Hawthorn flowers, made into a strong infusion of a good spoonful per cup, can be drunk two or three times a day at the onset of angina. A cupful of the same infusion can be taken at night to ease insomnia.

The flowers are used in decoction to heal facial blemishes and acne:

> The fair maid who the first of May,
> Goes to the field at the break of day,
> And washes in dew from the Hawthorn Tree,
> Will ever after handsome be.
>
> ANON

BERRIES

Hawthorn berries, dried and crushed and made into a decoction, ease diarrhoea and dysentery, kidney inflammations and disorders. This same decoction, when mixed with honey, is good as a gargle for sore throats and any resultant infection.

SEEDS

Hawthorn seeds, taken from the berry, cleared of down, bruised and boiled in wine, can be drunk to calm inward pains.

MAGIC

IRISH/GAELIC	*Huathe*
OGHAM	ꓵ
RUNIC	h
RULING PLANET	Mars
ABILITIES	Fertility. Guardian. Cleansing. Door to the Otherworld. Happiness. To do with the element of Fire.
SEASONS	Spring (Beltaine); Autumn

In ancient Greece and Italy hawthorn was regarded as the symbol of marriage and fertility, and in France, England and all Celtic countries it is still bound up with the pagan Mayday rites, which use the blossoms of 'the May' to symbolize love and betrothal.

All the community helped with preparations for the Beltaine festivities. Early on Mayday morn hawthorn blossoms were gathered and woven into garlands by the children of the village, who took the greatest pride and joy in their creations. The garlands were then worn by all the people in the festivities, and they also decorated houses, dairies and cattle sheds to bring prosperity to all aspects of life. The greatest care was taken in the weaving of an especial garland which crowned the maypole, the central point of all the festivities.

Beltaine is a festival of birth and bunches of flowering hawthorn were always carried in wedding processions to give fertility to the marrying couple and hope to their desires, while in Ireland newly married couples still dance around thorn bushes to gain extra blessings on their marriage.

During May the strength of the rising sun's energy also gives impetus and effect to any healings performed with hawthorn. This effect is especially powerful in healings worked at wells and springs, and whatever is begun at such a time and place will gain most benefit from the naturally occurring patterns of growth in the natural world, for it utilizes the tides of the seasons.

A beautiful spring-time custom of old was to plait crowns of hawthorn blossoms and to leave them for the angels or faeries who came at night. The people who made the offerings believed that if the faeries chose to dance around the crowns, blessings would be showered upon them. This custom is still practised in many parts of Ireland and Wales.

Old Midsummer's Day falls on 5 July and at this time the hawthorn trees themselves were decorated. The custom of blessing and adorning thorn trees is called 'bawming the thorn'. Flower garlands and red ribbons are attached to a tree, then children dance around it. This custom possibly derives from the reverence shown to guardian trees of early settlements. Until recent years it was performed regularly on certain trees such as the Appleton Thorn in Cheshire, planted by Adam de Dutton in 1125 and thought to be an offshoot of the Glastonbury Thorn.

Upon farmsteads the farm kitchen was given protection from fire by a charm created from hawthorn. A globe was woven from hawthorn branches and twigs, and this was hung in the kitchen at new year to protect the place until the following new year, when it was replaced by a new globe. The old globe was then ritually burned and scattered on the fields before sowing the seed, in order to protect and encourage good growth of the crops.

Hawthorn was intimately connected to all aspects of village life, especially that conducted around village wells. Many thorns still thrive near old wells, as if the magnetism of such places holds them spellbound. Old well-trees take on great character, in some ways embodying the old women who met under them and talked as they gathered water, or those who have whispered their spells into the water's reflective depths as they healed or charmed, blessed or cursed with their magic might. The potent energy of wells and springs bubbles up from the earth to weave and distort the trees into crazy primitive shapes. So full of character become these trees, that many were likened to certain individuals and were named accordingly. Thus we hear country tales of trees with names like Sally, Old Sal or Sally Hawthorn, in which the energies and qualities of the tree and the person have become so intertwined as to be one. This must be one of the nicest ways to be remembered by future generations.

As a faerie tree the hawthorn's work is to guard the wells. Springs and wells have always been held as sacred by mankind, for without water there is no life. They are also places where people feel that the veil between spirit and matter is thin. Many shrines exist where ancient thorns still stand sentinel and they are still visited by those who look to the trees as intermediaries between themselves and the higher realms. Such visitors leave wish-rags and offerings tied to the tree's branches in order to attract luck, love, healing and success.

Full of ancient memories and mysteries, evocative of spells and faerie tales, the hawthorn is the tree most associated with fertility and fulfilment in the hearts of the people, and its beautiful blossoms were thought to help prayers reach heaven. Sick children were traditionally carried to hawthorns where pagan prayers were said for their healing, and hawthorn blossoms were attached to a baby's cradle for similar healing and protection.

Properly evoked, the hawthorn spirit has the power to protect on many levels. It can be used by direct contact meditation to cleanse or rid us of inner problems of a vital or sexual nature. A very simple way to gain such healing and a quick way to gain a magical contact with the tree is to eat a few of its leaves, slowly chewing while concentrating upon the contact being made with the actual substance of the tree, its spirit and its physical presence. By eating part of a tree we ingest all that that tree has to offer, to most of which we are as blind. And yet if we could but see, as did the ancients, we would realize why it has always been said that a high price would be demanded by the higher powers on those who cut down hawthorn needlessly.

Folklore abounds with tales about those who would fell a hawthorn. As was mentioned earlier, a Parliamentary soldier was said to have been blinded as he tried to fell the Holy Thorn at Glastonbury. In another tale, a certain farmer, annoyed by visitors to a flowering hawthorn on his land, tried to cut the tree down but saw blood flowing from its trunk. Yet another farmer felled a hawthorn and immediately broke his leg and had his farm burn down. Thus in country parts it is still traditional for a prayer to be said before even taking a branch from a hawthorn.

To carry a sprig of hawthorn was to have proof against storms at sea and lightning on shore, and in some regions hawthorn was taken into the home and placed in the rafters for protection against spirits, ghosts and storms. Superstition engineered by the Church led to the belief that this was unlucky. However in 1350 John Mandeville wrote:

> And therefore hath the white thorn many virtues! For he that bearest on hym thereof, none manner of tempest may dere him: be in the hows that yt is ynne may none evil ghost entre.

Hawthorn's protective qualities against lightning are shown in this traditional rhyme:

> Beware of an oak,
> It draws the stroke,
> Avoid an ash,
> It courts a flash,
> Creep under a thorn,
> It will save you from harm.

The young girls of the northern counties of Britain eagerly awaited the first blossom of hawthorn, and the girl who found it would partly break it from the branch and leave it hanging. That night she would dream of her future husband and if the next day she found and gathered up the broken twig of blossom, it could be kept as a charm until her husband appeared.

Hawthorn's planetary ruler is Mars, which gives it a fiery nature full of lusty qualities. The deities associated with hawthorn are Flora, Olwen, Blodeuwedd, Hera, Cardea and Hymen, the god of marriage, who carries the bridal torch made from hawthorn, and who was invoked by the bridal song called 'The Hymeneal'.

INSPIRATION

To many country people and travellers throughout the ages, hawthorn is known as the 'bread and cheese' tree. This is because leaves eaten from the hawthorn were reckoned to give as much sustenance as a plate of bread and cheese. This is the name I knew it by as a child, as I nibbled its leaves to stop my tummy rumbling for food when playing or sitting in the shade of the hedgerow. Eating the hawthorn's leaves became a special thing to me, my cherished communication with the tree, during which we shared secrets that no one else knew. Even before I knew the origins of the 'bread and cheese' name I knew the daydreams that came to me from hedgerow trees, memories of people on journeys upon paths and trackways of long ago.

Upon long journeys, Nature's food picked from the trees and hedgerows gave travellers comfort and strength when they were far from habitation. As well as a food, hawthorn was also a friend and confidant to the traveller, for certain trees that grew at meeting points along the routes not only provided nourishment for weary people that rested by them but also aided them spiritually and replenished their energy. It would seem, by the memories contained within trees, that they retained impressions of communications between themselves and the people which could later be recalled by another person of the same family or tribe, or by a sensitive who actually tuned into the tree in the same manner as the original impression maker. This capacity kept the wandering tribes in close communication on a spiritual level, and thus kept them healthy and strong. To me all this 'travelling' energy is symbolized by the hawthorn's way of making you feel as though you have faerie feet, through which you are pulled by the lands of vision, knowing where you are going even though you've never been there before.

These traditions are illustrated in a song entitled 'The Hawthorn and the Clover' written by Mic Darling, a travelling man whose poems and songs reflect his observations of life. The song is taken from his tape *My Pony and Me: Songs of contented travelling*, and within it today's realities are presented, for the hawthorn which feeds the people and the clover which feeds the horses are both very much at risk:

> *Good luck to the tent and the old caravan,*
> *The tinker and the gypsy and the travelling man,*
> *Good luck to his horses, his kettle and his pan,*
> *Good luck to the hawthorn and the clover.*

> *I have travelled this land, I've been near, I've been far,*
> *I won't swap me horse for a new motor car,*
> *Good luck to God's children whoever they are,*
> *Good luck to the hawthorn and the clover.*

> *Good luck to the tent and the old caravan,*
> *The tinker and the gypsy and the travelling man,*
> *Good luck to his horses, his kettle and his pan,*
> *Good luck to the hawthorn and the clover.*

> *With me horse and me dog I can go a long way,*
> *I don't listen much to what them politicians say,*
> *We know what's wrong, but they say it's OK,*
> *Good luck to the hawthorn and the clover.*

> *They can drag empty tractors to mess up the ground,*
> *They can speak really nice but that's not very sound,*
> *They call it redevelopment but they seem duty bound,*
> *To destroy the hawthorn and the clover.*
> *They'll destroy the hawthorn and the clover.*

> *O good luck to the tent and the old caravan,*
> *The tinker and the gypsy and the travelling man,*
> *Good luck to his horses, his kettle and his pan,*
> *Good luck to the hawthorn and the clover,*
> *Good luck to the hawthorn and the clover.*

We have already discussed how hawthorn's spiritual contact in the season of sexual interaction was outlawed by the Christian Church, which saw any fertility celebration as being under the power of the devil. This later became the typical puritanical response to the procreative energy. In order to frighten and control a pagan populace, the Church claimed that the Lord of Nature with his animal horn crown was the devil incarnate. Yet the ancient pagan gods were depicted with horns to show their divinity and their one-ness with Nature, for when wearing them such a god was seen to possess all the natural qualities and strengths of the most noble of beasts.

When we look at the associations hawthorn has with all this we come to the touchiest point for the Church, for the perfume of the tree's blossom encouraged, by its female scent, the most potent attribute of the Nature-god, his blatant sexuality. To counter this it was proclaimed that sex was sinful and an affront to morality. Compare this to the following pagan prayer to the goddess of fertility:

> *O mighty Mother of us all,*
> *Giver of all fruitfulness,*
> *Bring us fruit and grain, flocks and herds,*
> *And children to the tribe,*
> *That we be mighty!*

There is no doubt that the Mayday festivities and love-making in the woods were a great aid to the contentment of the community, for they ensured that all could feel the touch of love and laughter, no matter how high or low their rank or status. At the first sign of the blossoming hawthorn the expectant people felt their hearts a-beating and their pulses racing. In the words of Swinburne:

The coming of the hawthorn brings on earth heaven,
All the spring speaks out in one sweet word,
And heaven grows gladder, knowing that earth has heard.

Now let us approach the hawthorn of the hedgerows. The art of hedgerow laying, training small trees and bushes to form an impenetrable barrier, is sadly dying as our hedgerows disappear. One of my strongest childhood memories is of spending whole days with the hedger, chatting and aiding him in my small way as he inched forward along the lanes, 'laying' the hedgerow. It seemed a sort of magic as he spliced halfway through the branches and slim trunks of hawthorn, which he then coaxed to bend horizontally along the hedgerow, weaving branches and twigs, and staking all neatly into position with forked branches. At the end of his day you could look back at the way he had come in his back-bending labour and see the newly-formed hedgerow, Nature aided by a man with a love of his craft, enhancing the harmony and usefulness of the land. This is a much better way of tending hedgerows and preserving necessary wildlife than that of ripping them to shreds with mechanized hedge-cutters.

Nature responds quickly to sympathetic treatment, for the splices of the branches heal within a couple of days and the whole structure sends forth new leaves in an almost miraculous fashion. Farmers knew a good hedger could bring magic to their fields, for by an understanding of the energies of the plants and the land he did not disrupt their flow but enhanced it.

However, little did I realize in my childhood days why so many of Britain's hedgerows contain hawthorn. It was purposefully adapted from being a tree which grows upwards into a hedging plant which is made to grow sideways when the peasants were thrown off their 'inherited' land by landowners, following the General Enclosures Act of 1845. To ensure enough hawthorn to construct the miles of hedgerows needed, millions of quick-growing hawthorn seeds were planted. Thus the peasant's tree, the faerie hawthorn, was turned into an instrument of division and derision by political and money-minded barons, a barrier hedgerow to keep people off the land.

John Clare, a poet who witnessed the peasants' passing life-style, tells of the changes he saw as the hawthorn trees were adapted to new uses and the spirit of the people was crushed:

> *Ye injur'd fields, ye once were gay,*
> *When Nature's hand displayed,*
> *Long waving rows of willows grey*
> *And clumps of hawthorn shade,*
> *But now alas, your hawthorn bowers*
> *All desolate we see!*
> *The spoilers' axe their shade devours,*
> *And cuts down every tree.*

And yet, as people were forced to travel great distances in search of food, shelter and work, did not the hawthorn give them strength with the sustenance of its leaves...?

PHYSICAL USES

Hawthorn wood is hard-wearing, but as the tree is small it only provides enough wood for small things. Anciently it was used to make handles, particularly (because the wood was considered lucky) handles of personal things necessary for protection, like knives and daggers. The hawthorn's root wood, because of its beautifully fine grain, was used to make combs and small boxes for ladies.

No wood burns more readily than hawthorn, even when green, and it is known as the hottest firewood, better even than oak for oven-heating. Excellent charcoal is made from hawthorn.

In Scotland hawthorn bark was used to dye wool black and in most country places hawthorn leaves were used to make a refreshing tea. Nowadays, if we mix equal quantities of dried hawthorn leaves with our ordinary brand of tea-leaves, we have a vigorous blend of tea which not only does us good but helps save money. Hawthorn flowers can be added to syrups and can make a spirituous wine by following a basic wine recipe.

Hawthorn berries are also useful. They can be made into jellies and wines, and the following recipe makes a good chutney which livens up meats and cheeses:

Pick 2 lbs (900 g) (8 cups) of haw berries, snip them from their stalks, wash them and put them in a large saucepan with 1 pint (½ litre) of cider vinegar and 1 teaspoon of salt.

Bring to the boil and simmer for one hour. Take a good sieve, and rub the boiled haws and vinegar through it into another saucepan.

To this pulpy mixture add ¾ lb (350 g) (1½ cups) brown sugar and the following ground spices: 1 teaspoon ginger and 1 of nutmeg, ¼ teaspoon each of allspice and cloves, and plenty of fresh black pepper. (An optional additive is ¼ lb (115 g) (1 cup) of dried fruit.)

Bring this to the boil, stirring all the time, and then heat slowly until the mixture thickens. Pour into jars and seal.

As mentioned earlier, hawthorn was also used widely for hedging. It is Britain's most prolific hedgerow bush and makes a good barrier, for its fast-growing habit allows an intense tangle of branches and spines to form quickly. Another type of boundary was enforced with hawthorn, for in Cornwall a clod of earth and a sprig of hawthorn were placed on each boundary stone of a parish in the beating of the bounds.

Having hawthorn in the fields was known to make cattle thrive; and if the birthing of a calf was premature, the afterbirth was hung upon a hawthorn tree so it could magically protect the young calf and give it quick growth.

Hawthorn trees provide safe havens in thunderstorms, and along with the ash, apple and sometimes oak, it bears the mistletoe. Hawthorn was also used as a 'stock' tree, having fruit trees grafted onto it.

Hawthorn has always been used at weddings, as already discussed, being used to decorate the wedded couple and the nuptial bedchamber and at the celebrations it was added to the incense, food and drink.

THE ASH TREE

BOTANICAL

ASH. *Fraxinus excelsior*. Deciduous.

Ash is one of the easiest trees to recognize, especially in winter before its leaves appear, for its branches are arranged opposite each other as they grow up and out of the trunk. They then curve gracefully downwards and rise again so their tips reach up towards the sky.

The ash tree has toughness, strength and elasticity, and can grow up to 150 feet (45½ metres) high. It is a native of Britain and grows throughout Europe and America, being often found in ancient fossil beds.

142

BARK

The trunk of the ash can often be sensuously curved. Its bark is ash-grey in colour and smooth to the touch when the tree is young, but it grows more irregularly ridged and cracked with age. The upright ridges of old ash trunks resemble the impressions of wave 'edges', formed into sandy beaches as the tide recedes.

LEAVES

A few weeks after the flowers have opened the leaves appear on the tree. Sooty-black leaf-buds grow at the end of ash branches on stout grey twigs which are flattened at their tips. These buds are phallic in appearance and are unlike the buds found on any other tree. Their blackness is caused by bud-scales which are covered with flattened hairs and contain a dark resin. In some instances this resin is plentiful and the buds ooze its stickiness. Ash is one of the last trees to leaf, and country-lore watches for this and compares it to the leafing of the oak to determine the coming weather for the planting of crops: 'If the ash leafs before oak, we are in

The leaf-buds, leaves, male and female flowers and winged fruit of the ash

for a soak, but if the oak leafs before ash, we are in for merely a splash.' When ash leaves appear they are beautiful, feathery and graceful. They are of a light green colour which goes darker as they progress through their first month, during which time they also become a lot tougher.

The strong leaves of the ash are compound, made up from four to eleven pairs of leaflets with toothed edges placed opposite each other on a central stalk, with a single leaf at the end. They droop gracefully from upturned branches and form quite a dense crown to the tree. Ash leaves are often mistaken for rowan leaves, but they are quite different (*see also p.226*).

By being made up of leaflets, ash leaves allow for minimum damage from rain or hail. The leaflets have a conduit for water running down their centre stem, which is triangular in shape and is almost closed over. Hairs in this channel absorb moisture as it trickles down the mid-rib of the leaf. Water-absorbing structures are a feature of the ash tree, for it loves water.

The ash is not in leaf long, for as well as being virtually the last tree to open its leaves, it is often the first to let them fall in cold winds or at the first sign of frost. After a leaf has fallen, a small horseshoe-shaped scar is left where the leaf stalk was joined to the twig. From this scar next year's black flower-buds will form. The leaves turn quite yellow before they fall from the tree.

FLOWERS

Ash flower-buds open in April before the tree shows its leaves and they reveal thick bunches of purple-headed stamens. There are no petals or sepals to ash flowers, only stamens.

The seed vessels, which are green and shaped like small bottles, stand between two stamens where they can be fertilized by the wind distributing the pollen. Generally each flower is complete in its male and female parts, but sometimes there are no seed vessels produced by the tree or only one set of the male/female parts functions, and because of this the tree will not develop fruit, and will often appear as more male or female in character.

FRUIT

After a few weeks the stamen-flowers shrivel and fall off to reveal the seed vessels, which have changed into flat, lime green 'wings', hanging from long stalks at the ends and from the sides of the twigs and branches. These seeds are often called 'keys', for in their winter state they were likened to bunches of medieval lock-keys. They have also been nicknamed 'spinners', for when they fall from the tree they spin in the air, an effect enjoyed by children when they throw them into the air during play. This spinning motion is due to the shape and weight distribution of the seed vessels, for by being notched at their outer end and containing the seed at the end closest to the stalk, they are weighted at one end and light at the other, and this allows for the spin as they fall through the air.

Throughout summer and autumn these bunches of seeds grow and turn a dark green. Eventually they become hard and brown, and often remain clinging to the bare branches of the trees for most of the winter, until they are torn off by strong winds upon which they spin to earth. Once in soil, they will not begin to grow until their second year, but once quickened their growth is vigorous.

ROOTS

The ash is deeply rooted, which ensures that the tree stands firm in mighty gales and enables its life-span to be of several hundred years. At 40 or 50 years old it is mature and will only then produce fertile fruit. The roots of the ash spread out for some distance from the tree and tend to exhaust the soil. They sour the earth somewhat, which discourages other plant life to grow around or under the tree.

CUSTOM & LEGEND

The belief that the essence of humankind originated from the ash tree was extant in many ancient world cultures. From Greece to northern Europe, the ancient myths of the gods and goddesses associated with the ash tree colour that belief, and show us the strength of the tree's role within the inner and outer worlds of humans.

We are told that the ancient Greek goddess Nemesis carried an ash branch as a symbol of the divine instrument of the justice of the gods. She epitomized the female fates or furies who dispensed justice under and through the ash tree, and she measured out mortal happiness or misery, ensuring that fortune was shared out amongst the people and not cossetted by the few. If a man whom the goddess of fortune had favoured boasted of his abundant riches, or didn't sacrifice part to the gods or alle-viate the poverty of his fellow citizens, Nemesis stepped in and took back what had been given. In this respect the ash scourge dispensed justice through humiliation.

Nemesis was also associated with the seasonal changes and the mythical annual death drama of the divine king, which portrayed the due enactment of the seasonal rites. The wheel of Nemesis originally conceptualized the solar year, its spokes showing the required seasonal changes or transformations necessary to acknowledge in order that life unfolds continuously.

In her lighter character Nemesis was identified as Andrasteia, daughter of the sea-god Oceanus, by the later Greeks and was a pastoral goddess known as 'Nemesis of the rain-making ash tree'. In this instance her scourge was used for ritual flogging to fructify the trees and crops, and besides the scourge, wheel and ash bough, she also carried an apple bough as a reward for heroes. This bough was also the king's passport to Elysium, the Abode of the Blessed.

The title Andrasteia was also given to an ash-nymph who became the foster-nurse of Zeus. Some legends recount that Zeus fell in love with Nemesis in another of her nymph forms, Leda, and he pursued her all over the earth and through the seas. Leda escaped from Zeus, but eventually he won her by changing into a swan, a form sacred to the goddess which Leda could not refuse. It is said that Leda laid an egg from the coupling with Zeus, from which was born the beautiful Helen of Troy.

From the earliest of days the ash tree was regarded as one of the seasonal guises of the goddess. It was also of importance to pastoral devotees of the goddess, for it was associated with thunderstorms which watered the earth and with the birthing season of animal life. Nemesis as daughter of Oceanus strongly emphasized the connections between ash and the life-sustaining qualities of water.

The Greek god Poseidon was also associated with the element of water and strongly identified with the ash tree. His palace was in the depths of the ocean, and there he kept horses with brazen hooves and golden manes, which pulled his chariot across the waves of the sea. Poseidon was believed to have taught mankind the art of managing horses by the bridle, and to have been the originator and protector of horse-racing. He was also able to metamorphose into a horse. Similar associations between the ash tree and gods with horses are found in the northern European myths of the god Odin, as told later. The symbol of Poseidon's power was the trident, with which he could shatter rocks, call forth or subdue storms, shake the earth, etc. Poseidon is also represented by a dolphin. He was later called Neptune by the Romans.

The Greek legends of Achilles tell of a wonderful ashen spear, a gift from the gods which was ritualistically handed down from father to son when the child became a man. Achilles' father Peleus was King of the Myrmidones. When he married the immortal goddess Thetis the gods blessed the marriage, giving Peleus divine protection with a wedding gift of an ashen spear whose shaft had been polished by the goddess Athene after it had been cut from the summit of Mount Pelion. The blade of this spear was forged by the old god Hephaestus. Along with this gift came a magnificent suit of golden armour. Poseidon's wedding gift was Balius and Xanthus, two immortal horses from the west wind.

Achilles was the seventh son of Peleus and Thetis. Unbeknown to Peleus, Thetis, who wished her sons to be immortal like her, had successfully destroyed the mortal parts of each of them by every night placing them in a magical fire. Peleus finally discovered her doing this to Achilles and such was his anger that Thetis fled. The child Achilles was entrusted, still mortal, to the learned centaur Chiron, who instructed him in the healing arts.

Another account tells that Thetis tried to obtain immortality for Achilles by dipping him in the river Styx and that she succeeded with the exception of his heel, by which she held him, which ultimately led to his death in the Trojan Wars.

It is said that Thetis was gifted with great foresight, and that she had seen that Achilles was fated to gain glory and die early, or live long but ingloriously. On being given the choice Achilles chose the former fate and thus became the hero recorded by Homer in the *Iliad* as 'the handsomest and bravest of all the Greeks'. Achilles was educated by Phoenix, who taught him eloquence and the arts of war. Before entering war at his coming of age he received his father's wedding gifts: the ashen spear, golden armour and immortal horses. This tradition of the child receiving arms upon reaching manhood appears the world over.

However, as a solar hero, Achilles was beautiful and in his youth, like other solar heroes, he was hidden amongst women so his beauty would not reveal his true identity. In such cases liberty and arms could not be given to the child until the priestess-mother deemed the time was right and this often caused great arguments to rage.

In a Western version of this tradition we find Gwydion having to trick the priestess-mother Arianrhod to release her powerful hold on the young solar hero Llew Llaw Gyffes. To do this Gwydion created the noise of battle outside the castle, which forced Arianrhod to give a shield and sword to Llew Llaw to defend himself, an act which also gave him his liberty.

Achilles is mythologically accepted as a sacred king destined to become an oracular hero. His role – birth, youth and death – was enacted by many other Bronze Age heroes. As the sacred king of Olympia he was mourned at the Summer Solstice when the Olympic Games were held in his honour. At his death his ashen spear became the talisman which allowed entrance into and exit from the Underworld, the realm through which he travelled as sun-god to ensure that the correct solar cycles continued.

Achilles' mother Thetis was a legendary seal-priestess, who came forth from the sea to marry a mortal and returned to the sea again. At her wedding to Peleus 50 seal-priestesses danced the rituals of the Nereids, immortal seals believed to become beautiful dancing women when upon moonlit shores. They epitomized the ancient seductive female qualities, guises and associations of the ash tree.

In northern European legend ash stands supreme as the World Tree, a symbol of universality which spreads its limbs over every land and forms a link between the gods, mankind and the dead. This link was visualized as a road, bridge or ladder which reached from the Underworld to heaven. In early Germanic tradition, the World Ash Tree is sometimes referred to as the Tree of Mimir, being named after the giant of the Aesir who forged the magical sword Mimming. The World Tree concept, coming to the fore quite late in European myth, was possibly an extension of the ancient traditions of World Pillars, which were associated with early northern European cults of the supreme sky-gods. Such pillars, made of wood and used in temples, were thought to contain the essence of a god. In this context there are similarities to Egyptian myth, for Osiris was ritualistically entombed within a pine tree *(see p.51)*.

Throne-like 'high-seat' pillars evolved from World Pillars, and these were taken to new lands as the tribes moved and settled, ensuring that the essence of the god and the might of his worship travelled with the people. The pillars in Odin's temples were likely to have been ash, considering his link with the tree, whilst those of Thor's temples are reputed to have been oak. Having mentioned Odin, let us now look at his associations with the ash tree.

Odin hung himself on the Great World Tree to receive illumination in the form of the runes and so the tree became known as Askr Yggdrasill, Odin's magical steed, for Yggr was one of his titles. In hanging from the tree Odin made voluntary sacrifice in order to acquire hidden knowledge and wisdom.

The practice of hanging from a living tree was associated with Wodan from very early times, as with initiatory ceremonies of almost all early shamanic races, for it has always been believed that before mortals gain true healing abilities and enter the realms of spirit and the gods, they must undergo ritualistic death. In many ways the Christian concept of the crucifixion is a poor copy of these ancient customs, a cross of dead wood being substituted for a living tree. Yet in hanging from the ash tree Odin does not share the suffering of the world as did Christ. Instead he receives the hidden knowledge of the runes by which to aid mankind.

We are told that Yggdrasill constantly suffers anguish from the life it hosts, life symbolically portrayed by animals. The serpent at its roots represents the ancient earth (female) energies, whilst the eagle at the top of the tree is associated with the energies of the sky (male). These two interact continuously, causing stress to the tree. Shamanically, the squirrel who runs to and fro between the serpent and the eagle is likened to the human, moving between heaven and earth via lifetimes. Four deer live in the tree's branches, continually gnawing it on high, providing moisture from their antlers which falls as dew on the earth below. The leaves of Yggdrasill never wither and the divine goat of Odin feeds upon them, providing in turn the 'drink of the gods'. This drink is given to the warriors of Valhalla, where in the Great Hall of Odin, dead warriors are refreshed and brought back to life for their next ritualistic combat.

Yggdrasill was the epitome of a guardian tree, and its legends strengthened the traditions of planting such trees near settlements, homes and sacred sites. Conceptually it marked the centre of the universe around which everything flowed and it united the cosmic regions. When the end of the world threatened, Yggdrasill reputedly trembled and shook, and it was believed by many tribes that souls were born in its branches. As the tree's life was constantly renewed, it was symbolic of the constant regeneration of the universe by which mankind can attain immortality.

Like all such sacred trees, Yggdrasill had a spring at its roots, the Spring of Fate, which was also called the Well of Urd, a name referring to destiny. The guardian of this spring, from which Odin drank, was Mimir, whose oracular head Odin consulted as the source of wisdom and inspiration. Near the Spring of Fate dwelt three legendary maidens called the Norns, who ruled over the destinies of men. They were called Urdr (Fate), Verdandi (Being) and Skuld (Necessity). They watered the tree daily from the spring and whitened its bark with clay, thus preserving its life. The Norns were associated with childbirth, aiding it by taking the healing fruit of the tree, burning it and giving it to women during labour.

In the northern creation myths the gods created humans from two trees on the seashore (or a block of ash, according to the Scandinavian Edda), and placed them onto the earth. The earth itself had been created from the body of Ymir, a giant who appeared from the initial fusion of fire from the south and ice from the north. The original natures of man and woman were created through the World Tree (or Pillar), and named Askr and Embla respectively. As a source of new life or life continuous, legend tells how a man and a woman shelter in the World Tree during terrible winters, feeding on the tree's mead-like liquid until they step forth to (re)people the earth in the following spring.

The World Tree symbolism is very shamanistic in its concepts and in true shamanic form Odin sought wisdom through contact with the dead.

The name Odin in Old Norse means 'intoxication, fury and raging', and his cult bore all these hallmarks. Odin was a late god who succeeded Wodan, the Germanic god of 'possession, intoxication and fury', also associated with ritual sacrifice by means of stabbing, burning, hanging or spearing. 'Wodan' literally means 'one who makes mad'. According to Chaucer, 'wood' or 'wode' expresses madness. Odin seemingly developed out of earlier concepts of a god who ruled over the battle-fields and while he had great strengths he was also known to be treacherous.

In Scandinavia Odin was a god of magic, poetry and the dead. In later folklore he was associated with the Wild Hunt, where lost souls, led by a demonic leader upon a great horse, are heard in the fury of the storm. Yet more often, as Lord of Hosts, god of hanged men, violence and battle, Odin was known as the 'spear brandisher'. Gungnir, his great spear, was formed from ash and he used it to stir up warfare in the world, a state through which his followers could gain ecstatic frenzy. Odin was able to grant trance-like states of intoxication, which filled men with such inspirational madness that they knew neither pain nor fear. It was through either such trance or battle or liqueur that they found a means to achieve forgetfulness of self whilst on earth.

In the Germanic and Viking worlds battle was very much an individual affair, as lands, homes and wives were fought for in an unsettled society which was ever open to invasions, feuds and wars. Odin protected in the hour of battle, yet blood was constantly demanded by him, along with offerings of swords, mail, spears and shields, which were either burnt on pyres or cast into deep lakes.

The warriors of Odin were known as Berserks, i.e., 'bear shirts'. They were heroes in life and guests of Odin at death, when they were prepared in the halls of Valhalla for re-emergence into life and battle. Such faith in a god gave supreme confidence and strength, the fury of possession. Berserk warriors took initiation by the mark of an ash spear consecrated to Odin. They were also known as 'wolf-coats' (the Franks wore wolf-skins even after their nominal conversion), and were seen as sacred to the god, able to shape-change into animal forms when enraged. The expression 'having gone berserk' is directly related to this change of form through rage. Such dominant companies of warriors existed well into the Viking period.

Odin's Berserks cultivated the art of terrifying their enemies. They dyed their bodies black, used black shields and fought in the black of night, their only protection coming from shields or magical cloaks. While in a state of frenzy they would be free from the laws which govern ordinary men.

Providing the link between Odin and the slain in battle are the Valkyries, female spirits who wait on those in Valhalla. They are described by poets as carrying out Odin's commands, dressing in armour and riding horses which can travel swiftly over land or sea into the rage of battle. They gave victory at the god's will and carried slaughtered warriors to Valhalla to be restored. Human princesses were believed to become Valkyries after death. Such priestesses of the gods of war were similar to the Norns, deciding the destinies of men, for as seers they could protect certain men in battle by the aid of spells. *Valkyrie* literally means 'chooser of the slain'.

In the Irish sagas the Celtic goddess Morrigu also bears a close resemblance to the Valkyries, for she appeared on the battlefield or in men's dreams before battle. Morrigu and the goddess Bobd were said to take the forms of birds of prey which uttered prophecies concerning battle and war.

The Swedish followers of Odin marked their dead with an ash spear and burned the bodies in homage to him. Sacrificial hanging of men and animals from trees, in copy of Odin's self-sacrifice, continued in Uppsala until well into the eleventh century AD, though by then the battle-filled cult of Odin had been well overlaid by the less bloody cult of Thor, the characteristic hero of the stormy Viking world.

In Viking times Denmark contained Norway and Sweden. It was a vast country. The official Christian conversion of Denmark was not until circa AD 960. Prior to this people acknowledged a pantheon of gods of which Odin and Thor were the most popular. The cult of Thor, less bloodthirsty than that of Odin, ruled the weather and sky and thus the crops. It was acceptable and long-lived in Western Europe.

Thor was the epitome of the patriarchy, a god of the sky mythologically born from Mother Earth. His power, which subsumed earlier gods like Frey, was symbolized by his ashen spear and enormous hammer, and extended over the community. Many of his roles, such as overseeing birth, marriage and death, were once the province of the goddesses, who would be forced ever deeper into the shade. Thor reigned over travelling, land-taking and the making of oaths between men who had powerful relationships with their weapons.

The Vikings' great speed over water made their massive ships their most potent weapon. They were fascinated by powerful ships and bedecked their graceful lines with prow heads and great vanes. Their magnificent vessels were ocean-going cargo carriers as well as war-ships, and while they were constructed of oak, all their magical parts were ash, for its sacredness to the battle-god gave great speed and control over water, along with an intoxicating physical prowess. The Viking ships rode the waves in similar ways to the horses of Poseidon.

The Vikings gained their title of Aescling (Men of Ash) because of their great reliance on the magic of the ash tree. Their paganism, more sacrificial and bloody than that of the countries they invaded, and their great sacrificial burial feasts, caused them to be greatly feared. Their largeness of stature, their enormous ships and their reliance on gods of violence and weapons did little to dispel such fear.

Through successive invasions the Viking culture came to dominate Britain. The first Danish ships reached England around AD 789 and by 850 the English were faced with invading armies rather than scattered raiders. The great influx of paganism brought by the Vikings, while it frightened the natives, also greatly extended the resistance to Christianity.

In Ireland the Viking culture rapidly established itself. It is relevant that to do so it used the magic of the ash tree, for in the early histories of Ireland it is said that three of the five magical trees which protected that land were ash, the other two being yew and oak. The magical ash trees were called the Tree of Tortu, the Tree of Dathi and the Branchie Tree of Usnech. The fall of these trees was said to symbolize the triumph of Christianity over paganism, and is most probably linked to St Patrick, who supposedly drove all serpents from Ireland with the aid of an ash stick in the fifth century AD. Unfortunately it also symbolized the descent of the values of the goddess in the affairs of man, for pagan associations between the ash tree and serpents have always been strong.

In ancient times serpents represented the wisdom of the earth-goddesses originally associated with the ash tree; they then became symbolic of lightning over which the gods reigned. The great archetypal tree Yggdrasill also had a serpent at its roots. However, the Christians revered ash as the only tree in the Garden of Eden that the serpent dared not approach, thus severing the ancient associations.

We have seen through legend how the ash tree became symbolic of the power of the sky and sun-gods, yet before such gods rose to dominion, the lunar associations of ash meant that the intuitional aspects of the tree were more pronounced, in that people viewed it from that perspective and thus associated it with feminine principles. This view was given strength by the tree's love of water. Many people today still consider the ash as essentially feminine, calling it 'sister', 'granny' or 'mother', and in folklore and woodman's tales it is known as 'the Lady (or Venus) of the Woods'.

In an ash leaf there is almost always an odd number of leaflets and in earlier days an ash leaf with an even number of leaflets was considered as lucky as a four-leaved clover, hence the country saying 'If you find an even ash or a four-leaved clover, you will see your true love 'ere the day is over.'

The ash tree seems to almost invite lightning to strike it, and for this reason when a storm is brewing, country people advise to 'Avoid an ash, for it courts a flash.'

The fruit of the ash, which often remain on the tree throughout winter, go by many names, some of which are: ash keys, ash chats, ash candles, cats and keys, and locks and keys. As already mentioned, they are called keys because they resemble the shape of ancient medieval keys, but a more romantic theory says that if a seed wing is inserted into the correct place on an ash tree's trunk, the tree will reveal all its historical wisdom. To enable such secrets to be unlocked, trust must first be achieved, for the dryad of a tree ensures its knowledge is not wasted.

As explained in the beginning of this book, get to know the tree and its spiritual entity, and let it get to know you. Then the tree will guide its own 'unlocking' and communication will begin.

HEALING

In early Britain the ash was associated with rebirth and new life, and through the tree sympathetic magic was attained. In this context ash was famous for its ability to heal children, who were passed through a split in the tree's trunk in order to be cured of ruptures, hernias, rickets, warts and similar afflictions. From the earliest of days the action of crawling or passing through 'openings' in the natural world, whether in stone, earth, trees, water or vegetation, conveyed the action of rebirth in the minds of the people, or the passing from one dimension into another.

To make such an opening, the trunk of a young ash tree still living and rooted in the ground was split, with due ritual. After the children were passed through the split, the trunk was bound together as prayers were sent to the powers of Nature for help in the process. If the tree healed well, so would the child, and it was deemed a great gift from the goddess of the ash tree. Trees used in such a way had many offerings carefully buried around their roots, including gold coins and small pieces of coal.

A very old method of healing was to create a 'shrew ash', in which a live shrew was buried, with many incantations, in a hole made in the trunk of an ash tree. Once the shrew was packed inside, the tree was believed to have specific healing qualities, and leaves and twigs from it were used to cure paralysis and painful cramps in humans and cattle, for as they were placed on the afflicted areas, the essence of the shrew in the tree was believed to run 'magically' over them, causing movement within the patient's body and thus providing relief from cramps and paralysis. Such a tree is supposed to stand by the church at Selborne, Hants., though it may not be still alive. Rows of pollarded ashes were also said to grow in the same area, the 'seams' down their trunks bearing witness to past healing given to children who were passed through splits in them.

The juice from an ash stick was customarily given to newborn children in order to protect them from harm. To do this one end of an ash stick was placed in the fire, and the liquid which bubbled out of the other end of the stick was caught and placed in the baby's mouth or rubbed onto its body.

BARK
The bitter bark of an ash branch was used to ease intermittent fevers. It was more potent when cut in the spring when the sap rises in the tree. The bark from the root is even more potent, and in early medicine was used for its tonic and astringent properties in treating arthritic rheumatism and liver diseases.

LEAVES
An infusion of ash leaves gathered when they exude their sticky substance in May or June, and powdered after drying, can be used to alleviate rheumatism. The leaves are more active dried than when fresh. They are also, if taken every morning in an infusion, said to give longevity. They are believed to reduce fatness, but this may be due to the fact that they are both laxative and diuretic, so go carefully if using them in this way. Ash leaves are an alternative to senna pods, and gypsies use an infusion of ½ a cup of leaves to 2½ cups of boiling water, taken over 24 hours, as a gentle laxative.

Ash is also used to remove unwanted energies, spells and hexes, which in ancient times were thought to appear in the shape of warts. To cure a wart, a pin was stuck into it and then into an ash tree, as the following words were recited: 'Ashen tree, ashen tree, pray take these warts off me.' Judging by the amount of references to this healing 'spell' in old books, ash would seem famous for its wart cures.

However the greatest healing provided by the ash tree is on the subtle planes, for it helps us balance our inner and outer selves by educating our reaction to the world. It also heals the isolation within the human psyche caused by the severing of its intimate contact with the natural world. This began long ago as the patriarchal age gained momentum, and subsequent religions and politics forced changes in people's spiritual values. In order to establish a precedent for these healing capacities of the ash tree, these points are given fuller treatment in Inspiration (*see pp. 161–9*).

FRUIT

The seeds of the ash were anciently believed to 'provoke lust and make men more spirited with the ladies', and decaying ash wood was used as an ingredient in a powerful aphrodisiac powder. Ash keys keep all the year round if gathered when ripe.

MAGIC

IRISH/GAELIC	*Nuin*
OGHAM	ᚅ
RUNIC	ᚾ
RULING PLANET	Sun
ABILITIES	Inner and outer worlds linked. Marriage-bed of opposites. Quick intellect. Clarity. 'Aquarian Age' energy. To do with the element of Water.
SEASON	Summer

On healing and learning levels the ash tree acts as an assimilator, helping us absorb healing and knowledge from both it and all other trees. Assimilation means 'taking into', 'experiencing the full knowledge and effects of', etc., and as the ash helps us find our balance within the world, it also prepares us for such experience. Through ash we can translate the past and realign our realities of the present with a wiser view to the future. Through ash we become aligned with the world.

In a druidic sense the oak tree forms the entrance into the grove (or what may be termed the subconscious or memory) and the ash forms the exit back into reality (the conscious world of today), having assimilated the knowledge found within the grove into practicality.

Because of the reverence given to the ash tree by the Teutons, after the Germanic tribes entered Britain *en masse*, the ash replaced the birch as the species used for what would become called the maypole. Originally the birch and the young goddess expressed through it were the earthy central focus of the celebrations welcoming summer, yet the focus changed when ash became viewed in terms of the sky-god. The maypole then became extremely symbolic of the creative life-giving energy of the sun, the phallus of the god round which the sacred dance of life takes place. This is comparable to Eastern traditions associated with Shiva.

As a tree ruled by the sun, the ash was considered important at the agricultural seasonal celebrations. However at Imbolc its feminine qualities were honoured to gain protection for the newborn, the flocks of lambs and delicate young plants beginning to push their way through the earth. Ash's water-loving aspects were also invoked to bring the spring tides and showers so necessary for growing life.

Mayday songs tell of 'Oak & Ash & Thorn', and where these trees grew naturally together, it was believed possible to see the faerie-folk. The mix of these three tree energies was used by druids in certain forms of magical workings. The oak provided the rich male energy, the thorn the intuitional fertile female and the ash, because of its specific capabilities, blended the two and directed the energy wand-like (spear-like) via the minds of magicians to places where it must work. Many trees work together in such ways. Oak, ash and willow give incredible power in the visual sense, which is especially good for astral workings. Alder, ash and elder give access to the old, old magic of the land; while oak, ash and elm open doorways to the deep magic of the cultivated earth, the fields and hedgerows.

By midsummer water is precious, and at this, its most powerful time, ash's ability to absorb moisture makes it appear as a green oasis within the summer heat and draws life to its cooling shade. On Midsummer's Eve, those who ate the buds of ash were said to become invulnerable to the influence of witches and in ancient days garters of green ash bark were worn to protect against the powers of magicians. Staffs of ash protected against malign influences and leaves of ash attracted love and prosperity.

Norse myth tells us of the ash as the mighty World Tree which spanned the universe, with its roots in hell and its branches in heaven.

Earth was at the tree's centre, along the length of its trunk. These three positions were known to ancient druids as the 'Three Circles of Cosmology', which symbolized past, present and future. The past and confusion reigned in hell, the future and creative energy ruled heaven, and the present and earth were in between the two. In some traditions these forces are symbolized by upright pillars: a black one representing the past and darkness, a white one representing the future and the light, and the ideal position of the human, the present, being balanced between the two.

The druids carved magical images from ash roots, which they believed were every bit as powerful as mandrake. The human shapes formed by the roots make them ideal for use as healing images or 'fith-faths'. The druids' magical wands were also made from ash and they were traditionally decorated in a sunwise-spiralling pattern. Ash wands make excellent healing wands because the tree is ruled by the health-giving sun and the best time for cutting them is at midsummer. At this time also the magical fern-seeds of invisibility were gathered by druids. The ash and the fern-seeds were possibly worked together, the fern making the druids invisible and the ash (because of its associations with travel over land and sea) allowing them to travel great distances whilst invisible. In other words, they aided entrance to and work upon the astral planes.

A cross of equal arms carved from ash wood can be used in sea rituals, for ash represents the great power of water. Such a cross was carried by sailors to protect them at sea or by land-folk for health and protection against malign influences. The wassailing bowl of the druids, used to toast the harvest trees (see Apple, pp.116 and 122), was carved from the health-giving, protective ash; and ash was the traditional wood of the Yule log, burned to call back and celebrate the return of the sun-god at midwinter. If a log could not be found big enough to continue burning through Yuletide, bundles of tied ash faggots were used, and forfeits were enacted each time the ties burned through and the faggots blazed.

The use of ash in weapons, especially the spear, so beloved of the northern tribes of Europe, was deemed the highest protective magic, for lives literally depended upon it. The ancient custom of taking oaths on weapons was probably Germanic in origin. They were solemn affairs, for if the oath were broken it could result in failure at a critical moment and the weapon could turn against its owner. 'Take care lest your weapon turn against you!' was the greatest warning and curse to deliver to your enemies, for the power of the gods was intrinsically bound up in the composition of weapons on all levels. Weapon-makers, or smiths, were ranked highly, for they were trained in metal magic and the martial arts, and their ability to fuse the elements put them in a literally awe-inspiring position.

Many of the legends concerning ash refer to its speed over water and land, and its prolific use as spears and arrows testifies to its flight through air. Witches were said to fly on broomsticks with ashen handles – a polite way, perhaps, of referring to 'riding' the phallic maypole and entering the astral realms through sexual ecstasy. In modern times and with modern travel, placing an ash leaf in a car or on a motorcycle is believed to protect against accidents and bring you safely home.

To sleep with fresh ash leaves under your pillow brings psychic dreams, and if a circle is cast to the elements and ash leaves are scattered to the quarters, it is possible to invoke great powers. When doing this, similar words to these may be used at the quarters:

> *Elements of the East, Powers of Air,*
> *Bring to me Knowledge and Inspiration.*

At the South call on the Powers of Fire for Energy and Change; at the West on the Powers of Water for Healing and Love; at the North call on the Powers of Earth for Prosperity and Success. Ash leaves are thrown to each quarter as the words are spoken, and after completing any workings the elements are thanked and blessed for their aid. This ritual can be used to gain control and balance of the elemental powers within yourself, by substituting the given words with those more pertinent to the situation. Specific boons can also be asked for at the quarters, as can healing, as explained in Inspiration (see pp. 161–9).

Ash is the tree of balance, the marriage-bed of opposites which links our inner and outer worlds. Ruled by the sun, it contains the element of fire yet still responds to the subtlety of the more feminine water element.

Ash reflects the Aquarian Age energy of quick clear intellect and strength of purpose, aided by keen intuition. Wands carved from ash are used for healing and solar magic, and all parts of the ash are used for protection, health and prosperity.

The deities associated with the ash tree are Odin, Woden, Poseidon, Nemesis, Achilles, Andrasteia, Neptune and Mars.

INSPIRATION

Now we can look more closely at the ancient symbolism associated with the ash tree, for by illustrating the fullest expression of life, it stimulates the psyche into remembrance and cultivates a specific strength within us. This enables us to heal the past and reclaim our true spiritual heritage.

It is no secret that indigenous beliefs and practices have been consistently overlaid by invading cultures, politics and religious change. It is, however, rarely realized how deeply this affected the people, for their intimate and reverent contact with the natural world was severed, and their traditional values negated. This has great relevance on how we re-enact this in our world of today, for as a people we are unconsciously moved by our collective race memories.

Of all the trees considered within this book the ash has been most difficult to define, for as it touches the deepest primeval levels, it shifts the sands of time so dramatically that we become as our ancestors, moving through ages stretching back into infinity. As a tree of ancient lunar associations which became symbolic of the might of the solar-gods, the ash knows the changes wrought and our mix of genealogy. It is thus ideal to guide us back to ourselves.

The most powerful symbols associated with ash are the World Tree and the maypole, concepts which illustrate the pattern of life and our position within it, showing the forces which constitute living and aligning those forces within us. They illustrate Nature's blueprint. The ash shows us there are many levels of being and many worlds which parallel those levels. It is felt that our early ancestors were more aware of universal order than us and that by seeing themselves as integral to the flow of such order, found security in being part of the Whole. This is expressed by the intuitive lunar associations of the ash tree. The World Tree concept as we know it (*see pp. 148–50*) came relatively late in history.

The ash tree's energy expresses the life-force, which comes through as visual impressions or feelings of energy. To me this looks and feels like ribbons, which weave and flow, knot and tangle, according to the situation being expressed. Because ash is intimately associated with both lunar and solar, i.e., receptive and active, female and male, etc., qualities, it is ideal as an interpreter and aligner of energies. It shows us the world, educates our reaction to the world, lines us up as part of the world, and guides us into the world. So let us now, through the ash tree, look at the energies of life and ourselves as individuals.

We begin with the natural world. The only aim of Nature is to (re)create through an interaction of its forces and forms. This culminates on the physical plane in (re)production. This interaction is total and without it there would be no life. In animals and humans there is an obvious interaction of male and female in the sexual act, whereby, through physical conjoining and the sexual blending of their substances and energies, species give life to copies of themselves and maintain their continuance. The same is true of the vegetable world, wherein intermediaries, such as the wind and insects, introduce the pollen of one 'sexual' plant to another, enabling impregnation to occur.

However we humans are the only species in which this interaction is attached to the ego, intellect, emotions and personality. This presents difficulties, for in those areas we are open to such things as peer-pressure, restraints, conditioning and control, which increasingly remove us from interaction 'as Nature intended', and thus increase our separation from the primal source. As explained earlier, the suppression of the indigenous life-celebrating Nature religions began the isolating 'programming' of our ancestors, for not only did it forbid recourse with Nature, but also denied the sexual body and particularly negated the female. This overshadowed our sexuality and our connection with the life-force with fear and superstition, for by using the physical basis of gender to negate the spirit, the concept of unity was severed. The politician's favourite trick has always been 'divide and rule'.

As a consequence, most of our problems stem from superstition, deep-set conditioning and even fear of the parts of us that are closest to the procreating force of Nature. Raw elemental energy has little human control and can be observed in the movements of animals, shamen, aboriginals, dancers, lovers, artists, musicians, actors, street-fighters, etc., when they are 'taken' by the Spirit. Then we see power and magic and genius. However, when people are affected by such powerful energy the superficial world of human values falls away. They begin to operate on much deeper levels that do not sway in the face of rules and regulations concerning politics and religion. This is why we are still being suppressed.

These deeper levels concern our life-force, or more precisely how we interact with the world through our logical maleness and our intuitional femaleness. They bring understanding of the energies within us, leading us to the point of truth, as our egos, emotions, minds, bodies, spirits and souls scramble to assume their ancient order found only in the natural world.

So what is the ideal alignment of our energies and how do we (re)attain it? In oriental symbology the harmonious relationship of the forces of life is expressed by the Yin–Yang symbol. This shows the pattern of the meeting-point of life's energies, i.e., the curving line formed where darkness and light, lunar and solar, night and day, unconscious and conscious, receptive and active, female and male, yoni and lingam, etc., meet. It also shows the small amount of the opposite energy within each, i.e., the small amount of maleness within femaleness (the white dot in the black), and the small amount of femaleness within maleness (the black dot in the white). It is the alignment of these forces within the world and within ourselves that allows for correct ecology upon the planet, and competence, happiness and health within us, *not* the suppression of one force by another.

However in order not to suppress we require a deeper understanding of the forces in question in both their positive and negative states, as well as an ability to recognize the effects caused by their lack of alignment within us. So we need to look at the universal symbols associated with them, in particular the solar (male) and lunar (female) symbolism around which it is thought our ancestors built their Nature religions. Then we can use the ash tree's legendary associations with both to best effect.

We begin with solar energy. The power of the sun gives life. It reaches into every living thing, allowing it to move forward and progress. It provides our 'get up and go', and is essential to growth, health and happiness. We all know how good we feel when the sun shines, how vital and alive. Yet there is a negative side to solar energy, for if out of control this supreme element of fire can destroy life in a blaze of flame.

As it is with the world so it is with us. Within people the active solar energy can become unbalanced through a lack of compensation or an inability to use or transmute it, and this can build up within the body, causing an over-exaggeration which slowly turns its effects negative. We are all prone to varying degrees of this, from the lost temper on a hot day to the chaos of 'midsummer-madness' which often ends in violent acts. Severe build-ups of solar energy within the body are more liable to happen if a person is under severe stress, or if they are extremely tired, or if blockages exist which alter the flow of energies around the body. Added to this is a medical condition, where a lack of specific minerals in the body which normally counter energy intensity leaves many people (unknowingly) open to such effects.

The resultant symptoms of such conditions, when exaggerated by intense solar energies, are a loss of equilibrium and an internal growing 'heat', which confuses and over-stimulates the mind and, more often than not, the sexual appetite. If not corrected, such over-stimulation can lead to conditions of manic, aggressive, 'animalistic' behaviour, hyperactivity and a severe lack of contact with reality. Sleep is not possible when these conditions prevail, and in severe cases this results in an eventual burn-out of the nervous system and physical body. It is like when an engine is left running with the choke full out.

Too little solar energy, on the other hand, can cause depression, often so deep that the winter months are lost in uncreative darkness. Lack of sun also severely decreases the sexual appetite, making the person feel totally useless.

Understanding such conditions is increasingly important, for we have destroyed a great part of our planet's protective ozone layer, which is allowing unknown qualities and quantities of solar rays to descend upon us. The urgency of this is reflected in the growing number of people affected by what are termed 'manic-depressive' conditions, in which the sun, or the lack of it, seems to play a large part.

Modern medicine has provided us with some treatments such as lithium replacement therapy, which provides the necessary amount of the mineral to the body so it can function correctly during seasonal changes. Yet even as answers are found, conditions change around us, producing new effects. However, while scientists have been struggling in their laboratories, others have been looking to the world of Nature for understanding. They have seen that the heat of the day is calmed by the coolness of the night as the moon replaces the sun in the heavens, and they have recognized that likewise, our calm, intuitive, dream-like qualities soothe our hurly-burly rat-race stress, just as woman heals man. With such awareness we can, like our ancestors before us, prepare ourselves before the summer months by communing with Nature and letting ourselves become as one with its energy. We thus allow it to align us as it aligns itself for the coming seasons, for it is a much better judge than us of conditions in the world.

Meditating or working with the ash tree is excellent for this purpose, for it is ruled by the sun yet still retains its ancient associations with lunar energies. By tuning in to the natural world when intense conditions prevail we let the flow of energy within us compensate naturally, according to Nature's plan. Then there are no more battles within, for division and isolation fall away as we experience unity with our true legacy.

Now we can look at lunar energy. The ash tree's strong associations with the element of water are aided by the old lunar roots of the tree. This association shows that the ash has a great capacity to promote healing to and from the emotions. As humans we are around 80 per cent water and have a natural affinity to such a process, which will also put us back in touch with our receptive, intuitive selves. In this the ash prepares us to work from the heart, with concern and caring. It moves us from our individuality into the world, replacing subjectivity with objectivity, wherein the caring for others becomes, through the concept of unity, caring for ourselves as part of the whole.

The phases of the moon bear great relation to specific states of the psyche, affecting us very much as they affect the waters of the earth. Every single living thing is affected by the force of the moon, and like the sun it has both positive and negative effects.

The moon appears in the night sky and we are caressed by its rays during sleep. It has been proved that none of us can survive without the dream-world of our sleeping times, and that its detriment leads to a complete breakdown of the body's equilibrium, let alone the mind's sanity. We need to understand more about our dream-worlds, for we have moved so far from our aboriginal roots that we have forgotten their message, relevance and necessity. The ash-tree puts us back in touch with our dreams through its ancient visionary lunar associations.

We have discussed how unbalanced solar energies in the body lead to conditions of tension, aggression and depression; here we will see how unbalanced lunar energies can lead to lunacy, possession and obsession, conditions in which the dark unconscious mind overshadows reality, luring the conscious mind into states of paranoia, fixation and waking nightmares. In its positive state, lunar energy promotes loving emotions and stimulates the imagination. In its negative state, it twists the emotions and feeds subsequent delusions with an over-blown imagination. It is seductive and sensual, able to make us love or hate, affecting our beings more subtly than the solar forces, yet affecting them none the less.

Obsession and possession most often take the form of 'imprisonment' of the spirit, ensnaring it spider-like in a cocoon of misplaced emotions and fears. The spirit may be within another body, a child or a lover, or even within ourselves, and the cocoon is given many names, but is mostly born from fear. If we take, for example, the human family of mother, father and child, we see that for all the giving birth to, the feeding, loving, teaching and protecting we do for our children, our main responsibility as parents is to ensure the freedom of that child's spirit as it grows up and moves on from the family into the world. However letting go of the child is not always easy, for then we are made to face the world differently and this can raise the question of identity.

For the mother who has let her child become her only reason to be, re-entering the world as a woman is hard and often children are held back in order that such difficulties need not be faced. Yet so important is the release of the child, both for its sake and the mother's, that in Ancient Egypt it was considered a great initiation; for the child's spirit would then grow from experience in the world and thus add to its richness, and the mother would be freed into her full womanhood, having grown wise from her experience as creatress and thus able to help the world with such wisdom.

These points also have relevance to fathers and husbands. How many children's spirits have been harnessed, even before birth, by obsessive fathers intent on the continuance of family and 'empire'? How many artists and poets have been doomed to archaic uninspirational systems devoid of soul? How many spirits forced to live another's dream? And as the child grows and the woman emerges from motherhood into her own power, how many are swayed from expressing their own identity in the world? Yet is this not the time when mother and father may meet each other again as woman and man, to enjoy the fresh excitement their interests bring?

Possibly the strongest obsessions occur between lovers and these are born from the desire to possess. Then our fears of isolation need not be faced, for we hold them at bay by control over another. Then we need not acknowledge our responsibilities, for we have an excuse in another. Yet this is not love but selfishness, for it entraps another's spirit in order to hide our weaknesses. In women often the obsession to possess becomes so strong that they purposefully introduce the ultimate emotional blackmail by which to control and allow themselves to become pregnant in order to use the spirit of the child to suppress the spirit of the father. The only thing this guarantees is misery, for no inspiration can form from entrapment. It also lays great karmic debts upon the perpetrator, for it is tantamount to denial of the sacredness of the spirit.

Lunacy is also associated with the changing phases of the moon (Latin *luna*), the full moon being the characteristic 'mad' period. While shutting hysterical, violent lunatics away from the world belongs to a by-gone age of little understanding, it also reflects the intensity by which lunar energy moves us when our being is unable to control or compensate and our condition becomes negative. When such a condition prevails, we are looking, as it were, at the opposite end of the scale to the solar unbalance described earlier. The cold rays of moonlight can bring confusion, irrationality and madness as well as inspiration, ecstasy and vision.

People most prone to degrees of lunacy are emotional and suggestible. They have over-vivid imaginations, which, as the condition progresses, steadily build up fear images until the inner nightmare takes over reality. The negative side of lunar energy is ruthless, manipulative, heartless and cold, reminding us of the Three Furies of legend who at times dispensed cruel justice devoid of love. However, the line between inspiration and madness is thin, and at times of intense stress within our computerized and often troubled human world, many of us have felt ourselves approach it. And yet, as with solar energy, our strength and power of control can be aided by the natural world, and warmth and healthy activity can be found within the sun's rays to encourage us back to the joy of life, balancing the lunar energies within us, as does the mighty ash tree.

So it is with the forces of life, whose power affects us all. What we have looked at here is but a glimpse of such forces and if we learn from our ancestors how they maintained equilibrium through Nature, we see by their reference to ash as the World Tree, that it truly pertains to its attainment within the world.

Now we can look at the symbolism of ash as the maypole, where it represents the phallic, solar centre of the celebrations of life, around which the gaily coloured ribbons of the weaving, lunar energies are woven in dance. Such symbolism also reminds us that at specific times of the year as the solar energy grows, most especially when it peaks at midsummer, the calming lunar energy may cool and wisely direct its force. Alternatively, the sun can balance the introverting effects of the moon, its warmth bringing the spirit of life to the cold darkness of winter isolation.

In order to attain healing, keep the imagery of the ash maypole in mind, close your eyes and concentrate. See and feel the tree as your backbone, your spinal column which aligns your nervous system and directs the strong upward thrust of your life-energy. As such the maypole is your axis, around which the ribbons of your receptive, emotional, instinctive and intuitional energies are woven and wound.

The most fulfilling way to feel this alignment is to stand with your backbone against an ash tree, allowing your contours to fit in with its shape. Align yourself also to its inner contours, which is a sort of 'becoming as one' with its presence. To do this it is often easier to begin in the earth, by thinking yourself into the tree's roots which are below you and feeling what it would be like if you had roots which moved within the warm soil. Think of the flow of sap moving up from those roots, or the blood that flows up your veins, and feel it as it travels up your backbone, through your trunk, or body, to your branches, or arms and head, and above. Feel the energy coursing up through you and then out, through skin and bark, hair and leaves, to be renewed again in ebb and flow. As your pulse beats side by side with Nature's, allow any pent-up emotion and tension to flow from you. Let it be carried out on the out-flowing energy as you become one with the tree and all around you. Take your time and go with the flow, your eyes closed and your body still.

As you form a rapport of interchange with the tree, remember its World Tree associations, for your ancestors regarded the ash as the axis of the world around which the universe found harmony. Feel this harmony within the tree and within yourself. Be part of it, allowing the energies to flow through you, revitalizing you. This is the unity which was severed long ago, the unity which is essential to your well-being and happiness in the world. This is your true heritage, your birthright. Blessed Be.

PHYSICAL USES

In country areas of Britain ash is still called the 'husbandry tree', a name which refers to the traditional economics of using ash wood, for it is quick-growing, does not split when worked, and is the toughest and most elastic of all timbers. An ashen joint will bear more weight than any other kind. It was thus used in the construction of wagons, coaches, fencing-rails, oars, poles, furniture and implements.

Ash wood is rarely used for actual building, for it decays on contact with the soil. It is, however, resistant to diseases and insect pests. Agriculturally, ash was used for more purposes than any other tree. It was believed to protect from thunderstorms and to guard birthing on the farm.

Ash was known to aid movement, and this applied to movement over-land, through the air and through water. On land axles of ash enabled a carriage to move faster and handles of ash on working tools enabled a worker to do more. Sticks of ash were used to drive cattle, and in Ireland and Wales as rods to manoeuvre horses.

Legend is full of witches riding through the air on ash and birch broomsticks, and in later years ash was the second most important wood used in aeroplane construction.

Because of its elasticity ash was occasionally substituted for yew in bow-making. It was also used for the shafts of arrows.

In ancient Wales and Ireland the water-loving ash was used for coracle slats and oars. The Vikings used it to give special potency, speed and protection to their boats and weapons.

In later Britain ash became the Yule log, for its burning was seen as beneficial to the future prosperity of the family. Ash is the sweetest of the forest woods for burning, giving warmth to many ladies' chambers of the past:

> Burn ashwood of green.
> 'Tis fire for a Queen.

Here is a method of making an ash walking stick:
Search for a straight stick on the tree (3–4 feet (around 1 metre) long for a walking stick, and 4–6 feet (1–2 metres) long for a thumb stick) and cut it when the tree is bare of leaves and flowers. The walking stick will be shaped at its end into a handle or knob-shape, and the thumb stick will have a Y-shaped end for hooking your thumb in. These points should be borne in mind when cutting your stick.

Once you have cut your stick, trim off its side shoots, but not too close to the stick – leave them 2 inches (5 cm) long. Also trim the top and bottom, adding 2 inches (5 cm) to the overall required length. Don't peel the stick. Leave it to season for 6 months in a shed or garage. Then fully trim off the side shoots close to the main stem and trim the handles or thumb-rest to the length needed.

Shape the handle or thumb-rest with a file and sandpaper, and then polish the stick repeatedly with furniture polish until it gleams. When polished, ash has a lovely silvery-grey sheen.

THE
OAK TREE

BOTANICAL

ENGLISH OAK. *Quercus robur*. Deciduous.

The oak is a tree of great longevity and imposing stature, taking some 60 years to produce its first full crop of catkins, and gaining heights of 110 feet (33 metres) and girths of 30–40 feet (9–12 metres). There are over 400 species of oak in the world, ranging from trees to bushes, both evergreen and deciduous.

The English oak is known as the common or pedunculate oak, and is found in fields, hedgerows and woods. Along with the Sessile (or

Durmast) oak (*Quercus petraea*), it is a native to Britain.

The Sessile oak is most prolific in the forests of central France and the west of England. Because its leaves are bigger and on a longer stalk than the English oak, it produces a better canopy. Its male catkins are very yellow and obvious, and its acorns are on twigs instead of stalks like the English species.

The Holm oak (*Quercus ilex*) is common to the south of England and to Europe. 'Holm' is believed to be Anglo-Saxon for 'holly'. The tree adds to this association by its fondness of growing near holly, as well as by having holly-shaped leaves. Holm oak is more or less evergreen and because of the toughness of its leaves gives good shade. In

The leaves, flowers and acorn fruit of the English oak

June its male and female catkins appear, along with any new leaves, and the resultant acorns, which take 18 months to ripen, are ⅔ hidden by their very deep cups.

The Turkey oak (*Quercus cerris*) is by far the most prolific of the species introduced to Britain. It is a tall tree and when fully grown takes two years to develop its acorns, which grow in very mossy cups. While it is beautiful, the Turkey oak attracts the gall-wasp.

Of all the homes built by insects on oak trees the most harmful are the galls produced by gall-wasps, for they grow from the life-giving sap of the trees. These galls (or oak apples) can be seen on the bare branches of the trees in winter, looking like hard brown balls at the ends of twigs. Very often they have a small hole in them where the grub-turned-wasp has emerged and flown away. All galls are formed by the tree's defence mechanism, for when insects lay eggs in the bark of a tree they cause great disruption to the tree's flow of sap, forcing it to go on the defensive and produce a growth, rather than doing its proper work of feeding the tree.

Insects also attract birds such as nut-hatches, flycatchers, warblers and woodpeckers to the oak tree, and its acorns provide food which attracts many other forms of wildlife. The tree's shade also encourages the growth of wild flowers like bluebells, primroses, wood anenomes, foxgloves and wood sorrel. On the trunk of an oak tree fungi and lichen grow alongside tendrils and boughs of ivy, and oak woodlands are abundant homes to stinkhorn fungi. An oak may host the mistletoe and become sacred under druidic lore, but this is rare.

The oak may live to well over 700 years, outliving all except the yew. Even at death it retains its dignity, for its bare twisted branches rise high into the sky like a crown of antlers.

England was once covered in oak forests. In the time of Henry VIII's reign, one third of the land was still oak, but this has gradually declined over the centuries, mainly by man's hand. However with its strength to endure the winter gales, the oak has a noble dignity and is still known with affection as the 'King of the Forest'.

BARK
Oaks are broad sturdy trees with grey-brown distinctly gnarled and extremely furrowed barks. Their waisted trunks broaden out to divide into heavy branches which resemble big crooked arms, growing horizontally and seeming to defy gravity. The smaller branches and twigs are knobbly and crooked, and throughout winter they bear the closed buds of next year's leaves and catkins set in a spiral.

LEAVES
In late April or early May the soft tender tufts of new oak leaves appear. They are feathery, pale green and (on the English oak) short stalked. By June they have become dark green and thick, with a strong centre vein and deeply lobed edges. This gives them a distinctly crinkled appearance.

All through summer the leaves do their appointed work of breathing, perspiring and light-perceiving, by which they aid the tree's nutriment.

174

An old country observation states that 'the last leaf never falls off the oak', and this may refer to the fact that the oak, like the elder, has the capacity to releaf itself if its young leaves are caught by frost or destroyed by insects.

Oaks are known for their production of 'Lammas shoots', which appear as we move into August and the heat of the summer. These new leafy shoots make the oaks glow with fresh colour at the time when all else seems to wilt from the heat of the sun. They are pinky-golden when young and turn from pale to dark green as they harden. With this production the oak can retain strong leaves until late in the year, and because of this the tree provides extra shelter for animals and the 200 or so species of insect it houses.

In autumn oak leaves change colour dramatically, moving from dark green to yellow, orange, russet and pale brown. They sometimes remain on the tree until the next spring or until the buds forming for next year push them off.

FLOWERS
The male catkins appear on the tree with the leaves in April. They become long, pollen-filled and pendulous by May. Then the female catkins open as upright flowers, which await the touch of fertilizing pollen from the males. The female catkins are made up of two or three small cups. They hold the seed vessels which will become acorns, the fruit of the oak tree.

FRUIT
By autumn the acorns have ripened. They have changed in colour from green to pale yellow to dark olive brown. Now the oak drops its fruit. The acorns which fall and cover the ground beneath the tree are food to many animals such as pigs, deer, squirrels and dormice, and even man when times are hard. If they remain uneaten, they send out tiny shoots which root into the earth and produce a sapling tree.

Acorns hold a great reserve of food for a young tree and once this store is used up it will be strong enough to survive. The main enemy of young oak saplings are field-mice, which relish eating them.

ROOTS

The trunk of an oak is wide and spreading at the bottom to give its many roots a good grip in the earth. Oak roots go deep into the earth to compensate for the heavy branches above and the tree grows quickly (about 25 feet (7½ metres) in 15 years).

CUSTOM & LEGEND

The oak hosts many different forms of life. It is called a 'garden and a country', and because of its warmth and friendliness to man is regarded as an emblem of hospitality and strength. In the legends of many cultures acorns are said to have been man's first food. Traditionally, couples were married under oak trees long before the Christians substituted marriage in church. Because of the all-encompassing power that oaks express, ancients the world over regarded it as symbolic of the gods, believing they resided in the tree or were cradled in its shade.

The oak is possibly the most widely revered of all trees. The earliest spirits of Greek mythology were oak-tree spirits called dryads, and it was believed that oak was the first tree created by God from which sprang the entire human race.

According to Herodotus the sacred oak grove at Dodona had the greatest reputation for the gift of prophecy. Dodona was the oldest and most hallowed sanctuary in Greece and the goddess Dione (Diana) had an oak cult there. In earliest legend two black doves flew from Egyptian Thebes, one to Libyan Ammon and the other to Dodona. Each alighted on an oak tree and began the oracular oak cults.

In ancient times all oracles were delivered by the earth-goddess, but eventually her authority was so great that the power-seeking gods seized her shrines and appointed priests, or retained her priestesses, into their service. Zeus seized the oracle of Dodona from Dione and proclaimed it to be his, just as the Hebrew Jehovah took the willow from Anatha and Ishtar's oracular cult (*see also p.262*). Apollo wrested the shrines of Delphi from the earth-goddess, and Argos from Hera, the daughter of Cronos.

Amongst the Gauls of Galatia oak was sacred to the goddess of heaven until the change of rule went from women to men, when it became sacred to the god. Thus eventually at Dodona, priests and priestesses listened to the cooing of black doves, the rustling of the oak leaves or the clanging of vessels hung in the tree's branches and proclaimed that within the sounds was found the voice of Zeus.

The oak grove of Dodona was situated at the foot of Mount Tomarus, and it contained a far-spreading oak tree with evergreen leaves and sweet edible acorns. We are told that at this shrine an old woman named Pelias became the most famous interpreter of Zeus's messages to mankind, and that at the foot of the tree a spring of cold crystal water gushed and from its murmur inspired priestesses prophesied. The voice of Zeus also came in the form of thunder and it is said that more thunderstorms raged over Dodona than anywhere else in the classical world. Thunder-gods in particular are associated with oak, for as the tree's electrical resistance is low, it is struck by lightning far more than any other species.

Jason's legendary ship, the *Argo*, was built from the trees of a sacred oak grove and the goddess Athene fitted an oracular beam into the ship's prow, cut from Zeus's oak at Dodona. This beam whispered to forewarn the Argonauts whenever danger threatened. Athene was a daughter of Zeus and Metis, and was a goddess who reflected the harmonious blend of power and wisdom. As 'preserver of the state' she maintained law and authority. In her warrior aspect she wore a mask of the head of Medusa upon her breastplate to protect her virginity. She is likened to the Roman Minerva and was worshipped throughout all Greece. Her gentler side made her patroness of all the useful arts such as spinning and weaving.

Jupiter, Zeus's Roman counterpart, was worshipped as a god of rain and storms as well as thunder and lightning. Jupiter revealed the future to mankind by the flights of birds, which were thereafter called the 'messengers of Jupiter'. As lord of the heavens he was also prince of light, and the colour white was especially sacred to him. Esus, the druidic god of oak, shared all the attributes of Zeus and Jupiter.

According to legend, Dionysus saved the lives of the Maenads, the frenzied priestesses who were fleeing the wrath of the gods, after he had lured them into destroying Orpheus and his sun cult under Apollo. To do this he turned them into oaks rooted in the ground.

Fire has always been associated with oak. In Rome the vestal virgins used oak wood for their perpetual fires and in later years the fires of St Briget's retreat in Ireland were kept alight with acorns, as is discussed later *(see p.180)*. Oak was one of the traditional woods used for the Yule log and the midsummer bale-fires, or any fires lit for need.

The Bible is full of references to oak. To the ancient Hebrews it was sacred and Abraham supposedly received his heavenly visitors under an oak. Jacob buried all the idols of Shechem under an oak, and under the Oak of Ophra Gideon saw the angel who advised him how to free Israel. Saul and his sons are said to be buried under oaks, and when Augustine preached Christianity to the ancient Britons he stood under an oak tree.

Great oak forests once covered much of western Europe. The Celts with their thunder-god Taranis (*taran* is modern Welsh and Breton for 'thunder'), the Germans, the Baltic tribes and the Slavs all worshipped within oak forests, forming holy groves in which to contact their awesome gods. Growing in close proximities, the forest trees were often struck by lightning, and when this happened, a stricken tree was visibly and audibly wrought with the fire from heaven. In Tolstoy's words from *Anna Karenina*: 'Suddenly there was a glare of light, the whole earth seemed on fire and the vault of heaven cracked overhead.' So in the eyes of the ancients the mighty oak provided a channel through which the power of the sky-god might reach down to the world of men.

In Scandinavian myth, Thor was champion of the gods and chief defender of Asgard, the realm of the Nordic gods known collectively as the Aesir. As a sky-god Thor drove his chariot across the heavens, grant-ing good weather and favourable winds. In north-west Europe the oak was especially sacred to Thor, and Tacitus mentions groves held sacred to him at the end of the first century AD, many of which were felled by Christian missionaries, for example the Donar oak at Geismar, near Frankfurt, cut down by Boniface.

Thor the Thunderer was pictured as massive and red-bearded. He was armed with a hammer, iron gloves and a girdle of strength. Outspoken, indomitable and full of vigour, with a strong right arm and simple weapons, he is symbolic of 'action man', a mighty god with mighty appetites, typifying the characteristic Viking.

Thursday (Thor's day) was the day dedicated to the 'Thunderer' throughout the Germanic world and was kept as a holy day. Thor's hammer, named Mjollnir and reputedly made by dwarves, was not only symbolic of the destructive power of the storm (the fire from heaven), but was also protection against the forces of evil and violence. As a ritual object in common use, its derivatives were used at weddings and funerals and for accepting newborn children into the community. In symbolic form the hammer shape was used extensively on decorated amulets and jewellery, and similar 'throwing' hammers are still used in the Highland Games of Scotland.

The Anglo-Saxon god of thunder was called Thunor, but as the Vikings invaded Britain they brought their beliefs and culture with them, and these mingled with those of the natives. The Forest of Thor, on the north bank of the river Liffey, near Dublin, was in existence as late as AD 1000. Its great trees and lordly oaks were revealed, along with the protective power of the god, when the legendary King Boru tried for over a month to destroy the forest to little avail.

When Thor's followers settled in Iceland they took oak there in the form of high-seat pillars (see p.149) which they used to hallow new ground, enabling the god to protect his people in new lands. Most of Thor's legendary battles were against frost giants and giantesses, and he defended men rather than gods. It is said that his greatest adversary was the World Serpent which coiled around the earth.

Throughout the world, myths and legends describe the protective qualities of oak. In Britain, the oak still stands proud as the 'Father of Trees'. From Celtic times certain oaks were carved with a protective circle divided into four equal parts, symbolic of the earth, in order to magically prevent the tree from falling. This was most possibly a druidic custom, but was still practised long after druidism had fallen in the face of Christianity. The druids revered the oak above all other trees, because they believed it contained the energy, power and strength of their mighty god Esus. When it accepted the mistletoe upon it the oak became especially sacred, for the white berries of the mistletoe were seen to represent the sperm of the god. Thus the oak tree was likened to the male procreative force of the universe.

St Briget founded a retreat called the Cell of Oak for holy women at Kildare in Ireland, where it is said nuns burned acorns on perpetual fires. She evolved out of the goddess Brigid (Bridhe, Brig(antia), Brigadu, Brigit) and was originally a solar-goddess who prophesied and healed by virtue of the waters of inspiration. Brigid was specifically associated with the oak and the rowan, and she carried three fiery arrows with which to defend the land against invasion. As a saint Briget embodied the 'fire of faith' and her cauldron contained the 'milk of human kindness'. So popular was St Briget that by circa AD 452–525 the early Christian monks were forced to identify her with 'Our Mary Queen of Heaven'. Traditionally she is celebrated at Imbolc, the first Celtic fire festival of the year, and she is discussed more fully in the chapter on Rowan (see pp.229–30).

There have been a great many famous oaks in British legend. The wizard Merlin worked his enchantments in a grove of oaks and supposedly used the topmost branch of an oak tree as his wand. In the Welsh version of the story Merlin was born at Carmarthen. The Welsh name for the town is Caerfyrddin, which means 'Merlin's fortress', and the words of an ancient spell still resound:

> *When Merlin's Oak shall tumble down,*
> *Then shall fall Carmarthen town.*

The tree credited to be Merlin's oak was in Priory Street, and in recent years was little more than a trunk of oak bound with iron hoops and reinforced by a concrete pavement. Yet what little was left of this tree was recently stolen, precipitating the rapid planting of a new one in another location. It is to be hoped that a plaque will be placed in the original position of the legendary oak, given that a new tree cannot be now planted there, in order that the landmark remains consonant with the legend.

King Arthur's Round Table was reputedly made from one slice of an enormous oak tree and remains uncovered in a hollowed-out oak coffin in Glastonbury Abbey were believed to be Arthur's. This may or may not be true, but Arthur, like the oak tree, has always been regarded as a magical protector of rural England. Oaks were commonly planted as boundary markers between shires, and in the Domesday Book, wooded land was assessed in value according to the amount of pannage (feeding from acorns and beechnuts) it provided, rather than its acreage.

The oak tree has always been preached under (or in), and trees used specifically for this purpose became known as gospel oaks. Edward the Confessor preached under a gospel oak in Hampstead to gain support for his kingdom. His shrine at Westminster Abbey is of Purbeck marble and the tomb-chest, circa 1510, is of oak which is as sound as when erected.

Oaks are believed to have shielded many a hero. In Sherwood Forest, Nottinghamshire, Robin Hood, who protected the rights of country people, formed his life around and within great oaks. The great hollow Major Oak, in which it is said he held meetings with his merry band of men, still stands today, keeping his spirit alive, though the tree now needs support to prevent its collapse. The Major Oak is 64 feet (20 metres) in girth and is capable of holding 34 children within its hollow trunk. Unfortunately the shrine-like atmosphere of the place has been somewhat spoiled by the addition of tourist attractions.

The spirit of Herne the Hunter is believed to still inhabit an ancient oak tree. According to eighteenth-century manuscripts Herne was an oak-god of southern Britain 'whose antler-horned spirit still haunts Windsor Forest'. He is comparable to Hermes the god of shepherds, Mercury and Pan. In the Welsh tradition he is most comparable to Gwynn ap Nudd (the 'White One'), whose hounds, the dogs of Annwm, hunt souls across the skies. There was a supposed Gwynn cult at Glastonbury, where the Tor provided the gateway to the Otherworld kingdom. In this context it is Herne who leads the legendary Wild Hunt.

History tells us that Charles II hid in an oak tree following his defeat at the Battle of Worcester in 1651, and the tree was then named Royal Oak. Thereafter, 29 May, being both Charles's birthday and the day on which he returned to London after having taken refuge, became celebrated as Royal Oak Day, and during the festivities on this public holiday, oak sprigs were gathered and worn in hats and placed on all door-knockers. The oak was revered as a happy symbol, and people bedecked themselves with its leaves and boughs, which they were given permission to pick from certain woods. This celebration is thought to be a continuance of an older druidic Oak Apple Day and is still being celebrated in certain parts of Wiltshire.

Over time the Royal Oak Day celebrations became absorbed into the Mayday celebrations at the beginning of the month, where the Oak Man or Jack in the Green (the May King), wreathed in oak and hawthorn leaves with only his face left exposed, danced symbolically through the streets before claiming the May Queen. This enactment is a possible survival from the ancient goddess religions; customarily oak boughs have been used in wedding processions as a symbol of fecundity.

In honour of the oak as the Tree of Britain, a spray of oak leaves was engraved upon one side of sixpences and shillings, the coinage of the realm.

The counties of Hereford, Worcester, Shropshire and Staffordshire produce the finest oaks, and etymologically the oak has given its name to many towns. In this context the Anglo-Saxon root-word *ac* means 'oak', its seed being *accorne*. Place-names which reflect this are Auckland, Accrington and Acton. Another derivative is found in Okehampton.

HEALING

The oak tree has a wide range of qualities suitable for healing purposes. These also aid the spirit and soul of the patient, especially when their vital forces have become strained and unbalanced. The oak gives form and structure to these forces. It is especially good as a tonic for adults and as a strengthener for growing children. Specific healings obtained from parts of the oak tree are as follows.

BARK
Gypsies use oak bark as an astringent, antiseptic and tonic. It is stripped from the tree in April or May, and is dried in the sun, chopped and made

into decoction. (Use 3–3½ ounces (80–100 g) (¾ cup) to 2 pints (1 litre) of water and boil for 10 minutes.) This can be used as a gargle mouthwash for inflammation of the throat and the mucous membranes of the mouth. It can also be used in hot baths for chilblains, frost-bite, etc., or on hot compresses for hernias, inflamed glands and haemorrhoids.

If ground into a fine powder, oak bark can be taken like snuff to stop nosebleeds. It can also be sprinkled onto sheets to alleviate the discomfort of bedsores.

A strong decoction of oak bark is a good remedy for chronic diarrhoea. Put 1 ounce (25 g) (¼ cup) of bark into 1 quart (1 litre) of water and boil down to 1 pint (½ litre) of liquid. This can be taken by the spoonful or watered down and drunk. The same decoction can be used straight to staunch bleeding gums or haemorrhoids.

For women with menstrual disorders, a composition of oak bark, nettle flowers, shepherd's purse, marjoram seeds and yarrow (ingredients which can be obtained from most health food shops or herbalists if you can't get out to pick your own) can be added to bathing water or made into a tea, which is a good woman's tonic. If heavy menstruation problems exist, a pinch of bark powder can be mixed in honey and taken in the mornings, though it is also wise to see a doctor if the condition persists.

LEAVES

Young oak leaf-buds were prepared in distilled water and taken inwardly to assuage inflammations.

Bruised oak leaves are used outwardly, being applied to wounds and haemorrhoids to ease inflammations.

Oak leaves also make a good tonic wine (see p.196).

ACORNS

To carry an acorn was anciently believed to preserve youth and give protection, luck and a healthy life. Oak bark, leaves and acorns make an astringent tonic due to their high tannin content. This astringent quality was used in old remedies for diarrhoea, where acorns were powdered or grated and taken with water. A decoction of oak bark and acorns in milk was used as an antidote to poisoning from plants and bogus medicines.

An analysis of an acorn published in the *Lancet* stated the proportions of nourishment an acorn contains: 5.2 per cent protein, 45 per cent carbohydrate (in the form of starch) and 6.3 per cent water. This explains why acorns have always been prized as nourishing body-building food for animals and in earlier days for man himself.

Acorns still 'breathe' when off the tree and if they are to be stored a circulation of air is necessary. They can be used to make a rather bitter-tasting coffee which possesses nutritive properties and aids poor digestion, colic, diarrhoea and dysentery – a useful 'alternative' remedy once the taste is acquired.

OAK APPLES

The galls found on the ends of oak twigs are powerfully astringent, as though the essence of that quality of the tree has condensed within them in reacting to the insect which invaded it. They are botanically named *Quercus infectoria*.

Oak galls were formerly used to treat diarrhoea and dysentery. An ointment was made from them to treat haemorrhoids and haemorrhages from the nose or gums. An infusion of the galls was used as a gargle for sore throats and inflamed tonsils.

Toothache was said to have been cured by boring the tooth or gum with a nail until it bled, and then driving the nail into an oak tree. This method was also used with the ash tree. The oak is also used like ash in another method of healing, in that ruptured children were passed three times backwards through a split oak branch and if the split grew back together the child would be cured.

The Bach Flower Remedies recommend oak to treat the following conditions: despondency and despair of usually courageous people, nervous breakdowns and discontent with the self, annoyance on account of illness or feeling limited by illness. It helps perseverance in spite of set-backs, and is for those who never complain of others and tend to take all to themselves. Oak is calming when violence erupts through irritability, and as it centralizes energies it is good for those who struggle with life, and for those who are plodders and cannot find the way for direct action.

MAGIC

IRISH/GAELIC	*Duir*
OGHAM	=|
RUNIC	)
RULING PLANET	Jupiter
ABILITIES	Courage. Strength. Solid protection. Door to Mysteries. Health. Inner spiritual strength. To do with the element of Earth.
SEASONS	Summer; Autumn

In druidic tradition the oak is used magically at all major celebrations, for through its legendary associations with the sky and thunder-gods and with the goddesses of fire and fertility, it is closely aligned to the solar cycle, so much so that some would deem the sun its ruler rather than Jupiter. Throughout the vital solar cycle the oak-gods are invoked for their aid at the quarterly celebrations of Solstices and Equinoxes. The oak-goddesses are invoked at the cross-quarters, namely Imbolc, Beltaine, Lammas and Samhain.

At Imbolc oak is used for its feminine qualities and its nurturing abilities. It is associated with the goddess Bridhe who evolved into St Briget, as discussed in Custom and Legend.

At the Spring Equinox the oak is called upon to encourage the warmth of the sun for the healthy growth of young plants, animals and children. At this time bark may be easily gathered from the oak in order to store for healing purposes.

The Beltaine ceremonies celebrate the fertility of the land and the people, and the oak is invoked then for its ancient fertile character.

At the Summer Solstice when the sun is at its height in the heavens, the oak represents its strength and its powerful ability to ripen the harvests which will feed the people. This is the time of the sacred marriage between heaven and earth, when the power of the sun-god impregnates the earth-goddess with its future self. After this, as the sun begins to descend in the heavens, the sun-god gives his remaining strength to the crops of earth, his creations from his former self through last year's sacred marriage. As Father of Trees the oak represents the god's fatherly influence. The great fires of oak burned traditionally at midsummer celebrated his glory.

Quick-moving power is expressed by the oak at Lammas, the beginning of harvest-time. Now the woodlands are rich and abundant, and the oak-goddess Diana leads the hunt and harvest as stores are gathered in preparation for the changing seasons. As the gathering-in energy rises and humans, birds, insects and mammals scurry for bounty, the oak reflects their urgency by the appearance of its Lammas shoots, which seem to rush into being overnight from the ends of its branches. As all other vegetation is ripening under the heat of the sun the Lammas oak stands proud in a verdure of spring-like green, almost a verification of the continuing cycles of life.

At the Autumn Equinox the oak is ripe with acorns. Its rich harvest feeds the woodland animals as they prepare their larders for the coming cold of winter. So abundant are the species of life-forms dependent upon oak that it is revered at this time for its provision to life.

By Samhain the sun has declined in power and the sun-god is now believed to be entering the Underworld. At this time acorns represent the continuity of life through reproduction. Samhain was the Celtic new year and in order to see what was coming in the future year, oak apples or galls were used in divination, as discussed later. The oak also represents the unseen presence of the sun-god, who at this time draws back the veil between the worlds to enable the living to reunite with their departed loved ones. The divinatory aspects of the goddess Cerridwen, who undoubtedly used oak in her Cauldron of Inspiration, can be invoked at Samhain.

Having followed the cycle of the year alongside the oak tree, let us look more closely at its fruit, the acorn. That acorns were used magically and for religious purposes there is no doubt, for the phallic wands of all pagan faiths were tipped with an acorn or pine cone, both reminiscent of the glans penis in shape. Such fertility associations made acorns potent for use in love magic. Young lovers in ancient days placed two acorns in a bowl of water and waited to see if they moved together to seal the romance or if they moved apart as the young hearts would.

On a more serious note, an old magician's spell of the fourteenth century advised men who wanted their wives to stop erring while they were away to place two halves of an acorn in the woman's pillow. However, if the lovers were clever they could stop such a spell by finding the two halves of the acorn, placing them together, keeping them for six days and then eating half each.

An acorn necklace can be made and worn during magical workings, meditations or celebrations as an aid in contacting the graceful feminine energies of Blodeuwedd. Such a necklace can also be worn to invoke Diana, goddess of the woodlands, when we need to touch the 'survivor' strength of the feminine energies, or desire closer contact with woodland animals. Acorns can also be used to contact the high gods or any ruling deity. This releases strong energies for work needing physical endurance or inspiration from the ancients.

Gerard tells us of an ancient method of divination from oak galls which showed the nation where it needed protection. Galls were broken into at specific times of the year (probably spring and autumn) and what was found in them foretold the sequence of the coming seasons. If an ant was found inside the gall it foretold plenty of grain to come; if a spider, there would be 'a pestilence among men'; if a white worm or maggot, there would be a 'murrain' of beasts or cattle. If the worm flew away (presumably found at its metamorphic stage of becoming a gall-wasp or flying insect), it signified war; if the worm crept, it foretold scarceness of harvest; and if it turned about, it foreshadowed the plague. Such a record also gives us an indication of the harsh concerns of earlier times.

Diviners often used oak galls to discover if a child had been bewitched. Three galls were put into a basin of water under the child's cradle and if they floated the child was alright. However, if they sank the child was most probably afflicted, and further steps could be taken to free it from the fascination.

A healing 'oak-ball' was anciently made from oak bark or an oak gall. Once imbued with specific energies it was worn by those who needed healing. Because of its spherical shape the oak-ball represented healing associated with the moon.

When gathering plants that need to be free from the taint of human hands, it is traditional to use oak sticks to touch the herbs.

In country lore the leafing sequence of trees was watched carefully, for certain sequences foretold the coming weather (see p.143). This ensured that farming work was planned according to the signs of Nature, working with its rhythms and thereby gaining.

Because the oak is so deep-rooted it can aid the well-being of our feet, the point with which we contact the earth. Many old oak recipes are for ointments which heal weary feet. Likewise an oak foot-bath made with a decoction of ground oak bark or leaves will not only soothe feet, but will also help them find the right pathway through life.

Even without the use of such magic or medicine, contact with an oak tree brings a sense of well-being, security and sure-footedness. To continue this we can carry a twig of the tree with us. Cutting a twig from a tree is but a small act, yet as we handle that twig, communication with the tree itself develops and deepens. If two small twigs of oak are tied into an equal-armed cross with red cotton, it can be carried in a pocket and used to aid strength and balance, and as a talisman giving protection.

The deities associated with oak are numerous. The goddesses include Dione, Diana, Rhea, Cybele, Circe, Athene, Demeter, Brigid, Bridhe, St Briget, Blodeuwedd and Cerridwen. The gods are mainly rulers of thunder and lightning, including Zeus, Jupiter, Hercules, Pan, Jehovah, Esus, Odin, Thor, Dagda and Herne. Oak also represents any ruling deity.

Oak is ruled by the element of fire. Its ruling planet is Jupiter, though it is closely associated with the sun. It is used for health, fertility, luck, joviality and potency.

INSPIRATION

The druids were known as the 'wise men of oak', and the title 'druid' is most likely derived from *duir*, the old Irish/Gaelic name for oak.

According to Nature mystics of all ages, the oak is a doorway, like all other trees. Through these doorways we enter other dimensions where we perceive different realities and worlds. In physical reality the oak also provides real doors of incredible strength and beauty, and its doorways to other realms, both spiritual and psychological, have the same qualities. In such places we contact primeval strengths which give us the ability to overcome adversity. In much the same way oak overcomes lightning, by still growing even when 'blasted':

> *There is no crown to mark the forest's King,*
> *For in his leaves shines full the summer's bliss,*
> *As Sun, storm, rain and dew to him their tribute bring.*

ANON

Through worship and ritual, seeing the oak at times as the embodiment of the Godhead in Nature, druids celebrated the cycles of the year, not merely those of the seasons, but many more concerned with the life of the nation, such as the oracular rites at Dodona mentioned earlier. Today as we begin to gather more information about the natural sciences as they once were, druidic ways may seem eccentric. To those who believe superstition, they may be frightening. Yet theirs was a way of living that responded to the ways of the earth, respecting Nature's moods and acknowledging and working with its ultimate ruling power. Nature was regarded not only as divine but also as intelligible. To the druids the oak was at times the medium for interpreting the will of the gods. This implies a profound respect for the Spirit of God in Nature.

As a child growing up in the country I remember hearing in church that God was in everything. I still vividly recollect trying to work this out as I wandered hedgerows and fields looking at every single detail of

Nature, for I could not come to terms with the enormity of a world filled with uncountable things. That awe has never left me.

As the oak grows to such old age it enables us to focus on the concepts of time and memory. Within this book I have endeavoured to stimulate or reawaken memories and confirmation that I have been on the right track has come to me strongly during recent years.

One of my favourite druidic histories concerns a Welsh druid called Iolo Morganwg, who did much at the beginning of the nineteenth century to promote the re-establishment of Eisteddfod, festivals celebrating the ancient bardic arts and sciences. An eccentric, he was asked one day exactly what he considered he'd given to the people. Upon reflection he replied, 'Memory.'

When I heard this story and its simple druidic statement, it seemed to verify that I was using the correct druidic principles for the foundation of this book. However a year or so later even stronger confirmation came, for on asking my mother to illuminate the Irish side of my family, she offered, out of all the information she could give, illumination on my great-great-great-grandmother, stating that her maiden-name was Memory! Above all else this affirmed that my initial experience with the oak trees was valid and that the oak grove was truly open to me, as were the memories contained within.

Within an oak-grove is found protection and warmth, essential requirements for communication with the natural world, and for the successful invocation of gods and goddesses. The most famous ceremony performed by druids inside a grove was, and still is, that of the oak and mistletoe. Mistletoe has always been associated with the sun, and the traditional custom of gathering it at both the solar Solstices (the wood at midsummer and the berries and leaves at midwinter) associates the plant with the sun cults of Old Europe.

Mistletoe was anciently called *druad-lus*, the 'druid's plant'. It was regarded as the plant which 'falls from heaven upon the oak', the plant of peace. Druids saw their all-powerful god as primarily residing within the oak and they believed that the white berries of the mistletoe, which they called 'All-heal', resembled drops of semen, which carry the seed of life. Thus if the oak let the symbolic semen grow upon it and if the mistletoe accepted the tree as its host, it signified that the immortal Godhead had come that much closer to the mortality of all living things on earth.

This symbiosis of mistletoe and oak and the acceptance of one by the other was considered the highest magical phenomenon in Britain, for English oaks are not often accepted by the mistletoe, even though other oaks are. Thus the most powerful combination of oak and mistletoe is on English oak. To the druids, attainment of the 'marriage-proper' upon this species was seen as divine, brought about only by the aid of the gods.

The Godhead of the oak was regarded as akin to the Godhead of the sun, and the energy of the oak, like the sun, is at its height around midsummer. Mistletoe is ruled by the sun and wands are cut from it at midsummer. At the Winter Solstice ceremony the mistletoe, with its berries, is ritualistically lopped (not cut) from the oak tree, and is caught in a cloth so it never touches the earth. When laid upon the altar during rites, mistletoe brings fertility to the spirit of the earth by symbolically representing the semen of the oak/sun-god which is given to the earth-goddess, renewing her fertility.

At midwinter the holly tree also comes into full power with its resplendent red berries. In some traditions it is held that at midsummer the oak hands its power over to the holly and reclaims it at midwinter (see also p. 36). This interaction between the holly and the oak has passed down in folklore as a battle between rival gods for the hand of the earth-goddess. Traditionally this was enacted by mummers at fairs and festivals, with oak and holly knights competing for the hand of a fair maiden, enactment which, in spite of parody, kept alive the themes of the pagan religions. In druidic tradition the robin and wren are associated with these trees and also compete according to season, adding symbolically to the many connotations within this overall theme.

Throughout the centuries it has been said by woodmen and foresters that when an oak tree is felled it screams like a man. It was the screams of dying oaks which caused this book to be born, and it would seem from the following words of Mervyn Peake that he too was moved by such:

> *If trees gushed blood when they were felled,*
> *By meddling man, and crimson welled*
> *From every gash his axe could give,*
> *Would he forbear, and let them live?*

As already explained, given the amount of veneration shown to trees throughout myth and folklore the world over, it seems that ancient man never viewed trees as inanimate objects, but rather as a species of life-form akin to humans and animals. We would do well to do the same.

Oak spirits, or dryads, are usually depicted as wizened old men, as used to working underground in the earth and the roots of the trees as they are above in its branches. Oak dryads have a strong humorous presence which brings us a sense of release, showing that every problem is surmountable if we take nourishment from the earth.

I have a favourite oak tree in a nearby field which never fails to give me strength and a feeling of great security. Its spirit is very wise and patient, and no matter how stressed out I am when approaching it, I always leave with a feeling that life contains a richness that I have only just begun to touch and see. As that oak heals my spirit I feel a bubbling exhilaration flowing through me. This brings the knowledge that I am able to achieve all that I desire through the acknowledgement of life in all its forms.

An incredible example of an ancient oak grove is found on Dartmoor, unusual in that it is a miniature oak forest no more than 20 feet (6 metres) high. Wistman's Wood is centuries old, and exudes such a spooky energy that writers since the seventeenth century have evoked its qualities for their tales of mystery and superstition, Conan Doyle's *The Hound of the Baskervilles* being the most famous of these. Such is the impact of this grove that it demands explanation.

Wistman's Wood grows out of and between enormous lichen-covered rocks and boulders. It is visually unique. I visited it in early spring before the trees had opened into leaf, and felt an instant displacement of the senses even before entering the place, for the countless rocks and boulders are set so closely together around the trees, it is virtually impossible to set foot on the earth between them. The lichen colours on the rocks disguises their cool greyness with vivid splashes of yellow and blue-green. From out of these colourful stones rise the twisted trunks of the oaks, seemingly removed from the earth. They are embodied by weather, age and the energies of the place. Their trunks bend and weave into branches which become as lace set against the sky. Upon these branches grow 'floating islands' of moss and frilly ferns which fill the air with colour.

The main effect upon the senses comes from these mossy 'islands', for they are at eye level when you stand upon the boulders. This creates a very *Alice in Wonderland* effect, as though you are inside the earth with your head poking through the grass. The feelings this brings are difficult to describe, for its strength and strangeness move deep chords within. However the true spirit of a place is reflected by its visiting wildlife and on the day I visited, Wistman's Wood resounded with the songs of courting birds, their melodies lifting the heavy rumbling background noise of the nearby river Dart. This wood is a storehouse of ancient elemental power and such is the ancient wizardry it exudes that it is easy to surmise that its original name could well have been 'Wiseman's' or 'Wizened' Wood. A place once entered never forgotten.

Similarly magical are the two ancient oak trees called Gog and Magog that stand towards the back of Glastonbury Tor. These trees are named after the last two giants who inhabited Britain, the ancient father-god and mother-goddess of the pre-Christian pagan religions. They are the last survivors of an ancient avenue of oak trees which wound the druidic processional way up the back of the Tor. Gog and Magog live up to their giant names well, for they are supremely majestic. The old female tree Magog appears at times formidable, at others more kindly. Like an old granny, she is stooped with age. Gog is very strong and king-like in his proportions, solidly standing tall and proud as he has for centuries. Side by side like husband and wife they represent the male and female energies of Nature which always guide the human race to fulfilment in life.

PHYSICAL USES

After its first century the oak only grows about 1 inch (2½cm) a year and this matures the wood as it grows, so that in great age the oak becomes virtually indestructible. Because it is so hard and close-grained, oak wood lasts for centuries, and as it does not rot it was anciently used for bridges, piles for waterbreaks, and walkways over marshes.

The wooden walls of England's houses gave rise to the term 'hearts of oak', for the Englishman literally made oak his home. Oak wood was also used in the creation of churches and cathedrals. The roof beams of Westminster Abbey are 'Durmast' timber from Sessile oaks.

The oaks of the Forest of Dean became many a wooden wall and ship of England. They became so famous for their quality of wood that after his defeat by English ships in the Battle of the Armada, Philip of Spain declared that every tree within the forest should be destroyed, as he would have liked to destroy the heart of every Englishman. Other oaks which formed the ships of the victorious English fleet were from the mountains of southern Ireland and still have not been replaced. The Forest of Dean was not destroyed by Philip's declaration, but by two centuries later so many of the trees had been felled for timber that Nelson asked the Crown to replant it with new oaks. Oak woodland on the Surrey–Hampshire border was also replanted at Nelson's request and has associations with naval history right back to Roman times.

As well as having incredible strength, oak wood is renowned for its beauty of grain and texture and its rich colour after polishing. For these reasons it has always been a prized wood for furniture. Oak tables, cupboards, chests, doors and chairs solidly survive centuries of use. They add warmth and a feeling of security to any home. In colour oak wood is pale brown, but darkens with age.

Fighting clubs were made from oak wood, and roots of oak were used to make hafts for knives and daggers. The twisted 'knees and elbows' of the oak tree's gigantic branches were prized by old shipbuilders for the shaping of their boats.

Oak trees of today are small compared to the earlier giants and this has been verified by the unearthing of a prehistoric boat of bog-oak at Brigg, Ireland, which had been dug out from one huge oak log, some 48½ feet (14½ metres) long. The durable qualities of oak are also shown by excavations in the Ouse valley, for traces of five successive oak forests have been found, the earliest being around 70,000 years old.

The Vikings made their magnificent longboats from the giant oaks of European forests. The graceful lines of these boats gave them speed through water and their dominating giant carved prows announced their prowess to any people they invaded. Viking spears were made from ash but all other weapons, especially hammers, were made from solid oak.

The British and Danish practice of burying people in oak coffins used large sections of tree-trunks, which were split lengthwise and hollowed out to contain the body. This was usually only done for great persons.

As oak wood is impervious to alcohol it has always been used for casks in which to store liqueur. Many taverns and old pub-signs still express the ancient associations of oak trees, such as the 'Royal Oak', the 'Oak and Acorn', etc.

BARK

Oak bark is often called 'tanner's bark' for it is used world-wide for tanning leather. The bark contains 15–20 per cent tannin, and is most easily stripped off the trees in April or May, before the leaf-buds open and the tree's flow of sap seals the bark to it.

The bark is also used for dyeing. An infusion of bark and copper is used by Scottish Highlanders to dye wool a purplish colour. With alum a brown dye is obtained, and with salt of tin, yellow. Native Americans dyed their skin red with the bark of a species of oak, *Quercus prinus*.

An acid used in the making of ink is found in oak bark, and old oaks found in peat-bogs with an iron content in the water have been surrounded by inky liquid caused by the acid's reaction with iron.

Gardeners make a decoction of oak bark which adds warmth to the soil to encourage plants. Unfortunately it is also known to encourage the growth of fungi, which may be harmful to some plants.

LEAVES

Throughout many centuries the leaves of the oak have been used to make good wines. For a medium-dry wine of good flavour the leaves should be picked in late spring or early summer. For a fuller flavour they can be picked around autumn as they change colour. Only fresh-looking leaves should be used and none which have been nibbled by insects or contain insect galls.

Here is the recipe:

To 1 gallon (4½ litres) of leaves use 1 gallon (4 litres) of water, 3 lbs (1½ kg) (6 cups) of sugar and 2 lemons.

Wash the leaves and put them in a large basin, and pour 4 pints (2 litres) of boiling water over them. Cover with a clean cloth and leave for 12 hours.

Put the sugar in a large saucepan with the remaining 4 pints (2 litres) of water and bring to the boil, stirring until the sugar dissolves. Take off the heat and add the strained lemon juice.

Strain the oak leaf infusion into a fermentation jar, add the water, sugar and lemon mixture and some activated wine yeast according to the instructions on the packet, and shake well.

Ferment, rack and bottle as other wines, and if you can keep it for a year before use, you'll be rewarded with excellent flavour.

ACORNS

Acorns are believed to have been one of man's first foods. It is written that the ancient Romans roasted acorns on embers and served them as a course at feasts, and that they also made bread from them.

At the end of seventh century in Britain special laws relating to pannage were issued. Land was measured and valued according to its swine-feeding capacities, all of which is recorded in the Domesday Book. Acorns have a large proportion of carbohydrate and fat and have been used to good effect in the past for fattening up livestock. However it is now realized that other vegetable matter should also be given to stock to stop the acorn's binding effects.

GALLS

Oak galls are used for a black dye, though it is not durable. They are also used commercially to obtain gallic and tannic acids for tanning processes and the preparation and manufacture of ink.

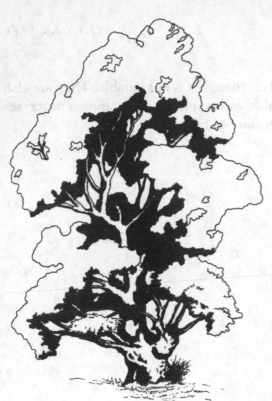

THE ENGLISH ELM

BOTANICAL

ELM. *Ulmus campestris*. Deciduous.

The family *Ulmaceae* contains around 16 species of elm which are found throughout Europe and Asia. There are two kinds of elm in Britain: the English or common elm and the wych elm. Both are lofty and noble. The English elm is one of Britain's tallest trees, reaching heights of 150 feet (45½ metres) in a century of growth.

The shape of the elm tree is distinctly waisted and its branches fan out broadly into a magnificent canopy which acts as a massive receiver of light. The branches have a zig-zag appearance and are twisted and knotted; when elms are seen growing in line, as they notoriously do, their branching is hypnotically repetitive as fan after fan reach for the skies like misty haloes. The twigs on the branches are short, more like bushy sprays growing close to the branch, and they bear many small bead-like buds in early spring, which open into flowers.

Some people doubt that elm is truly native to Britain, yet it is mentioned long ago in legend and is known to have formed part of the old woods and forests of centuries past. It was so prolific it was called the 'weed of Gloucester', and was a very common tree of the hedgerows and fields until recent times, for 70 per cent of hedgerows were said to have been elm.

However, Dutch elm disease, brought into Britain from Holland in 1919, has claimed all the mature trees. Now when a tree reaches 30 years old it becomes vulnerable to the disease-carrying ambrosia beetle, which burrows into the bark and destroys the flow of life-giving sap. The first sign of this is shown in the crown of the tree, where a mass of dead twigs and leaves appear, while other parts of the tree appear healthy and green. The leaves then start to fall and slowly the tree dies. The effect is cumulative, for the fungus caused by the disease gets blown as spores from tree to tree, passing on the disease. When dead, the trees stand as gaunt giant skeletons.

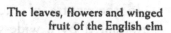

The leaves, flowers and winged fruit of the English elm

Since 1927 the import of live elms into Britain has been prohibited, yet this measure has not saved the trees, for all the mature elms are now gone. From noble trees living 400 years or more elms have become hedgerow trees doomed to die at 30.

Many insects are attracted to elms. The tortoiseshell butterfly uses the tree as a nursery, laying its eggs upon it and ensuring a good food supply for its caterpillars. Insects which bore into the wood of elms are loved by woodpeckers, which are able to detect their presence with relentless beaks. Other birds love the not too dense shade of elms, rooks being the most noticeable, and grass grows freely under the trees, allowing many other forms of life to survive.

Many artists have captured the beauty of English elms midst the harvest fields. A good example of this is Constable's picture 'The Hay Wain', for it portrays the true essence of agricultural England.

BARK

The trunks of elm trees, which can attain girths of 6 feet (2 metres), grow very rugged, furrowed, gnarled and knobbly with age. The English elm is recognized by its rough dark brown-grey trunk which has many surface furrows. As the tree grows, the trunk can become covered to the ground with dense brushwood. This is like a forest of small branches which entangle with stool-shoots springing up from the tree's roots. The leaves of this brushwood open before the leaves on the tree, and the shoots, if they can be separated, can be replanted.

FLOWERS

Elms are usually the first trees to flower in the spring. They flower and form their fruit well before their first leaves open. Elm flowers are crowded tufts of reddish coloured stamens with large purple heads, and when they are open and the sun touches the tree, it appears to glow with a distinctly fiery look of misty crimson.

In the centre of each flower is a tiny flat green ovary. This is surmounted by a wide-spreading forked stigma which collects pollen from the red stamens of the same flower. Elms have the capacity to release pollen when needed, for the stamen heads can open or shut according to the weather.

LEAVES

All elm leaves are lop-sided at their base. The leaf-buds open in May to reveal leaves folded up like miniature fans, their beautiful pale green colour co-ordinating with the opened protective scales which are fawny-brown on the outside and pink on the inner. When the leaves open out they become soft green, which by summer turns a dark bluish shade. They are rough in texture with many hairs which may irritate sensitive skin and they grow to about 2 inches (5 cm) in length, in comparison to the wych elm (*Ulmus glabra*) which has leaves up to 7 inches (17 cm) long.

By October the elm's leaves turn light gold and they begin to fall after the first frost of winter.

Black spots may appear on elm leaves. These are made by a minute plant which in time destroys the leaf.

FRUIT

In time the flower stamens shrivel and fall away to reveal bunches of flat green wings, each with a seed in the centre. These winged seeds quickly dry and turn light brown and paper-like. They are blown away on the wind almost at the time when the tree begins to open its leaves. Elms are some 40 years old before they begin fruiting, and even though their seeds are produced in vast amounts, they are rarely fertile, for the elm has evolved into reproducing via shoots and saplings which grow from the roots of old trees. While this method of reproduction has kept the elms' bloodline pure, it has not protected them in other ways (*see above*).

CUSTOM & LEGEND

Ancient elms were part of the superstructure of the massive forests which once covered England. They dominated the landscape, standing proud and tall. Even as late as the seventeenth century, when the forests had all but disappeared, Culpeper stated elms were one of the 'most commonest English trees, overlooking Nature's seasons'.

In legend the elm has always been associated with death, the grave and theories of rebirth. In the Greek legend of Orpheus, when he returned to the upper world from Hades he began to play a love-song to his Lady Eurydice, whereupon the first elm-grove sprang into existence:

> *The Thracian bard a pleasing elm-tree chose,*
> *Nor thought it was beneath him to repose*
> *Beneath its shade,*
> *When he from hell returned.*

ANON

Ancient Italian traditions encouraged a physical partnership between elms and vines, for elm trees were planted in vineyards to shade and protect the plants, and to give them a naturally branching structure to grow upon. This arrangement mixed the elm and vine legends, especially in themes referring to Bacchus, the Italian god of intoxication. In the words of the poets, the elm and the vine were 'wedded'.

European legends concerning elms often refer to their associations with elves. If we look at the elven world we can touch the magical atmosphere that our ancestors associated with both them and the elm tree.

Tolkien's *Lord of the Rings* depicts the atmosphere of elves and their magical realms particularly well, and it weaves such a descriptively rich tapestry that we are inclined to wonder how much elf and how much man was within Tolkien himself:

> *And see ye not yon bonny road*
> *That winds about yon fernie brae?*
> *That is the road to fair elfland,*
> *Where thou and I this night maun gae.*

J. R. R. TOLKIEN, TREE & LEAF

Elves have always been acknowledged in Scandinavian and Celtic countries, and the myths and legends of northern Europe are full of reference to them, especially their intimate associations with burial mounds. This is particularly interesting, for it connects with the later English tradition of using elm wood for coffins; and, as there are few remaining legends about the elm itself, it also gives clues to the position the tree held in our ancestors' lives.

According to Germanic legend, the realm of the elves was called Alfheim and lay beyond Asgard, home of the gods. There were light elves and dark elves and they helped or hindered man accordingly. In Scottish folklore elves are called the *Seelie* ('Blessed Ones') or the *Unseelie* ('Unblessed Ones').

The light elves were believed to have great associations with the sun and to propitiate them people carved cup-marks (associated with sun-wheels) into mounds, rocks and stones covering tombs, into which they poured milk as an offering, a practice still continued today in many country regions of Sweden. In the minds of European people a strong link formed between elves and the dead in the mounds.

Elves were believed to have the power to harm humans, but were also known to provide healing and aid during childbirth. In a legend of heathen Norway, King Olaf the Holy (*olaf* meaning 'elf') gave great concern at his birth, for his delivery was long delayed and the life of his mother was severely at risk. To remedy the situation a magical belt, ring and sword were fetched from the elves of the burial mound of Olaf, Elf of Geirstad, predecessor of the king. The magical belt was fastened around the stomach of King Olaf's mother and greatly aided with his birth, after which the sword and ring transferred the power of kingship upon him. King Olaf the Holy and his ancestor Olaf, Elf of Geirstad, became gods of fertility after their deaths, and ceremonies were performed where people asked them for fertility in life and ultimate rebirth.

In Britain elves were believed to give protection against lightning strikes and to help attract love. Such was their connection to elms that the trees gained the folk-name of 'elven' and such was their association with burial mounds that elms became incorporated into the death cycle, being literally made into coffins which housed the bodies of the dead:

> *Beneath those rugged elms, that yew tree's shade,*
> *Where heaves the earth in many a mouldering heap,*
> *Each in his narrow cell for ever laid,*
> *The rude forefathers of the hamlet sleep.*

GRAY

Elm groves have always been associated with superstition. The Saxon King Edgar provided evidence of the ancient elm groves that our forefathers worshipped in, for he decreed that 'every priest shall anxiously advance Christianity and forbid tree worship, divination with the dead, omens and charms with songs which are practised on Elms and various other trees', thus forbidding converse with the natural world. Yet in later years at places such as Lichfield (which means 'deadman's field' or 'corpse field'), elm branches were carried in procession by the clergy and choir of the cathedral during the annual beating of the bounds ceremonies. The gospel was read at eight places where wells once existed and the elm branches were then placed near the font in the cathedral.

The elm was integral to the farming calendar. The timing of its leafing was important, for it showed farmers when the season was right for them to sow crops:

> *When elmleaf as big as mouse's ear,*
> *Then sow barley and never fear.*
> *When leaf as big as ox's eye,*
> *Then hie boys hie.*

The elm also forewarned, for when its leaves fell out of season it was taken as a sign that disease might come to cattle. This belief was particularly common in Devon, along with that which claimed that lightning would never strike an elm tree, although this has been difficult to verify since the introduction of Dutch elm disease.

Elm trees once lined the hedgerows or grew in copses and all work of the farmers within the fields was influenced by them. Within the villages judges often dispensed justice from under the shade of elms. In parts of Cornwall elm was used as the maypole, being brought home on 30 April to be painted and decorated in preparation for the coming celebration.

Elms have always been a favourite tree for rooks, whose untidy nests and raucous shrieks would no doubt have boosted the dramatic imaginations of story-tellers as they spoke of brooding elm groves and the colonies of large birds which claimed them, for birds were regarded as either containing the spirits of the dead or being totemic symbols of the mighty gods. Yet the closest observers of the relationship between elms and rooks must be the ploughman and the sower, for they have always been followed by these raucous birds, which dive through the air to grab at grubs or seeds in their wake.

Elm's Latin name, *Ulmus*, refers to an instrument of punishment, for elm-rods were anciently used for whipping slaves. In Germany and Scandinavia the elm is known as *alm, ilme, olm, elem* and *helm*.

HEALING

Elm is a tree used to obtain purification. Physically it is used for cleansing the skin and making soaps, due to its astringent, anti-inflammatory qualities. Spiritually it is used for cleansing the spirit via meditation and use as an incense. Through this it also induces faith in yourself.

The Bach Flower Remedies advise using elm to alleviate feelings of failure, moods of discouragement, despondency and inadequacy. Elm's greatest healing lets you know that you are truly worthy.

BARK

Elm bark is collected early in spring and may be dried rapidly for storage. The inner bark was used to treat skin conditions and to alleviate rheumatism. It was either ground and made into decoction and applied to the skin, or placed whole, inner side to the skin, when still moist.

Ulmin, a gummy substance which exudes from the bark in summer, was used as an astringent and for treating ringworm.

A decoction made from the bark of the tree's roots, when fomented, was used to soften hard tumours.

LEAVES

The leaves or bark of elm, soaked in vinegar, clear scurf and it is recorded that they also treat leprosy.

Bruised elm leaves were used to heal wounds, the leaves being packed around the wound and bound with elm bark.

A decoction of elm leaves, when used like a warm poultice upon specific parts, is said to help broken bones mend.

The moisture found in blisters which sometimes appear on elm leaves (caused by a leaf-louse), if applied fresh, will 'cleanse the skin and make it fair', according to old recipes.

MAGIC

IRISH/GAELIC	*Lemh*
OGHAM	᚛
RUNIC	ᚲ
RULING PLANET	Saturn
ABILITIES	Purification. Love. Light. Elves. Wisdom. To do with the element of Earth.
SEASONS	Summer; Autumn

As shown in Custom & Legend, the elm was anciently called the 'elven' tree, and this association was enhanced by the inherited race memories of the people, their legends and practices. This is especially so with the people of northern Europe, for they consciously worked with the elves who guarded the burial mounds of their dead.

The Kormaks Saga of ninth-century Iceland describes a sacrifice to elves of the mounds in order to obtain healing. This involved painting the outside of the mound with the blood of a sacrificed bull and leaving the flesh for the elves to eat. Similar sacrifices were recorded in the eleventh century in remoter parts of Sweden.

In Britain the elf-dwellers of the mounds were approached for inspiration, and by interaction with them kings reputedly received wisdom and counsel from dead kings within the burial chambers. In similar fashion poets received inspiration from the tombs of dead poets by sitting upon mounds and employing the correct meditations.

In magical work today meditation with elm aids the development of our communication with the devas, the spirits of the herbs, and by pricking an elm-leaf with a pin before placing it under the bed-pillow, divinatory dreams can be obtained. Through meditation with the elm tree we can also contact the elves, who, whilst they guard the dead, also have a lighter side which attracts love, luck and merriment. For this reason elm leaves and twigs were carried by people when such qualities were needed in their lives.

The light elves are best contacted in the light part of the year, from the Spring to the Autumn Equinox, and they are friendly, tolerant and gentle. Not so the dark elves, who show no tolerance, are harsh and often ferocious. They are best contacted during the winter months and great care must be observed if you do, for psychic if not physical harm may ensue through calling up such forces. This is no doubt why severe sacrifices were used to appease them in the past.

Through its associations with funerary matters the elm was regarded as a tree that ultimately all would have to face – a tree of destiny. Possibly this is the origin of the saying that 'elm hateth man, and waiteth', or perhaps it came from the elm's habit of dropping branches suddenly and without warning, and that accidents happen around elm trees. Or maybe such superstition arose from deliberate manipulation designed to keep people away from all contact with Nature and their native traditions. Whichever, in the following quote Kipling did little to allay it:

> Ellum she hateth man and waiteth
> Till every gust be laid.
> To drop a limb on the head of him
> That anyway trusts her shade.

Yet to those who understood the ways of the natural world, death was regarded as a doorway to birth into another way of life, which is a far less sinister theory than that of Christian hell and damnation. Thus the elm tree, whilst being approached with respect, was also approached with reverence, hope and humbleness, for in the minds of the people any communication set up with the tree would be reflected in their passage from one life to another. No doubt in this context the elm also provided a 'confessional' quality, giving rise to the role which was later taken over by the Roman Church. This may explain why the elm and the theories of rebirth around it were particularly outlawed by those who ruled by the fear of death.

The elm trees and their elven companions watched over great realms in ancient days, for there were vast areas of growing trees. As the land was cleared and the fields were born, so the elms became integrated into the agricultural cycles, becoming guardians of the fields.

In the Irish Brehon Law elm was referred to as a 'peasant' tree, one round which country people lived and which became part of their lives. Elm was also connected to the afterlife, as the bridge between lives. These points are discussed more thoroughly in Inspiration, see pp.208–10.

INSPIRATION

In Britain elm is the hardest tree to portray in its fullest sense, for with the demise of all the ancient elms our innate contact with the memories they hold from the past has almost gone. A few young elms survive but they do not as yet, nor will they ever, fulfil the ancient archetypal reality of the magnificent elms which once dominated our landscape.

In looking at the relationship our ancestors had with elm trees we have seen how they were regarded with great spiritual respect, for the elm's link with the elven realms via the burial mounds and their subsequent use as coffins gave people a sense of security when they viewed the end of their days – an ideal that every religion has striven to attain. However the living relationship between elms and the people developed in the fields, where they formed a partnership with a fruitfulness which was harvested within the people as well as upon the land.

In my childhood days, majestic elms towered over ripened fields where the autumn light was filled with the dust of the harvest haze in the rays of the setting sun. Then, as the last sheaves of the day were hoisted upon the cart, the harvest moon rose into the sky. When beginning this book it was relatively easy to find other mature species of indigenous trees to communicate with to bridge the gap between childhood memories and the present day, but with the elms' demise the mature link between past and present has been destroyed. Feeling that this was very symbolic of the ecological mess we've made of our planet, I endeavoured to understand more of what we've lost through this destruction, opening myself up to memories held within me and within the earth. In part I became as an elm tree, my roots in the earth, my body above and my head in the heavens, just as the ancient druids had taught, for the life-form of a tree is humanity's bridge to the stars.

We begin within the earth and the ancient elms' roots. Knowing that English or common elms evolved to reproduce specifically from their roots (by forming suckers which become new trees but which still remain attached to the parent tree via the root system) prompted meditations of times when elms were extremely abundant in the land and made it easy to visualize them all linked together, inseparable below the ground. This is fascinating imagery, especially if you view our planet as a giant body which, like us, has veins, bones, nerves, a heart, lungs, etc., for surely such an enjoined root system added to the complex structure of the land, perhaps acting like its nerves. Our own veins and nervous system are incredibly like the root systems of plants in structure.

That the roots of elms are beneficial to the soil is agreed by folklore and botanists alike, for the trees' health-giving qualities are reflected in the lush vegetation found growing around them, vegetation which houses many life-forms essential to the eco-system of the land.

The branches of mature elm trees reached high into the sky, as long rows of waisted trees, joined by their roots below ground, formed lines like dancing sisters, each hypnotically following the other across an undulating landscape, their mesmeric crowns fanning out into patterns like antique lace. The abundant canopies of ancient elms attracted light and the trees actually radiated, for while they drew light to them they also sent it out, encouraging the growth of living things around them. Meditation upon such light-attracting qualities shows a flow of light around the tips of the branches within the crown of the trees which is so strong that it appears as vibrant rainbow arcs. To me these rainbows symbolize the bridge that elms provided between heaven and earth. They also show the life-spirit of the elms, which is no longer strong and cannot help us balance our future.

So the death of ancient elms has robbed the earth of an integral part of its precious life-sustaining structure below ground and ecological balance above. The roots of ancient elms no longer move to the heart-beat of the earth, nor do their branches illuminate the music of the spheres.

Between the life-sustaining roots and light-bringing branches are the 'waisted' trunks of the trees, around which so many forms of life may flourish. Man has also conducted his life around elm trunks, generation upon generation. Sadly it is also through the tree's trunk that his mistakes culminated in the death of all ancient trees of the species, for the disease introduced from foreign lands destroyed the vital flow of sap within mature trees.

It is to be hoped that the elms outsmart their virtual extinction, as trees often do by evolving new defences or by becoming immune. Yet even then we will never again have the companionship of our lost ancient trees. It is also to be hoped that what remains of our countryside will blossom anew, as Nature and we humans outsmart the destructive elements of money-making barons. The elm is extremely symbolic of that strife.

PHYSICAL USES

Elm wood is very tough and durable and does not split when worked, though it does have a reputation for warping. Because of this, the majority was used for rougher work in the construction of barns and houses. If seasoned well, however, it can be used for furniture. Cabinet-makers love it, for the rough bosses of its trunk form beautiful veins in the wood. It was also the wood used for coffins.

Elm wood is very durable in water, and as well as being used for ship-building, it was made into keels and bilge planks and was used for water-pipes before cast iron.

It was sometimes used as a substitute for yew in long-bows and its sawdust was taken as snuff.

Woodmen's tradition advised felling elms at the very dead of the year (31 December and 1 January) when the sap possesses least vitality.

In Italy, as already mentioned, young elms were (and possibly still are) planted in vineyards to encourage the growth of vines. The trees allowed the vines a strong foundation and protected the grapes from the burning sun with their foliage.

Farmers in Britain encouraged elm in hedgerows and many elms were specifically planted as windbreaks. Cattle love eating elm leaves and in times of famine its leaves were collected as fodder for milk-producing cows. Dairy churns were made from elm to protect the milk from nega-tive influences.

The inner lining of elm bark is very tough and fibrous and was traditionally made into ropes, string and mats.

THE
BEECH TREE

BOTANICAL

BEECH. *Fagus sylvatica*. Deciduous.

Beech trees form deep shady woods, for their thick leaves create layer upon layer of canopy which screens out the light. They may grow 140 feet (42½ metres) high, with canopies up to 130 feet (40 metres) in diameter and trunks over 20 feet (6 metres) round.

Beech thrives on chalky ground and improves the fertility of the soil. It shows beauty in all seasons. In mature trees massive boles rise like columns, and their smooth roundness and silky look invites the touch of hands.

Copper beech, with its beautifully coloured leaves, originates from Germany and has became a favourite garden or park tree in many parts of Europe.

BARK

In beeches the cambium layer (see p.315) is almost on the surface of the bark. This makes the tree very susceptible to injury, for all its life-giving functions are within this layer. It also makes beeches sensitive to light and trees which grow in the open branch low in order to give their trunks the necessary shade. When growing in woods beech trees shed their lower branches, for they then have no need to protect their trunks from light. This gives rise to their tall silvery-grey trunks.

Beech has the smoothest texture of bark and in colour is the lightest and most feminine of all the big trees, being dominant yet grace-ful in angles and movement.

LEAVES

The leaves of beech are also sensitive to light and always twist on their stalks to face the sun. Trees in the open have very tough leaves, while those of the woods and shade have an altered structure, being much more delicate.

The winter leaf-buds of beech are formed on dark purplish twigs and are long, pointed and chestnut brown. By April they have swollen and opened to reveal folded fan-shaped leaves of a beautiful soft, pale but vibrant green. As these leaves unfurl they seem to emit shafts of green light and appear as jewels set in leaf-bud 'tassels' of varying shades of red and pink.

The leaf-buds, leaves, male and female flowers, and nut fruit of the beech

By summer the leaves have hardened and turned a darker green. They are so abundant that often the stems and branches of the tree can hardly be seen. The canopy they provide makes the floor of the wood or forest cool and shady.

By autumn at the first touch of frost the beech wood becomes a place of immense colour, for the leaves turn from green to yellow, orange, russet and copper. As they fall they form a thick carpet on the earth which whirls and rustles at the slightest breeze. In sheltered places beech leaves may stay on the trees throughout winter, but if they fall the trees appear tall and graceful against the colourless winter sky.

FLOWERS

The beech tree's leaves open in April along with the male catkins, which hang like green tassels from long stalks. The female flowers grow on the same tree and are like bristly oval balls on a stem, from which slender pollen-seeking threads wave in the air. They appear by May and mature two or three days before the male flowers in readiness for the wind-borne pollen. Once fertilized, the female flowers develop into rough bristly brown husks containing two three-sided seeds which ripen by October.

FRUIT

Beech is not so long-lived as oak, but it is linked to both oak and chestnut by having fruit formed in the same way, for the woody bract of the female flower grows to form a husk around the seed.

Beech has a full crop of nuts every five years but does not really start producing a good crop until it's 50 years old. The ripe husks of the beechnut split easily into four sections to reveal three triangular nuts, originally green and now ripened to brown, inside a 'cup' lined with silky down.

Fagus, the beech's Latin name, is from *fagein*, the Greek for 'to eat'. However, while beechnuts are nutritious for humans, eating too many can cause headaches or giddiness, for vast quantities of potash are contained within the tree. The flesh of pigs fed only on beechnuts is said to be inferior to that of those fed on acorns.

Oil has been extracted from beechnuts since ancient times. It was used in the preparation of food and at times for lighting. So-called 'beech-mast' is loved by squirrels, badgers, dormice, blackbirds, thrushes, partridges, pheasants, deer and swine, as well as by humans. Good beech-mast is only produced in quantity from hot dry summers which promote the flowering of the trees.

The germinating power of the beechnut is lost if a suitable place is not found for it to grow within six months of leaving the tree. Beech saplings are slow starters, but at 20 years they begin to grow quickly.

ROOTS

The tips of all the roots and rootlets of the beech are clothed in a mantle of fungus which is very fine and invisible to the naked eye. This fungus attacks the tree when it is young and stays with it all through its life. It supplants the little root-hairs which forage the soil and takes on their work of absorbing salts in solution from the earth and passing them to the tree. For the price of a home it allows the tree to find food with ease. Such partnerships are also found with firs, poplars and oaks.

Other fungi are not so helpful. The tinder bracket (*Fomes fomentatius*) brings great destruction to beech forests, for it causes white rot in the wood of the trees. The giant polypore also attacks the trees' roots and the base of their trunks. This giant fungus forms large pale brown overlapping fleshy fans of up to a foot (30 cm) across, which cling to the base of the trees. Both these fungi cause tree trunks to snap off under the slightest of pressure.

Beech is also shallow-rooted, making it susceptible to being easily blown over in gales. Beech roots often appear on the surface of the earth, creating beautiful labrynthian patterns. Owing to the capacity of beech root systems to assist in the circulation of air through the soil and to the amount of potash contained in the leaves which fall to earth, beech trees conserve the productive capacity of the soil more than any other tree. They improve the growth of other trees beside them, though because of their deep shade they do not encourage the growth of smaller plants or grass beneath them.

CUSTOM & LEGEND

Beech is regarded as the 'Mother of the Woods', for it is protective and nurturing, giving shade with its canopy and food that can be eaten in its raw state. As a large tree of the broadleaf forest it is also known as the 'beech queen' who stands beside the 'oak king'.

Ancient Greek legend tells us that Jason used beech trees in the building of his ship the *Argo*, in preference to using oak, and that Helen of Troy, like many another lover throughout history, reputedly carved her and her lover's names upon the trunk of a beech tree.

However in European legend the beech has a unique place, for it is especially associated with ancient wisdom and knowledge. On a material level we are told that thin slices of beech wood not only formed the first book (as distinct from scroll), but were also the first prepared surface upon which words were written. This would seem corroborated by etymology, for the Anglo-Saxon for 'beech' was *boc*, which became 'book', the modern German *Buche* is 'beech' and *Buch* is 'book', and the Swedish *bok* is 'book' and 'beech'.

Books and scrolls are full of words, and in all ancient religions the god of learning or master of words was mighty. In early Egypt Thoth was scribe and messenger of the gods, the measurer of time and a great mathematician. In Greece Hermes was the god of writing and all its attributes. He eventually became Hermes Trismegitos of the medieval alchemists.

In Ireland, Ogma, the leading warrior of the Tuatha de Danaan, was credited with inventing the Ogham alphabet which was named after him. Originally this alphabet was used only for inscriptions, for there was druidic discouragement on the writing down of knowledge, but eventually through such vehicles as the Coligny Calendar it became more widely used. The attributes of Ogma became mixed with those of the Celtic god Ogmios, who was represented as having the sun radiating out from his face, gaining him the title 'Ogma Sun-face'.

In northern Europe Odin was credited with the first utterance of the runic system used for communication and divination (*see also Ash, p.149*).

These great gods with their invention of the art of writing were seen as benefactors to the human race, for they not only revealed ancient knowledge, but also gave ways to make that knowledge solid and tangible as marks upon a surface, thus preserving its wisdom for generations of the future. Whatever the word was written upon, be it wood, stone or hide, became imbued with the mightiness of the gods and the magic that they and their writing possessed. So beech received such reverence.

In an old tree alphabet beech is represented by the symbol of a crook, which may well indicate that it was seen to shepherd in all other letters, allowing them to group into words and sentences upon its strong foundation.

There is a Christian legend which tells of St Leonard, a hermit who used prayers to ensure his tranquillity and lived in a beech wood within a large forest on the Hampshire–Sussex border. As this saint could not sit and pray by day in the woods because of the abundance of serpents, and as he could not sleep at night for the sound of the many nightingales singing in the forest, he prayed most fervently that both serpents and nightingales would depart. This legend has always disturbed me, for it states that since that day no serpent or nightingale has re-entered the forest, a situation which is far from natural.

However, not long after writing the above, I was given a book which recounted an old county history concerning this particular wood and verified that at least one serpent did re-enter it. In the book, *The Mistress of Stanton's Farm* by Marcus Woodward, the main character and 'Mistress' was Grandma. She possessed a printed account of a famed 'dragon-serpent' of the forest of St Leonard, which verified the stories which occasionally arose in the area of some 'oudacious large snake'. The account had the following words on its cover:

True and Wonderful:- A Discourse relating to a strange and monstrous serpent, or dragon, lately discovered and yet living to the great annoyance and divers slaughters bothe to men and cattell, by his strong and violent poyson.

In Sussex, two miles from Horsam, in a woode called St

217

Leonard's Forrest, and thirtie miles from London, this present month of August, 1614.
Printed at London by John Trundle. 1614.

Many place-names are associated with beech, such as Buckingham, Buxton, Bicton and Bickleigh. Its folk-names include 'bok', 'buche', 'buk', 'fagos', 'faya' and 'heya'.

HEALING

Anciently it was stated that 'water found in hollow beech trees will cure both man and beast of any scurf or scab'. Coming closer to today, beech tar has been used as a medicinal antiseptic for eczema, psoriasis and chronic skin diseases. It is also an ingredient of an expectorant syrup used for bronchitis.

Beech leaves are cooling and binding. They can be applied to hot swellings as a poultice or an ointment. Dried leaves also aid patients when they are bedridden, for when put into mattresses or duvets they bring a therapeutic healing atmosphere to the sickroom, and a certain strength of Nature.

In the Bach Flower Remedies beech is used to treat arrogance, criticism, mental rigidity, fault-finding in others, pride, irritability and intolerance, tension from over-strong convictions, lack of sympathy and dissatisfaction with others, and an over-strong will which results in passing judgement on others. Beech also helps us to let go of 'fixed' ideas and opinions which are limiting to our progression through life and our personal development. Simply meditating with a tree can help here, or, even better, meditating in a grove of beeches.

MAGIC

IRISH/GAELIC	*Phagos*
OGHAM	ᚁ
RUNIC	ᛈ
RULING PLANET	Saturn
ABILITIES	Old writings and knowledge. Rediscovering old wisdom. Wishes. Letting go of fixed ideas. To do with the elements of Air and Earth.
SEASONS	Spring/Summer, Autumn

Because of its associations with the inception of writing, beech is linked to all written wisdom and we are aided in rediscovering the past through meditation with it. Indeed, when you feel drawn to beech, your subconscious is telling you to look to the past, for your answer to the present will be found there. Beech is the book of the past.

Through working with beech in meditation we can touch our ancient beginnings, the deep wisdom within ourselves which helps us formulate our ways of the future.

In its Saturnal connections beech pertains to written knowledge as recorded throughout time. The ancient materials used to write upon were primarily stone and wood, and thin boards of beech are known to have been used. These boards gathered information together and became pages grouped collectively into books.

Magically, beech is specifically useful for making wishes. To do this, simply write or scratch your wish upon a small piece of beech wood, or a piece of bark or a small branch, and then in an appropriate spot, bury it. A small spell or simple words can be said during this process. As your written wish is claimed by the earth in which you buried it, so it will begin to manifest in life.

Carrying a small piece of beech wood is also a traditional charm used to bring good luck.

INSPIRATION

The beech is one of our most beautiful trees. To stand within a grove of beech is to experience a magical grace which radiates from the trees themselves and the way they transform the air. This helps our senses to open, allowing us to perceive the elemental world of Nature. The ethereal atmosphere is made all the more intense by the tree's sensitivity to light, and its habit of using its branches and foliage to screen out any harshness. It brings a certain awe to humans that has moved artists and poets throughout time with its spirituality and inspiration. This sensation is felt as a sort of breathlessness as your being stills and you become quiet yet ever-watchful, aware of the magic that is Nature.

That men have always found beech groves inspiring is shown by their creations, especially cathedrals. These were designed with high arching vaults which lead the eye up towards heavenly realms, as is so emphasized by the lofty arching branches of ancient beech trees. Cathedrals also emanate the essence of awe felt within the beech grove, the closeness of Nature exemplified as a closeness to God. Such conceptions from the beech have woven magic and religion into its very fabric, acknowledging its magnificence on all levels. And as communication goes two ways, when we experience the supreme spirit from contact with beech trees, so the trees themselves respond to our emotion and an ever-growing rapport is found.

A beech wood is a magical place in every season, but is possibly most evocative when the sun shines down through the branches of the trees as their new leaves open. Then a breeze moves the newly forming vibrant-green canopies, allowing shafts of sunlight to flow through to earth, sometimes so quickly that the breath is taken away by their appearance.

So strong are these beams of sunlight when seen from within the shade of the trees that they resemble spotlights, anciently believed, perhaps, to have been turned on by the gods. The effect of these beams today makes it seem incredibly plausible that we could enter their shimmering rays and, upon utterance of the modern magic words 'Beam me up, Scottie', find ourselves transported to different dimensions. In *Star*

Trek, the television and film series associated with this magic phrase, the different dimensions are planets and galaxies. In the beech grove they are the spiritual realms of Nature.

Legend tells us many stories of serpents and beech trees. The poet Tennyson also referred to the 'serpent-rooted' beech, and this distinction is most often seen when a beech tree grows upon a grassy knoll or bank, for then its surface-hugging roots are uncovered by the erosive action of the elements and are revealed as scrawling patterns of intertwined snake-like shapes. I've never lost the childhood joy of finding such formations, which can become, through a child's eye, whole structured worlds in which 'little people' dwell. Trees which provide such memories act like mediums to the dream-state, which is made all the more real by the sureness that children throughout time have played, and will continue to play, around imagination-provoking trees. Serpent-rooted beeches are found at Avebury in Wiltshire, but my favourite glade is at Cerne Abbas in Dorset, down beneath the magnificent fertility giant.

In autumn days the shining green foliage of the beech wood is changed to gold, russet and brown, and, as some anonymous scribe observed, 'the low sun stares through dust of gold'. The fruit of the beech, now changed in colour to rusty gold, greatly enhances communication between people. When I had just started school I had to walk through woods each day to get to the village. Each autumn morning I'd gather pocketsful of nuts from under the giant beech which guarded the stream and the path through the woods. When at school I'd share the nuts with friends, chattering all the while as we concentrated on peeling the little kernels, eager to pop them into our mouths. As an adult I realize the virtue of this, for beech offers communal healing with its intimate involvement. Indeed, in times of stress, people once relied on eating beechnuts, not only to keep from starvation, but also as a collective action to strengthen communal or tribal ties. Nowadays, roasted beechnuts, prepared and eaten before a roaring fire with family and friends, evoke a warm glow of companionship.

Beechnuts can be collected from the ground beneath the trees in late summer or early autumn. It is best to gather a lot, for not all the bristly cases contain nuts. Once they have been indoors for a day or two, the cases open easily to reveal the kernels, three beautiful three-cornered nuts. With a sharp knife the outer skin of the small nuts can be removed. The peeled nuts are then spread onto a shallow baking tray and roasted in a hot oven for five to ten minutes, taking care they don't burn. When cool, the nuts are rubbed to remove their remaining brown skin and are then rolled in salt for tasty eating. While the process of preparing such small nuts is fiddly, the end result is worth it, for they're delicious. Collecting and roasting beechnuts is enormous fun for the family to do together, for it encourages communication between parents and children, it gets you all out into Nature and everyone works towards a delicious end result. It's a delightful enterprise for autumn weekends and holidays, entertaining young and old alike with little expense!

Children are also kept amused for hours by making beechnut necklaces. First they collect the nuts and bring them home. Then after the nuts are extracted they string them, using a large threaded sewing needle with which to pierce the nut and push it onto the thread. Once the thread is strung with nuts, the two ends are tied together to form a necklace which is beautiful to wear and is a good gift for a friend.

Because of the smoothness of their trunks, beech trees evoke a strong tactile atmosphere. We want to approach and touch them, which makes them ideal for healing. This atmosphere is especially felt by lovers, as is witnessed by the many hearts, arrows and names that have been carved upon beech trees.

Such is the magical power of the beech that beech groves crown many an ancient hill, guarding and intensifying the feminine qualities of these places and maintaining their queenly strengths. A powerful example of this is St Catherine's Hill near Winchester, whose aura is magnificent. Atop the hill, near its beech-grove crown, a maze is cut into the turf, which further emphasizes its power. It is extremely sad that this hill's protection, the horseshoe-shaped ridge of Twyford Down which flows around the hill, has been desecrated for the sake of a motorway and a lot of backhanders. May the eyes of governments be opened to the real power of the nation, and to its magical protection set down long ago by our ancestors, into the very earth itself. NO MORE ROADS!

PHYSICAL USES

Beech wood is yellowish-pink in colour. It has a close, hard texture and is used for parquet flooring, chairs and small articles of treen. As it is close-grained it provides a beautiful surface to write upon. From my own experience it also takes paint well, for it is not as porous as other woods. Beech trees reach heights of 140 feet (42½ metres), producing long lengths of wood. Because they last well underwater, these were ideal for shipbuilding in the past and in France peasant shoes (sabots) were traditionally made from beech wood to keep out the damp. However the wood is susceptible to the attack of a small beetle, which makes it brittle and lessens its strength and durability. This means that affected wood cannot be used for building purposes. In earlier days it was used instead to make charcoal for colour manufacture and gunpowder. It gives out great heat and is excellent for domestic fires.

In gardens beech is often cut and trimmed as hedging, and because it branches low it makes a good screen. As beech leaves preserve the productivity of the soil, they are used by gardeners as a mulch to improve the growth of plants.

The outer cases of beechnuts are often used in dried flower arrangements, for they split themselves into four petal-shapes as they dry and are easily made into 'flowers' when attached to a twig or 'stem'. Then their inner velvety lining reflects the light, adding another dimension to the arrangements. Similar effects are found with the autumn leaves if they are dried or preserved with glycerine. Such sprays of leaves are best collected before they are too far into their autumn colours, for if they are to drink up the glycerine mixture in which you place them, the sap of the tree itself should still be rising to some degree. As the leaves of a tree colour in autumn they provide an indication of the lessening flow of sap up the tree as it shuts down for winter. When gathered at their fall, dry beech leaves can be sewn into mattresses which stay sweet for seven years or more.

Here is a recipe for preserving leaves in glycerine:
Sprays of leaves should be prepared by stripping off lower leaves and twigs, and by crushing the bottom 2 inches (5 cm) of the stem.

Prepare deep jugs of glycerine and boiling water, approx. ½ pint (¼ litre) of glycerine to 1 pint (½ litre) of water (this is enough for a couple of jugs containing 6 sprays each).
Stand the sprays in them while it is still hot.
Leave for about two weeks in a cool place, until the undersides of the leaves look oily.
Lay the sprays flat on absorbent paper for a few days, then they can be used in flower arrangements.

In Europe pigs are still turned out to eat acorns and beech-mast, and in France beech-mast is fed to pheasants and poultry. In England mast is used to feed park deer and also for fattening poultry, especially turkeys. In times of famine it has been used as human food, but it should never be fed to horses.

In America the nuts are made into beechnut butter, and the oil is used for cooking and lamp-lighting.

THE
ROWAN TREE

BOTANICAL

ROWAN. *Sorbus aucuparia*. Deciduous.

The rowan is a small tree growing up to 30 feet (9 metres) in height, with slender branches pointing upwards. Rowan branches rarely die and this enables the tree to keep its graceful shape for the term of its life, which can be upwards of 200 years. Rowan is a species of the rose family, along with apple, hawthorn and wild cherry.

The rowan does not form woods or forests on its own account, but rather joins in with other species of trees, aiding them by shading new

225

saplings. Rowan is often planted in new coppices to protect young trees, but in time it becomes dwarfed and smothered by the very trees it sheltered. Rowan grows almost anywhere and tolerates poor soil and atmosphere. As it needs plenty of light and air, it prefers high altitudes like the wilds of Scotland and is known to grow as high as 2,500 feet (760 metres) and more, hence the name 'Lady of the Mountain'.

The rowan gives delicate grace to the land, which is why it is a favourite garden tree.

The leaves, flowers and berry fruit of the rowan

BARK

The bark of rowan is glossy smooth and can be varied in colour from grey-brown to almost purple. The trunk is scored with horizontal markings.

LEAVES

In spring rowan's leaf-buds are covered in grey cottony down and are pressed close to the tree's twigs in a spiral. The toothed leaves packed tightly inside the buds are also downy and when they open are seen to be compound, made up of many leaflets arranged upon a central stalk in up to eight opposite pairs, with a single leaflet at the end of the stalk. In this arrangement they are similar to the leaves of ash, which is why rowan is sometimes called the 'mountain ash'. In reality rowan is of a different family, fruiting with a berry rather than a winged seed. If the leaves of ash and rowan are seen side by side, rowan is obviously much more delicate in shape, size and colour, and it has no small stalk leading from the leaflet to the central stem as does the ash. When seen on the trees, the leaves of the rowan grow alternately on the twigs, whilst the ash's are set opposite each other. The rowan is noticeably far more feminine in all its features.

FLOWERS

Rowan blossoms in May. Its creamy-white clusters of scented flowers form masses over 4 inches (10 cm) across, which weigh down the slender branches. While they are very showy, rowan flowers lack the subtlety and whiteness of hawthorn blossom.

Individually, each tiny rowan flower is like a small apple blossom, with five petals and five sepals. Cross-fertilization of the flowers is aided by insects and once achieved the flowers fade, usually around the end of June. Then their petals fall in heavy showers, laying a creamy rich carpet upon the ground. Upon the tree we can see that the ends of the flower stalks have swollen to form small round green berries, very like miniature apples, which hang in dense clusters from the twigs.

FRUIT

As the season progresses, rowan berries ripen to a rich yellow-red, giving an incredible contrast of colour to the tree's green leaves. When looking at this red and green contrast it is easy to see how it became the inspiration of the tartan plaids of the Highlands, especially when you remember how profuse rowan has always been in Scotland.

Rowan berries are a favourite food for birds, especially song-birds. They sing for hours after gorging themselves, and aid the propagation and distribution of the seeds during their flights.

By autumn, when the berries have mostly been eaten, rowan's leaves begin their colourful transformation. As the first frost touches them they turn from green to wonderful shades of gold, pink and scarlet, in which state they remain on the tree until late October winds strip the branches. The new leaf-buds are in evidence well before the old leaves fall.

CUSTOM & LEGEND

The rowan tree is small yet incredibly bold, for its leaves, blossoms and berries make exceptionally colourful statements on the face of the land. The legends associated with rowan are also bold and dramatic, making it a tree you cannot ignore, whilst emphasizing why it was anciently regarded as the Tree of Life.

According to Greek legend the birth of the rowan was precipitated by the actions of Hebe, the daughter of Zeus and Hera and the goddess of youth, who had the power to make the old young again. She was cup-bearer to the gods and filled their cups with sweet nectar. Yet Hebe was lax in her duties and lost the cup of Zeus when it was stolen by demons. Great concern raged over this and the gods sent a special eagle to deal with the demons and recover the cup. A fierce battle ensued between the eagle and the demons, and wherever an eagle's feather or a drop of blood fell to earth, there grew a rowan tree. This is believed to be the reason why rowan has feathery leaves and berries like drops of blood.

The rowan is generally considered the feminine equivalent of the ash tree, and in Scandinavian myth the first woman was born from rowan and the first man from ash. Rowan is also believed to have saved the life of the great god Thor by bending over a rapidly flowing river in which he was being swept to his death and aiding him to get back onto land with its branches. It can be said that the rowan's attributes are like Thor's, for both help mankind.

In Icelandic myth rowan is particularly strong at the Winter Solstice, the beginning of the new solar year. At this time the tree is bare of foliage and when covered in frost appears as though covered in stars, powerfully expressing the outpouring light of the spirit in the darkest part of the year. It also shows the reflection of the moon's light and the myth of the star-dressed rowan possibly evolved from an ancient tradition of erecting 'moon-trees', an early representation of the sky-goddess energy. Moon-trees were actual trees or plants, or even wooden pillars or truncated poles, little evolved from earlier cone-shaped stone representations of the moon deity, which were covered with fruit and lights, and crowned with a crescent moon. In later years they were dressed with glittering objects to portray and reflect the light of the moon.

Yule legends say a special star glowed atop the mythical rowan tree, which heralded life returning to the world of darkness. The Christians later incorporated this star into their birth myths of Jesus and the starclad rowan became a forerunner of our modern Christmas tree (see also Pine, p.53).

In pagan eyes the wonderful red berries of rowan ensured the tree was held in high esteem, prompting myths and legends of its powers. As the mythological Tree of Life rowan bears special fruit every month and at each quarter of the year. This associates it with both the lunar and solar cycles. The berries of this tree were believed to stave off hunger month by month, to heal the wounded and to add a year to people's lives.

In Irish legend, the 'Quicken Tree of Dubhous' also had marvellous berries which, if three were eaten, could transform a man of 100 years to 30 years of age! Another magical tree had the power, through its berries, to refresh people with 'the sustaining virtue of nine meals'. This tree was guarded by a particularly strong dragon. Rowans are intimately associated with dragons and serpents, especially in regard to earth energies. This is discussed in Inspiration (see pp.237–8).

However in ancient world legend all red-coloured food – fruit, berries, nuts, fungi, crustaceans, etc. – was believed to be food of the gods, and thus sacred and taboo for commoners. Red was the colour of death, the colour of spilt blood, and red things were used extensively in burial rites. Red ochre found in Neanderthal burial sites and Bronze Age megalithic tombs on Salisbury Plain and in the Prescelly Mountains in Wales substantiates this, as does an ancient tradition of Ireland, in which a corpse is staked with a rowan branch bearing red berries to keep its ghost from wandering and to ensure its soul passes comfortably from its old abode to its new.

Rowan is under the planetary influence of the sun and is strongly associated with two ancient sun-goddesses: Brigid of Ireland and Brigantia of England. Both these goddesses headed river and water cults and protected pastoral people and their flocks and herds. Brigantia was known as 'The High One'. She was regal and influential. As patroness of the tribes of the north, she eventually became the titular goddess of the Brigantes who settled in Yorkshire. The Irish Brigid was the daughter of Dagda, one of the Tuatha de Danaan who brought four magical treasures to Ireland. She was renowned as a poetess, and in this visionary aspect was the Muse of the poetic and divinatory atmosphere which surrounds the rowan. This is especially enhanced in autumn when the song-birds are attracted by the berries. Specific ways to invoke the Muse of the rowan tree are discussed in Magic (see p.233).

Brigantia and Brigid were associated with spring, the season of birth when the warmth of the sun begins to oust the winter's cold. The arts they ruled over included spinning and weaving, and traditionally rowan wood was used to make spindles and spinning wheels. The spindle is very significant in world mythology, for its circular spinning motion is likened to the passage of the sun around the year, or to the 'spinner of the thread of life'.

These goddesses also possessed arrows made from rowan wood which could blaze with fire. The symbology of this is discussed in Magic.

In world concepts it can be noted that there are great similarities between the Western Brigid and the Egyptian goddess Neith, who is said to have ruled Lower Egypt while Osiris ruled Upper Egypt. Both these goddesses represented the healing greenness of Nature, for Neith was coloured green and Brigid dressed in green verdure. Like Brigid, Neith ruled over the arts of the spinner and weaver. Her symbol was crossed arrows. Both goddesses are said to have wet-nursed young sun-gods, Neith suckling Horus and Brigid the Mabon. In later years Christian legend follows the same concept, for St Briget, who evolved from Brigid, was revered as 'Mary Queen of Heaven', who in her role as midwife to the Virgin Mary suckled the infant Jesus.

The protective qualities of the rowan are illustrated in an old legend from Herefordshire, which tells of two famous 'hogsheads' of money hidden in a subterranean vault at Penyard Castle. The hiding-place was supernaturally protected, but a local farmer undertook to find the money. It took 20 of his oxen urged on by a rowan switch to partially open the great iron doors of the vault, which allowed him to see the two great chests within, upon one of which sat a jackdaw. The delighted farmer shouted, 'I believe I shall have it!' But immediately the doors slammed together immovably shut, as a sepulchral voice cried:

> Had it not been for your quicken-tree goad,
> And your yew-tree pin,
> You and your cattle had all been drawn in!

In Scotland the magical and protective qualities of rowan were recognized and utilized by Highlanders much as Lowlanders recognized and used hawthorn. The cross-beams of chimneys were often made from rowan and on Equinox and Solstice days rowan sticks were laid across the lintels to reinforce beneficial influences. In Devonshire and Worcestershire rowan was brought into the house on Holy Rood Day (3 May) to utilize its protective qualities.

The rowan goes by many names, such as 'mountain ash', 'roan', 'roddan', 'rantry', 'wild ash', 'quickbeam', 'quicken-tree', 'wild sorb', 'witchen tree', 'witchbane', 'witchwood', 'Thor's helper', 'ran-tree', 'sorb apple' and 'delight of the eye'.

HEALING

Rowan has been used since ancient times as an astringent and antibiotic. Through the visual senses it heals the human spirit. Meditation, or simply just sitting by a rowan (especially at its flowering or fruiting), lifts the emotions and allows mind and body space to relax and let go of stress and tension. The calm atmosphere and beauty of rowan, the gracefulness of its spirit and the energy of life it represents, allow us to find healing, strength and purpose. To sustain such qualities, on leaving the tree select a small twig or leaf to carry away with you.

BARK

A decoction of rowan bark is an ancient remedy for diarrhoea. It also eases the discomfort of vaginal discharge when used in bathing or washing water. Such a discharge should also be checked by a doctor to find its cause.

BERRIES

Warning: Rowan seeds are poisonous to children.

Rowan fruit contains tartaric acid before ripening, and citric and malic acids after ripening. The seeds within the fruit contain 22 per cent fixed oil, but children can be poisoned by them, so it is advised that they are not taken internally.

This said, rowan berries were prepared in decoction as a gargle for sore throats and inflamed tonsils. A strong astringent infusion was used externally to ease haemorrhoids and cure scurvy.

MAGIC

IRISH/GAELIC	*Luis*
OGHAM	⊨
RUNIC	ᚱ
RULING PLANET	Sun
ABILITIES	Protection against enchantment. Protection of ley-lines. Protection of stone circles. Highest pure magic. Control of all senses. Healing. Psychic powers. Success. To do with the element of Fire.
SEASONS	Spring, Autumn

As a magical tree, rowan is used for all kinds of protection and vision. Incenses made from ground leaves and berries from the tree help us banish undesired energies. The druids of old used smoke from fires of rowan to call up spirit guides and magical spirits, and in similar fashion on a romantic level, people have always used rowan smoke to aid divinations of future loves and soul-mates.

Because rowan has white flowers it was deemed a tree of the goddess and as a visionary aid it invokes her when we need her help in choosing direction.

Groves of rowan were preserved in ancient days as oracular shrines. Without doubt the priestesses of such groves imbibed the sacred rowan berry to gain the necessary trance-states by which to perform their arts. Nowadays, to contact the inspirational Muse of the rowan tree, take its berries to a place where the waters meet the land, a riverbank or the edge of a lake or stream. Then, by meditating on the Otherworldly meeting-point of earth and water, the correct state can be reached whereby the Muse will make her presence felt, especially in the musical or poetic sense.

Rowan was a sacred tree to the druids and therefore predominates in the traditions of Western Europe. It is said that wherever druidic remains are found, so also is rowan. Magicians of old recorded spells on rowan staves and in the thoughts of the people magic became inherent to the rowan tree itself. Any magic worked for the land benefited greatly from rowan's presence and the druids acknowledged this by planting rowan near all places of worship. This was done especially at stone circles, for rowan protected the energy of the circles and the ley-lines which linked them. In such a position rowan is at its most powerful and its energy was regarded as indispensable to the well-being of the land.

Irish legend is full of accounts of serpents and dragons guarding rowans, yet it goes unnoticed that the rowans themselves guard the earth dragons which express the life-force of the land. The later Christians, in suppressing the old traditions, created saints to 'kill' such dragons as they claimed the traditional sacred places as their own. As a druidess I feel the traditions of the land should be worked as of old, with adaptations to the present. During such workings, especially at stone circles, it would be advantageous to both ourselves and the earth if we remembered dragon magic and the ancient use of rowan to guard, for the land suffers greatly from our pollution. Meditation upon rowan's cleansing and protective qualities, and the planting of rowan saplings beside circles, will provide great benefit. This is especially relevant at sacred sites that have suffered from disuse, misuse and ignorance. It is a time-honoured method of ecology which positively affects all.

As we have seen, the traditional solar celebrations are magical times when the energies of the year announce the changing seasons. Then we can witness the outpouring of rowan's energy, which also runs concurrent to the phases of the moon. The cross-quarters of the year are specifically ruled over by rowan, and at these times women can make fullest use of it and of the sun's energy.

At Imbolc the goddess leads the long-awaited solar energies into the year to encourage the growing process of Nature. This is the time of the goddess (1 February became St Brigit's day) and she carries symbolic arrows to express the highest magic. These arrows are aimed towards the coming seasons and when released into the year represent the course of the sun in the heavens as it arcs to its height of summer then falls towards earth and autumn, to disappear beneath the horizon for winter.

In certain traditions the ancient solar-goddess had three arrows which were able to turn to fire in flight. It is possible that these arrows were the inspiration of the druidic Awen, the Three Rays of Light already mentioned in Apple (see p. 111), representing the knowledge, wisdom and inspiration of the Divine. This most precious of symbols, /I\ , is seen in natural manifestation and fullest glory within the Temple of Stonehenge, when at sunrise on Midsummer's day the first rays of the sun rise beyond the Hele Stone.

Then the rays are represented thus, \I/ , becoming the directional arrow, made up of three fiery arrows, of the Divine Spirit as it comes down from the heavens to earth.

In its other directional shape, /I\ , it is symbolic of our energy as it moves from the earth towards heaven and the Divine.

The druidic mantra of the West expressing the Three Rays was performed by the slow intonation of the letters IAO, all three in one deep breath so they become continuous and pronounced as 'eye-ay-oh'. It was especially intoned at sunrise on Midsummer's Day, for it opened the gateways of harmony both within an individual and throughout the spheres, aiding the 'marriage' of heaven and earth. Intonation of the IAO also promotes the 'marriage' of male and female within ourselves.

On 2 May it was traditional to deck the milksheds with rowan to protect the milk and cows from evil influences, and on this day also shepherds made their flocks pass through rowan hoops. So rowan was used to protect the opening senses of man and beast as they were swept along with the growing energies of the year.

At midsummer 'V'-shaped twigs of rowan were carried by travellers and it was advised that anyone travelling on Midsummer's Night should tuck a rowan sprig in his hat or horse's bridle lest he be transported to the land of faerie, for they are most active at this time. This custom was the possible forerunner of the 'rowan cross', which is two small twigs of rowan tied into a cross with red ribbon. These crosses were carried at All Hallows for protection. They can be used today for protection at all times.

Red, as well as being the colour signifying death, was also used to protect from evil. Red thread used to tie rowan crosses together strengthened the protective qualities of the red fruit of the tree.

In going out to cut rowan branches or twigs, tradition says that different routes should be taken when leaving and returning home, and that wood for rowan crosses should be gathered, and the cross made, without the use of a knife.

Lammas is a very powerful time for rowan trees. Then we are presented with the vivid splendour of their leaves and fruit. Nothing could be so 'dressed' and not be full of power. The orange-red fruit, as mentioned earlier, especially attracts song-birds. Field-fares, thrushes and blackbirds sing beautifully after gorging berries, and this link with the musical spheres is invocative of the inspirational Muse of the rowan. The power and effect of birdsong were recognized by the Celts, and in recent years science has acknowledged that birdsong sets up a particular vibration of sound which promotes the growth of vegetation. In spring when birds sing virtually all day, their chorus encourages the growth of new leaves and flowers upon plants. By summer, when the plants' main growth is formed, birdsong lessens during the day, being mainly performed at dawn and twilight. At these times a chemical change also occurs in the activity of vegetation, for as night falls all plant life begins to breathe in carbon dioxide and at dawn breathes out pure oxygen, which exhilarates birds into their dawn chorus. This process is essential, for it makes our air breathable. Without it we would die.

By Samhain the rowan stands bare of fruit and leaves, and as Nature prepares for winter sleep, it provides protection as the veils between the worlds open and we move from the past into the future.

Because of its protective qualities rowan was planted in many church-yards of Wales in preference to yew, to maintain peace for the dead. They called it the 'witchen' or 'wiggen' tree. Along with elder, it was also encouraged to grow near homes.

Rowan gives protection when carried in any form, and if kept in the house protects it from storm and lightning. Walking sticks of rowan are excellent protection for those who wander the fields and lanes, especially at night. Carried on board boats or ships rowan keeps storms at bay. Its branches were used by Norsemen as rune-staves upon which to carve runes of protection.

Such was the superstition surrounding the need for protection that old sayings still abound about the power of rowan, especially concerning the witches. It was believed that a witch touched by rowan would be the devil's next victim, when he came every seven years to claim his tribute, and that 'roan ash and red thread, haud the witches a' in dread'. An old Scottish ballad tells it thus:

> Their spells were in vain,
> The boy returned to the Queen in sorrowful mood,
> Crying the 'Witches have no power,
> When there is Roan-tree wood.'

Looking at the above superstitions it would be easy to think that witches avoided rowan trees, yet they did in fact use rowan in many of their workings, for rowan wands, rods and amulets aided their divinations and carved twigs of rowan helped them divine the whereabouts of metals underground. Rowan increases psychic powers, success and healing, and rowan berries and bark, when added to carrying pouches, bring good luck and quick recuperation from illness.

In the *Book of Ballymote* Morran MacMain sums up the rowan's qualities, calling it 'the poetical delight of the eye'. Because of its clear visionary qualities, this eye must be the 'third eye', which sees the astral or dream-time realms and feeds the soul.

INSPIRATION

According to legend, serpents or dragons guard rowan trees and from earliest times rowan has grown on or near sacred sites. Today we are witnessing the revival of that ancient body of knowledge known as geomancy, which is associated with the streams of earth-energy anciently called 'dragon-lines' and more modernly 'leys'. Through geomancy the Eastern peoples founded their temples upon places where they divined the earth-energies were most powerful. Celtic priests in similar fashion divined high energy places to erect standing stones, circles, burial mounds, groves of trees, etc. In many places throughout Britain where the erection of stones was not deemed appropriate, rowan trees were planted instead.

In Britain the ancient practice of placing stones upon powerful sacred spots has left us clues to the flow of the earth's energies, for a single stone was placed upon straight-flowing streams and circles were constructed upon coils or spirals. Spirals are the most commonly used symbol of the earth-dragon, for dragons were believed to coil themselves around hills. This gave rise to the theory that hills were formed by dragons squeezing their coils upon the landscape, forcing the earth to rise. Many hills today still bear such coil-marks. Wormington Hill in Gloucestershire and Glastonbury Tor in Somerset are two prime examples.

In the very ancient world the snake or serpent was symbolic of the earth-mother, for it lived in holes within the earth and continuously renewed itself by shedding its skin. It also had the reputation of immortality and wisdom. The dragon, as early goddess cults suggest, most probably originated from the serpent, the addition of horns, frills, ears, legs and wings empowering it with extra attributes. Of one thing we are certain: both serpent and dragon represented the power of Nature, the energy of the land that pagan tribes acknowledged so strongly.

Dragons were also believed to guard spiritual treasures. The Anglo-Saxons called their burial mounds 'dragon hills', and Viking longboats had prows carved into the shape of dragons, for they believed that they bestowed powerful elemental forces.

As a magical tree rowan guards the strong energy that the dragon represents. Dragon energy was also recognized in the sky in such phenomena as ball lightning. This possibly accounts for sightings of UFOs in more modern times. There are many legends of dragons with fiery breath which 'roamed and caused great chaos in the land', and these most likely showed places where the earth's energy was out of balance. To rectify this, dragon 'taming' was achieved by the use of stones or metal rods which were embedded into the ground at specific points. It was also achieved by the planting of rowan trees, for these aided the flow of energy back into harmony with the landscape.

It is told that the Christian St Patrick rid Ireland of serpents, as in England dragons were slain by Christian saints, St Michael, St George, St Mary and St Margaret being the most renowned. From such acts it can be concluded that dragons and serpents represented primal knowledge that empowered the tribes and encouraged pagan traditions, two aspects which the Church found difficult to endure. The 'killing' of dragons also occurred when Christian churches were built haphazardly over pre-Christian artefacts, for there was little acknowledgement of the correct alignment of the earth's energies.

Most imbalancing of the earth's energy is the result of human intervention, for mining, quarrying, road-cutting and buildings change or block the natural flow. Imbalance is the inevitable result of man's ignorance of ecology and his assumption of dominion over Nature rather than partnership with it. In legend we hear of great havoc reigning in whole communities because of such actions.

The druids, as initiated priests and priestesses, imbibed dangerous brews of berries and fungi during certain rituals in order to open pathways to Otherworld realms within themselves, and rowan berries were undoubtedly used in such brews. However the important thing here is that the druids were initiated in a lengthy and arduous way, which gave them the knowledge and experience to gauge the toxicity and actions of such ingredients, and the ability to discriminate between the magical realms they then entered. Most importantly, they knew how to earth themselves afterwards.

This is relevant to our drug-taking society of today, for a lack of earthing, i.e., being unable to return to everyday life with all faculties intact, can lead to physical and mental health problems. Often, unearthing produces delusions which are believed to be realities, and it is easy to become content with the resultant chaos which will in time affect the whole being and whatever comes into contact with it. The earthing process is begun by having a peaceful place to rest and by replenishing the body with wholesome food, water and fruit rich in vitamins, for the stabilizing of the body stabilizes the mind.

Druidic initiation takes some 19 years, for the magical realms need competent workers as it is through them that greater ecological balance takes place on earth. Anyone connected to chaos will manifest chaos on earth, and while 'chaos magic' is very much in vogue at present, using the theory that 'all is born from universal chaos, so let's continue that chaotic manifestation on earth', it does little to rectify our condition. *Chambers Twentieth Century Dictionary* has 'chaos' as the 'shape of matter before it is reduced to order', and while it is wise to acknowledge this, we should also look to its other meanings of 'disorder' and a 'shapeless mass', for the lines between all such states are thin. Chaos magic would seem the answer to the anarchist's prayer. But it begs a question from the world of Nature, for it would seem that its order is also threatened. An example recently heard during a chaos circle: the invocation of dolphins through the midsummer fire of the southern quarter, an act which brought shrieks of their pain to the circle rather than their songs! Given knowledge of and respect for natural lore (law), this act could have been performed correctly, invoking the dolphins through the watery quality of the west, their natural element. So whose side are these people really on?

'What about free will?' I hear, and that is a valid point. Free will is our birthright to use or misuse, given that we may become masters or mistresses of our own destinies, should we so choose. But the will is not free if it is bound by delusion. It is only free if it can see clearly and can then make true choices. And that is what initiation and instruction are about: seeing clearly the choices and then obtaining the trained ability to work them. The initiators of old were responsible for many lifetimes' care of those they initiated and many people waited great lengths of time before they were regarded as being ready to begin. In this day and age a little knowledge would seem a dangerous thing.

To gain more knowledge and understanding of natural lore we look to Nature and especially to trees, for they hold the secrets of our survival. Rowan itself is a symbol of the hidden mysteries in Nature, the energy dragons, standing stones and the ancient sciences. Through meditation with it we can become aligned to the hidden mysteries of life.

PHYSICAL USES

WOOD

Rowan wood is very tough. In the past it was used for ship masts and for poles and whips. Spindles and spinning-wheels were traditionally made from rowan wood cut between Beltaine and midsummer. Walking sticks can be made of rowan for protection while out at night.

Small branches of rowan were used to encircle milk and butter churns to protect the contents from thieves and evil, and goats were driven through hoops of rowan to ward off the 'evil-eye'. As already mentioned, rowan sticks were also used to divine the presence of metals underground.

The bark and fruit of rowan can be used to dye wool black. The bark is also used for tanning.

BERRIES

Rowan was often known as the 'fowler's service tree', for its berries were used as a lure to catch birds. When times were hard in the land and corn was short, rowan berries (without their seed) were ground and used as a substitute for flour. They can also be used along with crab-apples in jellies and chutneys. Rowan jelly, which goes with lamb, pork and game dishes, can be made in late summer:

Take 4 lbs (2 kg) (16 cups) of rowan berries and 3 lbs (1½ kg) (12 cups) of cooking apples or crab-apples.

Strip the berries from the stalks, cut the apples into quarters, add enough water to barely cover the fruit, and cook in a large pan until soft and pulpy.

When cold, pour into double-thickness muslin and leave to hang overnight to drip into a bowl.

Measure the caught juice into a pan.

Add 1 lb (450 g) (2 cups) of sugar to every 2½ cups of juice, and heat slowly to dissolve the sugar. Then boil rapidly for up to 10 minutes, until the liquid jells when dripped onto a cold plate.

Skim the surface of the jelly, then pour into warm jars. Cover with waxed circles and seal when cold.

In Wales rowan berries are renowned for their quality as a wine and in the Scottish Highlands, where rowan is plentiful, a strong spirit is made from them. The fresh juice from rowan berries can be squeezed into gin, giving it a bitter taste like Angostura.

Here is a recipe for a superb rowan wine:

Take 3 lbs (1½ kg) (12 cups) of rowan berries and strip them from their stalks with a fork.

To extract their juice, pour on boiling water to cover and leave to stand (loosely covered) for 4 days.

Strain the juice and add 3–4 lbs (1½ kg) (6–8 cups) of sugar according to taste, remembering that a fair amount of sugar may be necessary to counter the acid taste of the berries.

Add ½ lb (200 g) (1½ cups) of chopped raisins and the strained juice of 2 lemons.

Stir all ingredients and add them to already activated yeast, prepared

according to the instructions on the packet.
Cover and stand for 2 weeks, then strain into a fermentation jar and
allow to develop as with any other wine.

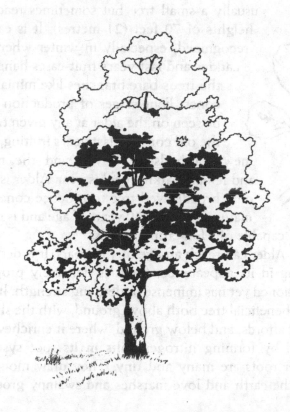

THE
ALDER

BOTANICAL

ALDER *Alnus glutinosa*. Deciduous.

The alder is native to Europe and Britain. It is found growing along the banks of streams and rivers or in low-lying swampy land. It is a cousin of the birch and hazel and often grows with them at the forest's edge, though, as its seeds don't have 'wings' to become airborne, it needs the water of a river or stream for their propagation.

The alder is a water-loving tree, and by bending its light branches gracefully over a stream or river it creates shade for plants and fish. It is usually a small tree but sometimes reaches heights of 70 feet (21 metres). It is easily recognized, especially in winter when its catkins and last year's fruit-cases hang on the tree's bare branches like miniature cones. Four stages of production can be seen on the alder at any given time: the old cones of last year's fruiting, the new leaf-buds or leaves, and the male and female catkins of this year. Alder is the only broadleaved tree to produce cones. It matures at about 30 years of age and is then capable of a full crop of seeds.

Alder can reach an age of 150 years. It is deceiving in its appearance, for it is delicately proportioned yet has immense underlying strength. It is a beneficial tree both above ground, with the shade it affords, and below ground, where it enriches the soil by forming nitrogen salts in its root system. Alder roots are many and tiny. They draw moisture from the earth and love marshes and swampy ground.

The leaves, catkins, cone fruit and empty cones of the alder

BARK
Alder has furrowed brown to blackish-grey bark. If an alder is felled, its inner wood is white at first then slowly turns a reddish-pink. This, in the minds of ancient people, elevated alder's sanctity, for it appeared to bleed like humans.

LEAVES
The short branches of the alder bear smooth twigs upon which buds on stalks are set in a spiral. These are leaf-buds and they are almost enclosed in a browny-yellow pair of bud-scales which peel back as the leaf unfolds. Only alder has buds set on short stalks from the bracket on which they grow. All other trees have buds set down upon their brackets.

244

Alder leaves are held out horizontally. They are rounded and of an inverted heart-shape, with the broadest part furthest from the stem. When young they are somewhat sticky, for a gum is produced by the tree to ward off moisture. Hence the name *glutinosa*. They grow alternately on their stems and begin life as a light rich green before developing into dark green, almost purply-black, heavy, leathery leaves.

FLOWERS

Alder catkins form in the autumn preceding their flowering. They remain dormant on the tree throughout winter and open in the spring before the leaves.

The pendulous male catkins are long (2–4 inches/5–10 cm) and are purplish to rich red in colour. The females are cone-like and grow on the same tree, hanging in groups of tiny green structures built of minute overlapping rough scales. They have threads hanging from them which catch the pollen from the developed male catkins, after which they grow larger and become dark reddish-brown as the seeds develop within.

FRUIT

By autumn the female flowers have become hard and woody, and the ripe seeds fall from them in October and November. They are either carried away on the waters to far-flung places or germinate in the boggy ground beneath the tree. Alder seeds have airtight cavities in their walls which allow them to float on water, along with a coating of oil to preserve them.

CUSTOM & LEGEND

Ancient legend tells us how alder and willow became trees of the waterways, the rivers, streams, ponds and lakes which give life to the land. At a great feast held for the fertility deities when all the life-forms of the natural world celebrated together, the alder and willow stood apart from

245

the others, gazing longingly into the waters of a flood. The mighty gods were angered by their lack of acknowledgement and declared that as they had shown their preference, there they should remain, binding them to gaze forever into the waters. However by such actions the gods gave a great gift to the land, for as king and queen of the waters the alder and willow reign supreme, enhancing the vital process of water movement which ensures that the life of the land is sustained.

The water-loving alder was especially revered by ancient man for, as already mentioned, it appeared to bleed when cut, its sap turning quickly red when exposed to the air. Through this quality it was esteemed sacred and was seen to represent the generosity of the gods and the health of the land. And yet with all its kingly qualities, alder is essentially a tree of the people. It is easily approachable and offers a safe haven. This is shown by the abundance of life beneath its boughs, where all is lush and fertile and the soil is enriched by its presence.

As we look at the legends associated with the alder tree we can wonder at the might entwined within them, for physically the alder is a small tree. Its associations with the ancient beneficent gods gave foundation to the very magic of ancient Britain. But first, let us look at alder's world associations.

In ancient Greece Cronos was represented by an alder tree. One of his epithets was *Fearinus*, which has been translated as meaning 'of the dawn of the year', i.e., the spring, when the sun, wind and rain bring on the growth of plant life. It is interesting to note that the Irish/Gaelic ogham name for alder is *fearn*.

In Italian tradition alder is also associated with the spring fire festivals and in Norse legends March was known as 'the lengthening month of the waking alder'. In Norse countries this specific time was called *Lenct*, and was a period of enforced fasting as the last of the winter's provisions ran low. When adopted by the Church and used for religious ideals, this time of fasting became Lent.

In Irish legend the first human male was created from alder, as the first female was created from rowan. Alder was anciently regarded as a 'faerie tree' able to grant access to faerie realms. It was also a tree which showed strong associations with, and visibly illustrated, the elements of life (water, fire, air and earth), almost as though it were an axis round which they flowed and formed.

Alder's associations with the element of fire are dramatic. In Ireland the felling of a sacred alder was said to result in the burning down of your home, in similar fashion to the burning of buildings built upon faerie paths. Alder's burning qualities have always been prized amongst metal-workers and smiths, for it was known for its hot charcoal, used to forge ritual weapons.

As a tree which 'bleeds', alder is bound up in the legends of the Rollright Stones in Oxfordshire, where the King Stone, which stands alone and some way apart from the other stones, was once reputedly associated with a grove of alder trees. According to ancient legend, ritu-als were performed within this grove in which the sacred alders were cut to make them 'bleed profusely'. When this happened, the King Stone apparently 'moved' in sympathy (for how the Rollright Stones were formed, see Elder, pp.279–80).

Alder also provides a fiery-red dye which was called roeim, a term which means, according to Cormac's tenth-century glossary of obsolete terms, 'that which reddens the face'. In The White Goddess, Robert Graves connects this term to the 'crimson-stained heroes' of battles past, recorded in the Welsh Triads as 'sacred kings and warriors of the alder cult'. If such a connection is valid, we may presume that alder dye was used in much the same way as the Celts and Picts used woad, to paint and stain their faces and bodies before going into battle, both as a protective measure and to put fear into the enemy.

Alder was anciently renowned as the best wood to use for whistles and pipes, and this use gave it great affinity to the element of air. Such was the reputed harmony of the music played on alder pipes that the topmost branch of the alder tree became known as the 'oracular singing head' of the raven-god Bran, of whom so many tales were told.

The alder was regarded as the sacred totem tree of Bran and thus figures in many ancient legends of the West. Bran was a much-loved pagan god, said to have been of such great stature that 'no house could accommodate him'. From this description we can surmise that in his orig-inal form he was possibly one of the race of guardian giants of ancient

Britain, who in the minds of the people became gods. He is especially associated with the Welsh tradition, wherein the *Mabinogion* speaks of him as the 'Crowned King', and celebrates his immense size.

Legend relates that Bran was sitting on the rocky shore of Harlech, when he viewed a fleet of 13 ships sailing from the direction of southern Ireland. The boatmen gave signs of peace and disclosed their purpose, asking Bran for the hand in marriage of his beautiful sister Branwen to the powerful Irish Lord Mattholoch. This Bran gave, thus forming an alliance between Wales and Ireland.

Great feasting took place at the wedding of Branwen and Mattholoch, but unbeknown to Bran, his half-brother Evnissien, because of his jealousy at not being asked about Branwen's hand, cruelly maimed the horses of the Irish and by doing so put the political alliance in a very awkward position. Bran offered the greatest apologies to the Irish, which he backed with gifts of an honour-bound staff of solid silver as tall as Mattholoch and a gold plate the circumference of his face. Even so the Irish faltered and Bran was forced to appease them with his greatest possession, his magic cauldron in which men killed in battle were revived overnight.

Branwen went to Ireland with Mattholoch and the Irish people loved her as their queen. But after a few years the councillors of the land remembered the insult delivered to Mattholoch in the maiming of his horses and forced him to relegate Branwen to the kitchen as a maid. While there, to take her mind off her humiliation, Branwen befriended a starling which she taught words and how to run small errands for her. One day she fastened a letter to the bird and let it fly away, and by good fortune it found its way to Wales and was taken to the court of Bran. On reading Branwen's letter, which described the harsh treatment afforded her, Bran decided on a war of revenge against Ireland.

In his anger he waded the seas from Wales to Ireland, his armies following in ships. From the Irish shore it is said that onlookers witnessed an extraordinary sight as the giant crossed the seas, for he created the illusion of a moving landscape containing a mountain, forest and lakes. Since this was coming from the direction of Wales, Branwen was asked what it could be. She explained that the forest illusion was made from the masts of ships and the lakes were created by the eyes of her brother Bran, who was himself the mountain moving through the water, since no ship had ever been built which could contain him.

The Irish retreated at such a sight and to stop the Welshmen from following, destroyed the bridge across the River Shannon. At this Bran declared, 'The man who would lead his people must first become a bridge,' and he prostrated himself across the river so his armies could cross over him. By doing such he not only helped his people, but also showed the principal quality of the alder tree, for its resistance to rotting in water has been utilized since ancient days in the construction of bridges.

The confrontation between Bran and Mattholoch raged over southern Ireland until Branwen was reunited with her brother. But again Evnissien upset things by throwing Branwen's son by Mattholoch into a huge fire, causing battle anew over the loss of the heir to the throne of Ireland. In this terrible fight great losses of men occurred on both sides, but the Irish made use of Bran's regenerative cauldron and brought their men to life again, vastly outnumbering the Welsh. On seeing how the balance was shifting, the enraged Evnissien threw himself into the cauldron amongst the Irish dead and stretched his giant body in four directions until he split the cauldron, and himself, into four pieces. As a result the Welsh won the battle, but only seven men escaped alive with Bran, who was grievously wounded in the foot by a poisoned dart.

On his death-bed Bran gave his last instructions to his men: to cut off his head and carry it to London, spending seven years with it at Harlech and 80 years in Pembroke *en route*. On re-entering Wales Branwen looked back over the sea and her heart broke with grief. The carriers of Bran's head, which remained vital and uncorrupted so it could advise them in song, followed his instructions and eventually buried the head in the White Hill of London, facing France, from which direction they were warned the next invasion would come. It is said that their journeyings took place in the realms of faerie.

Bran's shamanistic birds were ravens, which acted as his scouts and messengers. When his head was buried in the White Hill, his ravens stayed with him to carry out his desires and guard both him and the land.

249

The present day ravens at the Tower of London are possibly evidence of this legend, for it is said that Britain will fall if they ever desert the Tower.

Ravens' powers are oracular and prophetic when they are used as totems, and raven cults formed around many gods and kings of the ancient world. Bran, Cronus, Apollo, Odin, Lugh and Arthur are all associated with such cults. Because of their death connotations ravens were also intrinsically linked to the fate-goddesses, who in Britain formed the following trinity: Ana, known in folklore as 'Black Annis', who dropped spider-like from trees upon people; Badb, the Crow, also known as the 'Watcher at the Ford'; and Macha, the 'Red' or 'Raven', the battle-aspect, whose Poles of Macha had heads of slaughtered men stuck on them. These three goddesses were collectively known as 'the Morrigan' or 'the Great Queen'. She was invoked onto the battlefields by a warhorn sounding an imitation of a raven's croak. The Germanic equivalents of such goddesses, the Valkyries, are described in Ash (see p.152).

On a much lighter note, the association of alder and Venus aids the May-eve fertility aspects of the love- and death-goddesses, whose traditional chase through the year by the gods sustains the seasons of Nature. Such goddesses are seen to be in charge of prophetic ravens which the gods borrow from them, as did Bran from Danu, Odin from Freya and Apollo from Athene. After death and entrance into the Underworld, the gods use the ravens to keep contact with the upperworld.

Through its associations with Bran the raven became one of the primal totems of Britain and throughout Celtic history it was regarded as a guise of the goddess, a bird of wisdom whose appearance always announced great change. At the death of King Arthur, Morgan le Fey aided his changing into a raven.

Bran was a beneficial god who ruled his people well, just as alder is a beneficial tree to the land, its livestock and people. The purple colour of alder's leaf-buds is especially associated with Bran, and is called 'royal purple'. In pagan Britain, such was the deep strength of feeling for Bran that the Christian Church had to acknowledge him, eventually sainting him into St Brons or Bran the Blessed. The sacred head aspects of his cult, similar to those associated with Cronus and Orpheus, in which severed heads were retained as totems, oracles and guardians, became clearly incorporated into the Christian legend of St John the Baptist.

In Anglo-Saxon 'alder' is *alr*. Its Gaelic name is *fearn* and its Norse *olr*. Alder's Latin name, *Alnus*, is reputedly taken from *Alor amne*, which has a possible interpretation of 'I am nourished by the stream.'

HEALING

Alder has the ability to dissolve puffiness and the swellings of surface inflammation. Through its links with the element of water, it also has the capacity to heal our emotions. In almost all our struggles of life our emotions are involved and it is how we control them which decides our fate in any given situation. By 'bridging' the waters of the emotions through meditation, alder allows us to rise above the situation and thus become objective. Through this we become strong and centred, able to find a firm foundation upon which to stand. Above all else alder provides foundation. Its ruling planet Venus is reflected in the healing it can give, which particularly pertains to healing through the heart.

BARK
Culpeper recommended bathing in a decoction of alder bark to assuage burns and inflammations, and muslin soaked in the same decoction can be bound around the neck to ease inflammations of the throat. Alder bark gives much the same relief as alder leaves and is a good substitute during winter months when the tree is bare of foliage.

LEAVES
Our forefathers, without doubt greater walkers than ourselves, used alder leaves to refresh their weary feet, putting them onto their bare soles.

Huge beds of dry alder leaves were renowned for giving relief from rheumatism to those who slept in them. Today, when not all would relish a bedroom full of leaves, we can gain similar relief by loosely filling duvets or cushions with alder leaves, which can then be slept in or held on specifically painful areas for certain periods of time. The addition of aromatic herbs like lavender will enhance any healing.

Before the days of chemical preparations, alder leaves collected when the dew was still upon them were carried around houses to rid them of fleas, for the sticky gumminess of the leaves both attracted and trapped the pests, which were then carried from the house and burned.

MAGIC

IRISH/GAELIC	*Fearn*
OGHAM	ᚃ
RUNIC	ᚨ
RULING PLANET	Venus
ABILITIES	Divination. Oracular Heads. Protection of self and country. To do with the element of Water.
SEASONS	Spring, Autumn

Because of its ability to produce strongly coloured dyes (*see Physical Uses, p.255*), the alder tree is closely associated with the skills of dyers, spinners and weavers, wherein magical intent can be 'woven' into cloth and clothing. Such tasks were performed in the main by women and were held in the greatest esteem, for according to what was imbued in a garment at its making, so ran the protection and power of the wearer. Thus great trust was placed upon garment makers, for if wrong intent was put into the process, the wearer's life (and possibly soul) would be at risk. In Britain the goddess who ruled the spindle and loom was Brigid, her totem tree, the rowan, being used to make spindles and other such implements. Like the alder-god Bran, Brigid became a saint, as discussed in Rowan (*p.230*).

The appearance of alder's purple buds in earliest spring show that the tree is powerful from Imbolc to the Spring Equinox. At this time, as the strength of the sun is visibly growing, meditation with alder places our feet firmly upon the earth, whence we can discern the coming season of light and make wise preparation.

As the solar energy waxes into summer the fiery qualities of alder are used to propitiate the old gods, as did the smiths and weapon-makers of old, whose crafts were deemed the greatest elemental magic. This fiery element of alder can be used alongside the qualities of Venus, its ruling planet, to bring passion and an extension to healing abilities. This affects macrocosmic issues, i.e., world healing, etc.

Because of its associations with water alder is also powerful in the west of the year, particularly from the Autumn Equinox to Samhain. Then it can be used along with other divinatory herbs in incenses and decorations. Specific divination with alder at this time, especially when looking forward to the new Celtic year which begins after Samhain, pronounces its oracular 'sacred head' qualities, allowing us contact with the singing head of Bran to obtain divine specifics for the coming season of darkness. Thus the alder provides farsight throughout the year.

The alder's association with the water element is strengthened by the custom of putting sacred heads into wells in order to propitiate the land and people with their waters and inspiration. The fast-moving visionary qualities of the water-loving alder are specifically associated with Pisces, the zodiacal sign of the fishes.

The druids recognized alder as a sacred tree and with alder whistles 'enticed air elementals and whistled up the wind'. Old recipes say that to make such magical pipes several shoots of alder are bound together side by side, with one end stopped with plugs of clay or sealing compound. The shoots are trimmed to make the desired notes, similar to Pan-pipes. An old traditional method of preparing alder shoots for pipes or whistles goes thus:

Take green alder branches from the shrub alder species [possibly tag alder (*Alnus serrulta*)] and loosen the bark from the wood inside by tapping the shoots or branches with willow wood.

As the shoots dry, the inner-wood shrinks and can be removed, leaving the outer intact.

Witches were also said to use such whistles to conjure up the force of the north wind.

The old legends tell us that alder gives spiritual protection during disputes, so if you know you're heading for an unavoidable confrontation, carry a piece of alder with you.

In the Brehon Law tree classification of Ireland, alder is a peasant tree.

INSPIRATION

A distinguishing feature of the alder is that it's the only broadleaved tree to bear cones. These are incredibly potent, for they appear delicate and fragile yet possess amazing hidden strengths, as does the alder tree itself. Dried alder-cones, which become brown and hard after the seed has dropped from them, are very tactile, allowing sensory perceptions to come from touching them. The alder was anciently revered as a 'fingertip' tree used in certain forms of divination, and by handling its cones with the fingertips today it is easy to understand why, for by their very shape and construction they sensitize the fingertips, allowing them to feel much more distinctly the essence, construction and energy of whatever is touched. The blind make use of this sensitivity when using Braille, as do psychometrists, who have the ability to divine the properties and history of objects by mere contact.

To the artist such tactile aids are valuable, not only for realizing the construction of items, but also as a memory aid to recapturing impressions of the natural world. My work tables are cluttered with similar objects – rocks, bones, crystals, roots, earth-balls and amonites all help me remember and rediscover deep earthy things, while feathers, wings, butterflies, moths, leaves, thistledown and whirling seeds give me reference to things which are carried on the air or which fly through it. 'Mirrored' objects – shells, mother-of-pearl, sea-horses, seaweed, corals, driftwood and silvery things – allow me to visualize life within the waters, and dried flowers of red, gold and orange, ripe corn, cones and seeds, wood burnt into dragon-shapes, red jewels and candles show the qualities of fire.

When using these things, specific incenses can be burned to enhance the sight and it is remarkable how on a cold uninspiring day, meditations with Nature's tactile objects lift the emotions and spirit with the memories of seasons and places. From them comes renewed strength and inspiration.

Shelter, comfort and warmth are all reassuringly offered by the alder, and through these we can redefine our purpose and path through life. As guardian of the streams and rivers, the alder also watches over the life-giving waters that promote the health of the land. In this it guards the spark of wonder which is your birthright.

PHYSICAL USES

Alder is held as proof against the corruptive power of water, for its gummy leaves resist the rains and its timber resists decay when in water. Then alder wood becomes as hard and as strong as stone, and for this reason it has always been used to make bridges, platforms, jetties and piles of lasting quality. In sixteenth-century Venice, the city of Ravena and the Rialto Bridge were built upon alder piles, as were several European medieval cathedrals. Alder was also used widely in France and Holland as piles in foundation work. In the past alder was a favourite wood for boats and more recently it has been used in the construction of canal lock-gates. It was also used for pumps, troughs and sluices.

Out of water alder wood is soft and splits easily. It is of no use in the dry ground as posts and fences, for it decays rapidly.

Alder is a poor fuel but makes a favourite charcoal of smiths and potters. It was also used in the making of gunpowder.

Alder grown in England was used for making clogs, for it was soft, easy to work, warm and waterproof. Musical pipes, spinning-wheels and cart-wheels were also made from alder, and in Scotland it was used for chair-making and was termed the 'Scottish mahogany'.

Many beautiful dyes are obtained from the alder tree. From its flowers comes the green associated with faerie clothes or those worn by early tribes. Foresters and people needing disguise also used this dye, as possibly did the legendary Robin Hood.

Red dye is obtained from alder bark and if copperas is added the colour goes from red to black. The twigs of the tree provide a brown colour and the young shoots in March dye a golden cinnamon. The bark and young shoots, used with copperas, give yellow.

Leaves of alder were used to tan leather and are preferable to the bark and young shoots, which contain too much tannin.

Warning: While alder aids man in many respects it is nevertheless bad for horses to eat, for it makes them ill and turns their tongues black.

THE
WILLOW TREE

BOTANICAL

WHITE WILLOW. *Salix alba*. Deciduous.

Willows are common to watersides all over Britain and Europe and there are many species in the family: white, crack, weeping, bay, purple, almond, grey and goat willow, to name but a few. The white willow is largest and can reach heights of 70–80 feet (21–4 metres) and girths of 20 feet (6 metres).

Although willows are fairly large trees, they are rarely found growing to any great size, for they are mostly pollarded. Pollarding (*see Appendix I*)

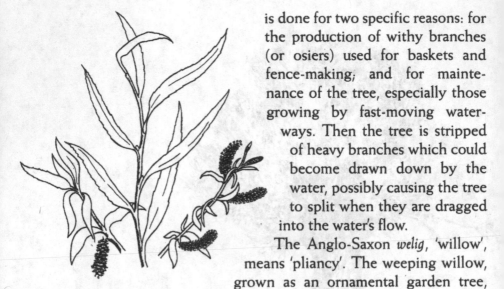

is done for two specific reasons: for the production of withy branches (or osiers) used for baskets and fence-making; and for maintenance of the tree, especially those growing by fast-moving waterways. Then the tree is stripped of heavy branches which could become drawn down by the water, possibly causing the tree to split when they are dragged into the water's flow.

The Anglo-Saxon *welig*, 'willow', means 'pliancy'. The weeping willow, grown as an ornamental garden tree, is native to China and was introduced to Britain in the eighteenth century.

The leaves and flower catkins of the willow

BARK

The white willow's trunk is thick and gnarled. It has rough and furrowed bark of a pale greeny-brown. From the trunk large branches rise into the sky and their many smooth slender twigs are so supple they tend to droop, especially when weighed down by leaves.

LEAVES

The majority of willow leaves are long and narrow, and the leaves of the white willow are of a greeny-grey colour on top, with an underside of ivory-white. They are easy to recognize from a distance, for when the wind moves them and their undersides are presented they appear as rippling silver waves, taking on the motion and appearance of water, to which the willow is closely allied.

FLOWERS

Willows flower and leaf in May, sometimes together or sometimes flower before leaf, according to the weather. The male and female flowers are on separate trees and willows rely on insects and the wind for pollination. Being reliant on the wind leaves a lot to chance, and the willow strengthens its odds of producing new trees by having the most easily propagating branches and twigs, which need only be stuck into earth to start growing.

Willows flower in the form of catkins, of which the males are the prettiest. They begin as small silvery-grey silky buds that feel like velvet and from these buds grow long green catkins rather like caterpillars, with tiny scales which open to allow the stamens to appear. The long stamens are in pairs, with a honey-sac between them to entice bees, and when the stamen-heads are ripe they burst to send showers of pollen into the air. On another tree the pollen lands on a female catkin and finds its way to the seed vessel where it begins to form the seed.

FRUIT

Along with poplars, which also have male and female catkins on separate trees, willows allow their seeds to be scattered to the winds in fluffs of cottony-looking down. Because they have to be so light to be carried on the winds, willow seeds are very small and have no endosperm (food supply). They thus have short lives, needing to land on moist ground where they can root quickly.

CRACK WILLOW

The crack willow has particularly rough furrowed bark and dark green leaves which are grey-green underneath. Its leaves turn a much richer russet-yellow in autumn than the white willow. Crack willow is so called because its branches and twigs are easily cracked or snapped, being decidedly less supple than other willows.

GOAT WILLOW

The goat willow is more a bush than a tree. It has large catkin-buds which burst open before the leaf-buds to reveal big beautiful silky globe-like catkins covered in silver down. These are the true 'pussy willows'. They grow in spirals on the branches and are irresistible to the touch.

The goat willow is one of the earliest plants to wake in the spring, not

259

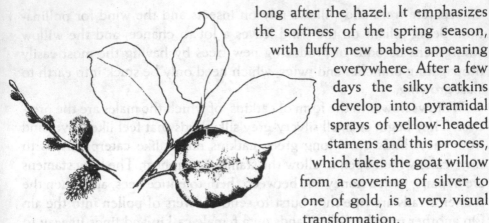

long after the hazel. It emphasizes the softness of the spring season, with fluffy new babies appearing everywhere. After a few days the silky catkins develop into pyramidal sprays of yellow-headed stamens and this process, which takes the goat willow from a covering of silver to one of gold, is a very visual transformation.

The leaves and 'pussy' catkins of the goat willow

Goat willow pollen is especially loved by bees. At night it also attracts many moths, which helps the distribution of pollen to nearby trees. After all the pollen is distributed, the catkins begin to fall. Then the goat willow's leaves open. These are not of the usual willow shape, but are more a broad oval with crinkled edges, with a dark shiny topside and a downy underside.

Goat willow leaves were customarily carried to churches on Palm Sunday, in remembrance of the branches of palm strewn before Jesus as he entered Jerusalem. The male tree gives the 'Palm gold' used on this day, which is why goat willow is also known as the Palm willow.

CUSTOM & LEGEND

It is believed that Orpheus, regarded by the Greeks as the most cele-brated of poets, received his gifts of eloquence and communication by carrying willow branches on his journeyings through the Underworld. Orpheus was presented with a lyre by the god Apollo, and he instructed the Muses in its use. He is said to have enchanted not only wild beasts, but even the trees and rocks upon Mount Olympus when he played music, so that, according to Dr Smith's *Smaller Classical Dictionary* of 1866, they 'moved from their places to follow the sound of his golden harp'. The ancient astronomers taught that at his death the lyre of Orpheus was placed amongst the stars by Zeus, at the intercession of Apollo and the Muses. A bas-relief in a temple at Delphi portrays Orpheus leaning against a willow tree, touching its branches.

Many ancient goddesses are associated with willows. Persephone, queen of the Underworld and daughter of Zeus and Demeter, the Greek goddess of the earth, had a sacred grove said to lie in far western Tartarus, which was synonymous with Hades. Robert Graves records that this grove was 'remarkable for its black poplars and aged willows'.

The Greek goddess Helice was associated with water magic and thus with willows. Because she was loved by Zeus, Hera (Zeus's consort) jealously metamorphosed her into a she-bear and Zeus placed her in the heavens under the name of the Great Bear. The priestesses of Helice were believed to use willow in every kind of water magic and witchcraft. In ancient times the willow-muse (or willow-tree faerie) was called Heliconian, after Helice. The willow-muse is sacred to poets, for the sound of the wind in willow trees exercises a potent influence upon the human mind which results in inspiration. 'Tree-top inspiration' was anciently deemed preferable to intoxication or trance, for it promotes clarity of mind.

The Greek sorceress Circe had a riverside cemetery planted with willows dedicated to Hecate and her moon magic. In this cemetery male corpses were wrapped in untanned ox-hides and left exposed in the tops of willow trees for the elements to claim and the birds to eat. Circe's cemetery shows the darker side of willow's usage, as do the Spartan fertility rites associated with the goddess Artemis, where a male celebrant was bound with willow thongs to a sacred image or tree-trunk and was flogged until the lashes produced an erotic reaction and he ejaculated, fertilizing the land with his semen and blood.

The ancient Sumerian goddess Belili was a goddess of trees, and willows in particular. She also ruled over the moon, love and the Underworld. As a willow-goddess she resided over springs and wells. Belili was dramatically superseded by her willow-god consort Bel, who became the supreme lord of the universe through a solar (patriarchal) revolt against Belili's lunar (matriarchal) order. In Europe the Celts honoured Bel as Belin the sun-god, and his worship as 'lord of life and death' slowly entered Britain during tribal migrations and eventually ousted the indigenous lunar worship. Belin's feast days were 30 April and 1 May. So these celebrations became known as Beltaine and during them great fires were lit in Belin's honour.

Another example of such supplanting is found in the legends of Anatha, a derivative goddess of Athena (or Anat) who had a willow cult at Jerusalem. Jehovah's priests not only ousted her but claimed the 'rain-making' willow as Jehovah's tree at the Feast of the Tabernacles, where to this day the time of the Fire and Water Ceremony is called the 'Day of the Willows'.

Hecate, the most powerful willow- and moon-goddess, was descended from the Titans, and was the only one of them to retain power under the rule of Zeus. Dr Smith describes her as 'a mighty and formidable divinity of the Underworld' who could send out terrible phantoms at night. She taught sorcery and witchcraft and haunted cross-roads and tombs. Her totem animal was the dog and her approach was announced when dogs whined at the moon, symbol of her strength. She is the goddess *par excellence* of the dark side of the moon.

Willows, water and the moon are a strong combination, with great implications with regard to deities associated with the sun. The Sumerian god Bel moved from being a local willow-god to a sun-god worshipped throughout the world, and young sun-gods in many traditions are set afloat upon water in baskets made from willows, from whence they are plucked by those who can best aid them to grow and reach maturity.

In the Bible we find reference to 'weeping' willows, which supposedly began drooping their branches in sympathy for the Jews in captivity:

By the rivers of Babylon, there we sat down, yea, we wept, when we remembered Zion. We hanged our harps upon the willows in the midst thereof.

PSALMS 137:1,2

262

Willow has many associations with funerary matters and has always been used as a funerary herb. Flints shaped as willow leaves have been found in megalithic tombs and old country lore advises to 'plant a willow and allow it to grow, to ease the passage of your soul at death'. Branches of willow were traditionally placed in coffins and young willow saplings were planted on graves. This is an echo of Celtic tradition, whereby the spirit of the corpse in the earth rises into the sapling planted above, which grows and retains the essence of the departed one. Burial mounds in Britain, especially when sited near marshes or lakes, were lined with planted willows in order to protect the spirits of the place. To 'wear the willow' once meant to grieve openly and garlands for mourning were traditionally woven from supple willow branches. The willow is still seen by some as an emblem of grief.

However, in Leviticus 23:40, we see how willows were used for rejoicing:

And ye shall take ... the boughs of goodly trees, the branches of palm trees, and the boughs of thick trees, and willows of the brook, and ye shall rejoice before the Lord thy God seven days.

Continuing from an even older tradition, in Europe on 23 April Rumanian gypsies still hold their festival of Green George. This character, very like the British Jack in the Green, is impersonated by a man wearing a wicker frame covered with greenery. Green George epitomizes the spirit of vegetation which brings fruitfulness to the cornfields, and unlike Jack in the Green, he specifically propitiates the water spirits through the willow tree. In order for this to be done properly everything is prepared meticulously on the eve of the festival. A young willow tree is cut down and erected in the place of festivities, where it is adorned with garlands in a lively party atmosphere. That same night all the pregnant women gather round the willow and each lays a garment of clothing beneath it. If overnight a single leaf falls from the tree onto their garment, it is taken as a sign that the willow-goddess is granting them an easy delivery of their child.

At dawn Green George himself appears. He approaches the willow and knocks three nails into its trunk. He then removes the nails from the tree and takes them to a nearby stream, throwing them into the water in order to propitiate the water spirits. This done, he returns to the willow and brings it to the stream, wherein he dips its branches and leaves until they are heavy with water. Then with the beneficent qualities of the willow and the water spirits evoked, the flocks and herds of the community are led towards Green George, who raises the willow on high and shakes water onto the animals in blessing.

After this the willow is again erected in the centre of the festivities and during the remaining celebration is approached for healing. It was considered especially favourable to the old and the young, giving comfort in the conditions of old age, such as rheumatism, and a vital energy to the delivery of the newborn. At the end of the festivities each old person would ask another boon, approaching the willow and spitting at it three times, saying, 'Willow tree, willow tree, you will soon die. Let us live!'

Pagan associations with willows have always been strong, for in the traditional sense they were revered as trees of the moon-goddess, she who reflects her moon magic upon the waters of Earth. In damp climates such as north-western Europe, willow was the tree most sought by the wise-women or healers, for it has great ability to ease rheumatism and other conditions aggravated by damp weather. Eventually the willow's medicinal and religious qualities fused and it gained the name 'witch's tree'. And for the superstitious came stories of willows visited by hunchbacked old women in the secrecy of night, under the watchful eye of the moon. These women resembled the shape of the trees themselves, with their crooked trunks and, especially on pollarded trees, their crazy mimicry of hair clawing erratically into the night sky.

Because of all these associations, the willow was regarded as a sacred tree and people have always been advised not to burn it lest grief befall them. It is thought that the origins of the saying 'Knock on wood' came from the age-old act of knocking on a willow tree to avert evil and bring good luck.

The vigorous growth of willows when propagated from branches and twigs was advantageous to the many cottage industries that once flourished. Economical use of undrainable land was also achieved by the planting of osier-beds to provide quantities of working material.

The seventh Duke of Bedford loved willows so much he made a Salicetum, that is, a collection of every known species of willow, at Woburn Abbey.

Willow is known by many folk-names, such as 'osier', 'pussy willow', 'saille', 'Sally', 'withy', 'witch's aspirin' and the 'tree of enchantment'.

HEALING

Willow has always been used to protect against diseases caused by damp conditions. The bark and leaves contain salicylic acid, which is a good painkiller and the source of aspirin.

Willow touches our deep subconscious as well as our deepest emotions. The Bach Flower Remedies advise using it to clear severe discontent, both with yourself and with others. Irritability, fault-finding, self-pity, unhappiness, resentment, jealousy and other such negative emotions are dealt with by willow.

The Chinese see willow as a herb of immortality, for it has the ability to grow from the smallest branch stuck into the earth. It is thought that the priests of the Greek healer Asclepius used a particular variety of willow (*Angus castus*) to cure barrenness.

BARK
Gypsies make a bitter drink from willow bark for easing rheumatism, influenza and headaches. It is also a good tonic, but it is advised not to take more than three doses a day. Decoctions of willow bark can also be used to treat chronic diarrhoea.

Culpeper advises to 'slit the bark of a willow in flower and collect the water from the tree', which is good for problems of sight, dimness and soreness of the eyes. It is also good for clearing spots from the skin.

Willow bark can be used as an incense to aid deep emotional healing, for it clears the head and uplifts the spirits.

LEAVES

When made into a strong decoction, the leaves and bark of willow can be rubbed into the scalp during hair-washing, before the final rinse, to eradicate dandruff.

MAGIC

IRISH/GAELIC	*Saille*
OGHAM	⊨
RUNIC	Y
RULING PLANET	Moon
ABILITIES	Dowsing. Psychism via water. Night visions. Lunar tides and magic. To do with the element of Water.
SEASONS	Spring, Autumn (Samhain)

As trees of enchantment, willows formed groves so magical that poets, artists, musicians, priests and priestesses sat within them to gain eloquence, prophecy and inspirational skills through meditation. Because of the willow's close relationship with water, the element pulled into tides by the magnetism of the moon, it has always been considered a feminine tree with a great effect upon the vision-producing subconscious.

The visionary aspects of willow are strongest at two points of the year. In spring they are ideal for workings of light and life, whilst at Samhain they are more suited to contacting departed loved ones and for deep psychic work pertaining to the subconscious levels which parallel the mythical Underworld. These workings are especially effective when willow wood is used as an incense or when meditating amongst flowering willow trees, and are discussed more fully in Inspiration (see p.270).

In the following recipe willow sticks (dried twigs) are used to charge a lotion made out of the herbs chamomile and eyebright, so it can be used to promote psychism, clairvoyance and clairaudience. It is also an excellent healing lotion.

Use 2 teaspoons each of chamomile and eyebright to just over ½ pint (¼ litre) of water. Put into a non-aluminium pan, bring to the boil and simmer for 12 minutes.

Then light the ends of 7 sticks of willow and plunge them, still alight, into the mixture. This charges the ingredients alchemically, the fire being the active boost to the visionary qualities instilled into the lotion by the willow.

Now, in order that all these ingredients manifest correctly on earth to fulfil the needs of our everyday world, the mixture is filtered through 4 squares of cotton material which represent the 4 elements of life: earth, air, fire and water. The fifth element, spirit, is resultant of the action of preparation: it comes from 'doing' it.

When cool, the charged lotion is poured into a cleansed bottle, and can be stored in the refrigerator for up to a month (a moon).

It can be used in the following ways:

HEALING Because the lotion is extremely concentrated energywise it aids in all healing, from the dab of 'magic lotion' on children's bruises and grazes to deep massage on specific points on the body. In massage it eases the 'knots' within us, aligning us so our stresses may be released. Because our intent was in the making of it, the lotion is still bound to that intent and allows us to exercise stronger healing. It is almost as if it awaits instruction and then comes up with the goods. And that is 'magic'!

PSYCHISM If massaged into the third eye area, between the eyebrows, the lotion stimulates the pineal gland. This gland has been called the 'seat of the soul', for through it we interact with the subtle vibrations of the cosmos, becoming aware and tuned in on psychic levels.

CLAIRVOYANCE In a visual sense the lotion promotes great clarity, whether massaged into the third eye as above or used, soaked into cotton wool, as eye-pads during meditation. This clears your physical eyes, first relaxing them, then cleansing them (through closed eye-lids) and focusing their energy. Weak eyes are strengthened by this and become alive and sparkling.

CLAIRAUDIENCE By now it must be realized that this lotion is like a condenser, attracting vitality when applied. It allows us to choose the areas we revitalize, and just as it is with the eyes and clear-seeing, so it is with the ears and clear-hearing. Cotton-wool ear-plugs, soaked in the lotion and placed in the ears during meditation, strengthen our audial senses and revitalize our hearing ability, tuning us in to clearer frequencies.

Other areas to be vitalized include the following: the throat, to clear infection, to improve the voice in song and speech, and to align the vocal chords for the intonation of the god-names; the chakra, massage or acupressure points, for healing and revitalization; the temples, as an aid in concentration. It can also be used on any part of the body that feels weighted down and sluggish.

The lotion has other qualities besides healing. It can be put onto objects to charge them magically and make them shine brighter in the home, onto good-will gifts to friends or onto important letters that have to 'move mountains' in your favour. Anything can be charged or blessed, for the lotion allows us the capacity to make changes for the better. You have only to apply your will to it.

The Celtic goddess Brig, herself a great seer, was celebrated at the Imbolc fire festival. At this time willows are beginning to show their flowering catkins, their power radiating outwards as they present themselves for pollination and fertilization. Such an outward-moving energy can be used to great effect in any visionary workings associated with the festival.

Imbolc was celebrated by the Romans as Candlemas, for thousands of candles were burned by them at this time to call back the warmth of the sun to earth. In Britain, while such concepts were celebrated, there were also indigenous qualities and traditions associated with the festival. However as the Roman Church became dominant these traditions were pushed into the realms of folk-memory, leaving a people disconnected from their roots and unable to resist foreign influences. Eventually Imbolc became better known as Candlemas, though more recently, hearkening back to its true concept, 1 February has been named Lady Day. *For the willow at Samhain, see Inspiration, p.271.*

In pagan religions, willow is a tree of fertility. It is used at the Beltaine festival in either wand or bough form. Wands cut from willow, called 'willie-wains' in the north of Britain, are said to contain the power of water which is never truly still. The druids used magical wands cut from goat willow as protective charms, the magical significance of which is discussed in Inspiration *(see p.272)*. All parts of all willows guard against evil and can be carried or placed in the home for this purpose.

In traditional spells willow leaves are used to attract love and one old custom for rejected lovers was to wear willow in their hats, not only to attract new love to them, but also to protect them from having jealous thoughts about their lost love. The Romanies still use willow to divine future husbands, for on certain propitious festival days the single women throw shoes and boots into a willow tree, and if one catches in the branches the owner is assured of being married within the year. As each woman has nine tries at this we can assume that the number nine has relevance to the spell, it being the number usually assigned to the moon, the agent of divination associated with the willow tree.

It is believed that in ancient days the ritual rain-makers of the tribes or communities were women. Today, when most of us have access to taps for water, we cannot imagine just how important rain-making was, nor the amount of reverence given to those who performed the art. In this context willow was especially revered, its love of dew and moisture and its associations with the moon (and thus the tides) making it a tree which greatly aided the rain-making process. In such magic the rain was regarded as the most precious gift, given by the moon-goddess herself.

Wishes are granted by the willow tree if they are asked for in the correct manner. Form your wish, and explain to the tree what it is and why you desire it. Select a pliable shoot on the tree and, without breaking it from the tree, tie a loose knot in it while expressing your wish.

Thank the tree before departing. When your wish comes true, return to the willow, untie the knot and thank it for its aid.

An old witch spell is related to have used willow seeds steeped in spring water. After a prescribed number of days the liquid was drunk by a man desiring great aphrodisiac powers. Through this he also became fertile, though it was warned that he would sire no sons but only barren daughters!

Magical witch-brooms are traditionally bound with supple willow branches, their strength binding the broom to the handle, their energy linking the broomstick to the witch-beloved moon (see also Silver Birch, p.100).

Willow leaves, wood and bark can be used in healing spells, especially as an ingredient of incense. Willow bark mixed with sandalwood can be burnt as an incense on outdoor fires. When burned at specific times of the moon, such incense attracts relevant spirits to the place of working.

The main deities associated with willow are rulers of the moon, sun and Underworld. They include the goddesses Persephone, Circe, Hecate, Hera, Belili, Artemis, Selene, Diana, Luna, Athena, Cerridwen and Helice. The gods associated with willow include Orpheus, Bel, Belin and Jehovah.

Willow is used for love, divination, protection, fertility and healing.

INSPIRATION

Willows look like ancient beings. It is easy to visualize them in days of yesteryear encircling vast marshes, their gnarled forms silhouetted by mists and moonlight. Arthur Rackman's paintings capture such trees and atmospheres at their most evocative.

The practice of pollarding willows accentuates the 'human' character-istics of the trees, and in times when much of the land still held waters from the Ice Age and willows were extremely prolific, the lunar, imagina-tive qualities of the trees, boosted by the reflective qualities of the water, would have had a great effect upon the spiritual and visionary senses of the people.

While willow is ruled by the moon, it is from its strong associations with Neptune that it gets its greatest visionary strength. Willows heal deep emotions and touch deep psychic levels within us, and because our deepest subconscious desires are difficult to face or deal with, especially primeval forces or 'raw' energy, it can be frightening to behold ourselves. That is why some have deemed willow to be 'under the power of the devil', though not, we may add, in pre-Christian times. In those ancient days the eternal pattern of life was understood: as light followed dark, day followed night, summer followed winter and life followed death.

When willow is used at the Samhain rites it is in this deep psychic and visionary sense, for it allows greater personal insight and easier contact with departed loved ones. Samhain is the only time of the year when the gateways between the worlds of the living and the dead truly stand open, and communication at this time is easy and natural. It needs no hocus-pocus and dramatic ritual: a lit candle, a thought and a touch of love are all that are necessary. No spirit need be disturbed or called from its domain, for it is possible to communicate easily as if in company with them. It is a time for memories, for messages and desires. It is a time for your world family and for gladness, for even after death we are never really parted. During such communications incense made from white willow wood guides the spirit and enfolds all in an atmosphere of protection. And when communication ends, it is time to close the gateways from this world to the next, saying farewell to loved ones with the witch words: 'Merry meet, merry part, merry meet again!' Then, to help earth us, apples are eaten, for as well as providing vitamins and minerals to nourish our bodies, they also allow us to retain the glow of spiritual contact. All altars are piled high with apples at Samhain, for they provide an excellent atmosphere (see also Apple, p. 116).

At Imbolc, as the first flowers and buds of spring begin to open, the willow of the woodlands, goat willow, is more appropriate as an incense, for it has strong associations with solar energies and will encourage the sun to grow and fulfil the year. Imbolc may be Lady Day, but it should not be forgotten that the earth-goddess must also lead the solar-god unto the earth, young though he may be at this time, in order to help life unfurl anew. At this time willows express fertility, guiding its flow upon the land as guardians of the waterways.

The goat willow is incredibly visual, its power shown to full radiance when it produces its catkin-flowers. This can be as early as February, and is a beautiful sight:

> *The woodland willow stands,*
> *A lovely bush of nebulous silver,*
> *There the spring goddess revealed.*

ANON

On female trees the silver catkins turn to grey spiky flowers, but on male trees they fill with pollen and turn to gold. 'His great attire of sunshine fire' is an old druidic phrase which describes the solar qualities felt to pertain to the male tree and the sun-god. Druids cut goat-willow wands from male trees, for the changeover from silver to gold was deemed very magical. The gold grains upon the silver were also regarded as a strong symbolic aid to the workings of the alchemists.

To understand the energies of willow is to understand the energies of the night. Magic mists, used for seership or as a barrier to hide things from sight, are raised by willow spells. It is a tree of powerful moon magic. Many a legend tells of willow trees uprooting at night to stalk unwary travellers and such spooky tales have ensured that willow gets due respect. Willow is a tree of mysteries and of witcheries.

The qualities of the element of water also affect the emotional side of our lives, for, as already explained, our bodies contain 80 per cent water. This links us with the moon's magnetic tides of ebb and flow, wherein we are moved by the strength of the primeval. The word 'lunacy' is rooted in *la lune* (French for 'moon') or *luna* (Latin) and is often associated with the intensity of the full moon, although the entire moon cycle is reflected in our lives (*see also Ash, p.166*).

When I see willows with branches arching over a stream, I cannot help but imagine the roots of the trees also, as they grow beneath the bed of the stream, 'mirroring' the branches above. If this image is viewed in section, the roots and branches form a sort of tube or tunnel through which the waters flow. This encasing effect prompts the recognition that willows help form the 'veins' of the land, as the ancient elms once did the nervous system, without which all would be dry and barren.

Lastly, mention must be made of a favourite book of children and adults alike. *The Wind in the Willows* by Kenneth Graham lovingly explores the nature of the riverbank and its occupants Ratty, Toad, Mole and Badger. In the words of its author, it is a book for those 'who keep the spirit of youth alive in them; of life, sunshine, running water, dusty roads, and winter firesides'. Inspiration indeed!

PHYSICAL USES

The wood of the white willow is light and tough. It was used extensively by builders for rafters and floors. The 'cricket bat willow' is a secondary species of white willow, and is used, as its name suggests, for the production of world-renowned cricket bats.

Willow provides a first-class timber of especially quick growth, taking approximately 15 years to gain heights of 70 feet (21 metres) and more, from the size of a branch. The branches used for willow propagation (called 'sets') can be up to 10 feet (3 metres) long. They are driven into the earth for half their length, and if planted in autumn, will be leafing by the following spring. Even if planted upside-down they grow, for the branches become roots and the roots become branches. Coppicing of willows cuts them down to ground level, and pollarding takes them off at shoulder height. Each method produces a mass of growth, used by its various sizes for all weights and textures of fencing, basketry, etc.

Willow is the native material for all kinds of woven basketry, for its supple branches are easy to weave and reliably strong. It is not easy to break a willow branch (apart from crack willow), for the bark is very thin and when split reveals the green pliability of a supple inner branch. All willow is stripped before use, its branches (called 'rods') being pulled through a stripping 'brake', a simple contrivance which scrapes bark cleanly off the branch.

Willows were customarily pollarded in order to produce enough material for the cottage industries, the like of which in these modern days of plastic we can hardly realize. The crafts of the willow-workers aided all walks of life. The most popular willow for baskets was the purple osier, easily recognized by its rich colour. The bulk of osiers were produced by coppicing plants in great osier-beds, making viable use of marshy land.

Because of the suppleness of its branches, willow was used by outdoor workers when straw was scarce to make hats used for protection from the weather. The branches were slit into long fine strips which were then plaited into shape. In days when nothing was wasted, the bark from stripped willow, which contains 13 per cent tannic acid, was used to tan leather.

Willow wood was used in the past in the construction of fast-sailing naval boats and for the bottoms of quarry carts which take a heavy, bumpy load. It is a strong wood. However, as a tree, willow is very liable to split in a storm, though this may be often due to the double beating it gets from both the wind and the waters, especially if it overgrows rivers or streams with fast currents, rather than from any weakness in the wood itself.

Willow was also used in the construction of coracles. These small keelless boats were so light in construction that they were carried home on the back instead of being moored. Each coracle was custom-made for its owner, taking account of their weight and size. They generally measured 6 feet (2 metres) in length, some 40 inches (102 cm) in the beam, and 12–15 inches (30–5 cm) in depth. They were used by fishermen on lakes, marshes and rivers, or in tidal bays. The rivers Spey, Dee and Severn were fished from such boats, as were the fenlands of East Anglia. As well as helping fishermen, coracles were also used to travel expanses of water which lacked bridges or fords.

Coracles are basically a large willow basket to which is attached a waterproof skin. Their framework is made from broad willow slats cut from stout poles and these are interwoven in an under-and-over pattern. The structure is usually formed from six slats running length-wise and eight or nine running cross-wise. No nails are used in the construction, for the tension of the woven slats holds them in place. The structure is further strengthened by two diagonal strips being woven across the floor and by the insertion of wood for a seat. The outer skin of tarred canvas (in ancient days hides or skins) is also secured without nails, by being wrapped over the gunwale and tightly bound to the plaited willow strip which forms and strengthens the top of the boat (see also Hazel, p.77).

As already noted, willow's unique medicinal properties have always been recognized and used by healers. It is considered the natural form and source of modern aspirin and thus is often called the 'witch's aspirin'.

THE
ELDER TREE

BOTANICAL

ELDER. *Sambucus nigra*. Deciduous.

The elder seems to love to grow wild. It is found in abundance on waste-land, in chalk-pits, woods, hedgerows and gardens. It likes chalky soils, and while it is rare in Scotland, is so common everywhere else that it is often ignored or considered a nuisance. It is anciently recorded that the trunks of elder trees grew to 6 feet (2 metres) in girth, though it is hard to visualize this when looking at our modern specimens. Today the elder is a shrub, bush or small tree which rarely exceeds 30 feet (9 metres) in height.

The elder has a peculiar method of growth. Several stems will appear at the base of a sapling, and each grows upright for a time and then droops over. The bud arising on the top of the curve created by the drooping stem will carry on growing upwards for a while, and then it droops over and growth continues from its upper-curve bud. By growing this way the elder trunk is not formed in one upward growing mass, as are oak and other trees, but is rather a patchwork of the curves of many drooping shoots, which is why the tree is never elegant nor of great height.

The elder sends up shoots anywhere, and will grow in dense shade and on a minimum of soil and still produce masses of fruit. Elder grows easily from cuttings, simply by a twig being broken off the tree and stuck into the ground. The elder always has stems at its base, and it casts its boughs crazily about itself. Sheep and cows eat elder leaves but they're not particularly liked by goats and horses. It is recorded that sheep fed on elder bark and the tree's young shoots suffer less badly with foot-rot.

The leaves, flowers and berry fruit of the elder

BARK

Elder bark is sandy in colour, with a surface which is rough and full of chinks. The branches are less rough and the smoother twigs are green, their surfaces marked with spots or brownish warts caused by the tree's lenticels, the pores through which it breathes. The wood of the main stem is heavy and hard, but elder twigs have merely an outer ring of wood, and are full of white pith. This can be easily taken out, as many a child has discovered.

LEAVES
Elder leaves consist of five leaflets attached to a centre stalk and they are set opposite each other on the twig or branch. Because elder-buds are not protected by a weatherproof bud-case, the elder produces another, smaller bud in reserve beneath each main bud. These second buds only open if the main buds don't, or if they are destroyed, and they can remain dormant on the tree for a couple of years until needed. In this way the wise elder ensures no loss of leaves if the seasonal climate suddenly changes.

FLOWERS
Not long after the appearance of the elder's leaves its flower-buds form. By June they have opened and the tree is laden with their flat-topped masses made up of millions of tiny creamy-white flowers. All elder flowers are alike, with five cream petals which have five green sepals behind them which look like stars on the back of each tiny flower. In between the petals are five yellow stamens and in the centre there is a cream-coloured ovary with a three-lobed stigma. The stamens and stigmas mature at the same time, allowing cross-fertilization to occur easily as insects (especially flies) are attracted by the fragrance of the flowers.

Elder flower clusters are built up from five very slim 'branches' arising from the end of the main stalk. Each branch then divides into five 'branchlets', and may branch again before reaching the flowers. Elder flowers are all at the same level, facing the sky. Seen from underneath they resemble small many-spoked umbrellas.

FRUIT
By late summer the fertilized ovaries of the flowers have developed into berries. These berries are green and hard at first, but as summer moves towards autumn they ripen, turning into juice-filled, deep purply-black fruit, hanging in heavy bunches called drupes. Birds love elderberries and will swoop *en masse* to strip a tree, often precipitating human needs. However this is necessary for the trees, for having eaten the berries

the birds void their seeds unharmed upon their flights, thus ensuring widespread propagation.

CUSTOM & LEGEND

The unique personality of the elder was anciently believed to come from the spirit of the 'Elder Mother' who dwelt within the tree. The Elder Mother, called Elle or Hyldemoer in Scandinavian and Danish myth, worked strong earth magic and according to legend avenged all who harmed her host trees. No forester of old would touch elder, let alone cut it, before asking the Elder Mother's permission three times over and even then he was still in dread of her possible wrath. Likewise, in many country districts of Europe and Britain, wise people still show respect by touching their hats when passing elder trees, in continuance of ancient custom. Certain North American tribes also believe that elder is the Mother of the human race.

According to legend witches would often turn themselves into elder trees, and one famous witch-tree turned a king and his men to stone, thereby creating the Rollright Stones in Oxfordshire. This ancient piece of folklore tells of a Danish king, on his way to battle for the English Crown with his warriors, meeting the witch and asking her what his fate would be. The witch replied:

> *Seven long strides thou shalst take,*
> *And if Long Compton thou canst see*
> *King of England thou shalst be.*

Because he was almost at the crest of a hill the Dane was confident as he strode forth, but unexpectedly at his seventh stride a long mound rose up before him, blocking his view. The old witch continued:

As Long Compton thou canst not see,
King of England thou shalst not be.
Rise up stick, and stand still stone,
For King of England thou shalst be none,
Thou and thy men hoar stones shall be,
And I myself an elder tree.

In an instant the Danish king and his men were turned to stone. Those warriors loyal to the king became the King's Men stones set in a circle; and those who had questioned his authority turned into the Whispering Knights, huddled together and apart from the others. The king himself became the King Stone, standing, still in shocked attitude, apart from all his men. The witch then resumed her guise as the guardian elder tree.

Many local customs and traditions arose from this legend. It is said that in ancient days on Midsummer's Eve people sought the elder witch-tree, dancing with elder garlands in their hair. Whereupon at midnight the King Stone acknowledged the proceedings and turned his head to watch the dancing. Unfortunately many of the customs associated with this legend were changed when religious laws forbidding paganism were enforced and we find that the majority of them showed condemnation for the pagan witch-elder tree rather than for the invading foreign king. Thus arose the custom of feasting around the King Stone on Midsummer's Night and of cutting the elder tree to 'bleed' the witch, when it is said the King Stone would nod his approval. Local superstition said that if you found the witch-elder and broke off a branch, you would have the chance to discover the witch's disguise. An added incentive to the witch-hunt was that if when you broke the branch it turned red and 'bled', you would be granted an extra boon.

However the Rollright Stones are also associated with powerful healing and divinatory qualities. The King's Men form a circle and prayers for the sick were reckoned more effective if offered up in the centre of it. It was also believed that barren women would be made fertile if they went to these stones at midnight and pressed their bare breasts against them. On certain nights of the year the King's Men are still believed to change into human form, in order to go dancing down to a nearby spring to quench their huge thirsts.

The King's Men have always seemed impossible to count, for each time you try a different total is reached, almost as if the stones move as you walk round the circle. This may be due to the effects of the energy of the place, or even to the legendary witch's spell! However there are known to be around 77 stones and according to custom, if anyone does get the same total three times, they will have great wishes fulfilled.

Since ancient days the Whispering Knights have been renowned for their ability to foretell the future, their secrets heard as the wind whispers through them. Thus, at midnight on Beltaine eve, local girls visited the knights so the stones could whisper the names of their future loves and husbands into their ears.

According to folklore, if ever Britain is in dire need the entire Rollright army will awaken into human form. Perhaps, as this army originally came to invade, this may refer to an escape clause set down in the witch's spell: that the king and his men could awaken, but only if they showed in their hearts they would truly aid the English.

The above legend illustrates the ancient associations between the elder and witches, and, as already stated, all witches were believed to be able to transform into elder trees. Folklore extensively embroidered this theme and it became the belief of the superstitious that if a transformed witch-elder were cut, the witch would return to human shape still bearing the marks and so could be recognized. Similarly, breaking a branch off a tree could be recognized in the human as a limp, or as cramps, etc. The paranoia arising from such tales is well illustrated by an old story from Northamptonshire, which tells of a man who cut an elder stick as a toy for his child, only to see blood flow from the tree. Later he met a local woman with her arm bound up and such was the hysteria of the times that the woman was ducked as a witch for the alleged offence.

In reality the elder provides excellent healing. Yet as paganism was being crushed by a Church no doubt eager for its priests to replace healers, this was denied. People were told that the only proper use for elder was to seek out the evil of witches. To do this a baptized person was to dab the green juice from elder onto his eyelids, which would enable him to recognize and see all the doings of witches in the community. This fallacy effectively boosted persecution. All healers, let alone unpopular women, took great risks to be able to perform their arts with elder, for they were ever open to the jealousies of others and the threat of diabolically rigged witch-trials.

In the legends of the Church elder was said to be the wood of the cross, even though the tree's peculiar growing habit denies it could be cut into straight, strong lengths of wood. Elder was also said to be the tree upon which Judas hanged himself after betraying Christ. Thus elder was deemed to be an invitation to the devil himself, bringing death to one of the family if it were brought into the home. This is a relic from the days when all things female were called 'devilish' by the Church and is in direct contradiction to the special qualities of the tree. Through these edicts of the Church elder became known as a tree of mixed powers, of good and of evil. A tree therefore not to approach!

In later years Saxon kings forbade 'vain practices' (i.e., divination) carried out with elder sticks and yet twigs of elder grown on consecrated ground were considered a counteracting charm, especially when tied into the form of a cross. Because of all the superstition attached to it, elder wood was never used for furniture, especially not for things that children used, in case the child grew sickly. It was also never used to beat boys or animals in case it stunted their growth.

Throughout the ages tales have surfaced about houses hemmed in by elder trees. The inhabitants of these houses died in rapid succession, and the places were only rendered healthy again when the trees were thinned. Yet conversely it was customary to place elder branches around the doors and windows of a house to protect the inhabitants from mischief.

Cornish folklore of 1816 tells of a farmer from Lostwithiel who used elder for similar protection. Every morning he noticed how one of his ponies was tired and travel-stained, and he suspected that it was being 'hag-ridden' at night. So he kept watch and saw five small men fighting in a nearby meadow. Eventually the victor of the fight jumped onto the pony and galloped it into a state of exhaustion. After seeing this the farmer pinned his stable door shut with green elder twigs and his pony was troubled no more.

Country folklore also states that those who sleep under an elder tree will never awaken, for the fragrance of the flowers will transport them to the Underworld. In reality the white pith inside the branches of elder contains a mild sleep-inducing drug, so this is probably responsible rather than the smell of the flowers. It is also possibly derivative of an old legend, which says that if you stand beneath an elder tree on Midsummer's Night and breathe in its fragrance, you will see the king of the faeries and his entourage. If you do not carry the necessary things to protect you from bewitchment, especially an implement of iron, you may disappear into the realms of faerie, perhaps never to return...

There are many superstitions about burning elder wood, especially on indoor fires, for it is thought that the Elder Mother within the tree will take great revenge for such a act, sending plagues of bad luck. Gypsies avoid burning any part of the tree.

The elder tree has been given this false reputation of shade and death, yet to our ancient ancestors it was a tree of great medicinal value. An elder in bloom was said to denote the true arrival of summer, which ended when its berries became fully ripe. Because the elder rejuvenates itself from shoots growing vigorously from its base, it also came to symbolize life itself by appearing virtually immortal.

The Anglo-Saxons named elder *ellaern*, meaning 'hollow tree'. It was also called *aeld*, meaning 'fire', a name no doubt connected to the use of hollow sticks of elder for blowing life into a fire like bellows. Elder's other folk-names include 'Lady Ellhorn', 'Old Lady', 'Old Sal' and 'the pipe tree' or 'bole tree'.

HEALING

Elder was used medicinally by the ancient Britons, Celts and Romans, for it was thought that the Elder Mother within the tree could cure 'all the ills of mankind'. Elder was known as the tree of regeneration, for it regrew damaged branches and rooted from any part of itself. Thus it illustrated the regenerative power of life.

Virtually every ailment of the body is cured by some part of the elder. Village doctors and herbalists throughout time have put their faith in the medicinal qualities of its roots, leaves, flowers, bark, fruit and spirit. The fevers and colds of winter months are appeased by elder's immense healing abilities, which is why it is most powerful from the autumn on, when its rich harvest of fruit provides strength for survival through the dark times of the year.

In the mid-eighteenth century John Evelyn stated of elder:

> If the medicinal properties of the leaves, bark, berries, etc. were thoroughly known, I cannot tell of what our country-men could ail, for which he might not fetch a remedy from every hedge.

Indeed, elder is the queen of herbs.

BARK
Elder bark is diuretic and as a strong purgative its use dates back beyond Hippocrates. In ancient days it was used to quickly evacuate and cleanse the stomach and system in cases of food poisoning.

The inner bark should be collected from young trees in autumn. To do this the outer bark is scraped off to reveal the green bark below, which is removed in strips. This is then dried in the sun.

SHOOTS
Young shoots of elder, eaten after being boiled like asparagus, clear the lungs and head of phlegm. The pith of the shoots contains a mild sleep-inducing drug. An elder shoot, tied in three or four knots, was carried as a charm of protection against rheumatism.

TWIGS
An elder twig carried in the pocket is a charm against saddle-soreness for horse-riders and elder attached to the harness will protect the horse in hot weather. A farm with elder trees growing on it is blessed, for they protect the livestock from lightning and promote their fertility. Elder twigs were tied into crosses with red yarn, and were

hung over the doors of barns, stables and homes for protection.

Toothache, however bad, supposedly disappeared completely if you held an elder twig in your mouth and said, 'Depart, thou evil spirit!' Lame pigs were reckoned to be cured by an elder peg being put through their ears.

Warts slowly disappear when rubbed with a green elder stick which is then buried in the ground to rot. It is recorded that at Waddesdon, Bucks., earlier this century, a young girl was seriously affected by warts on her hands. A neighbour secretly counted them, and without telling the girl, cut as many notches on an elder stick as there were warts and then buried the stick in the garden. As the stick decayed we are told the warts disappeared and the cure was complete.

Fevers were also cured by the 'rub with a stick and bury it' method, but there is a caution attached to this, for whoever digs the stick up will receive the fever!

In Ireland necklaces were made of nine sprigs of green elderberries (or a twig cut into nine pieces) and were worn by those needing a cure for epilepsy. Such necklaces were also worn by infants as an amulet during teething and elder was used in the blessing of babies.

FUNGUS

There is a type of fungus which grows on elder and elm which is purplish in colour. From its shape and the stories of the elder's association with Judas, this fungus is called 'Jew's Ear'. As well as being good to eat, it is used to treat throat troubles.

LEAVES

Elder leaves are used in both their fresh and dried forms. Gather them around midsummer, when they still hold the morning dew. Strip the leaves off the stalks, rejecting any damaged or insect-eaten ones, and if they are to be stored, dry them thoroughly in the sun. The juice of fresh elder leaves eases inflammations of the eyes, and if sniffed, clears a stuffy nose. It can also be used as a poultice for inflammations on the body.

Elder leaves are diuretic, expectorant and purgative, and care should be taken if they are used internally, for they are somewhat toxic and can cause nausea. To clean out the body and purify its fluids and blood, 6–8 leaves are chopped and boiled for 10 minutes. A small cup of the cooled liquid can be taken before lunch.

Leaves gathered from the elder on May-eve were thought best to heal wounds.

FLOWERS

Elder flowers are picked when fully open, preferably on the day of the full moon. They can be dried rapidly in the shade or used fresh from the tree. In days past elder flowers were pickled or salted for storing, or for use in health-giving culinary dishes where they were fried in batter.

Elder flowers are sudorific, diuretic, febrifuge and anti-rheumatic. They are also somewhat anodyne, in that they allay pain and have a cooling effect. Infusions of elder flowers were used to relieve many ailments: bronchial catarrh, bronchitis, eruptive fevers (scarlet fever, measles, etc.), rheumatism and gout. Elder-flower infusions were also used as inhalants to ease head-colds, a gargle for hoarseness and laryngitis, a soothing cleanser for conjunctivitis and as a compress for chilblains. They are a gentle laxative, a mild astringent and a gentle stimulant. At the first sign of a cold, a hot cupful of elder infusion, drunk before going to bed, will produce a heavy, cleansing sweat.

A volatile oil is distilled from elder flowers. This is valued for use in eye and skin lotions but is most often diluted to form elder flower water. This was much used by our great-great-grandmothers, when a bottle of it was part of every lady's toilette. It was regarded as 'Nature's gift to the complexion', whitening the skin and clearing freckles, soothing sunburn and tired or puffy eyes. Elder flower water was also used as a fixative in the making of cosmetics, creams and lotions, and its somewhat musty odour was said to improve with age.

Here is an old recipe for elder flower water:
Pick 5 cupfuls of elder blossoms when they are fully open but still fresh. Cut off the stalks and put the florets into a bowl and pour on 1¼ cups of boiling water. Cover and leave for two to three hours. Strain and pour into small bottles.

This needs to be kept in the fridge and will last no longer than two to three months. Here is a lotion for eyes:

To cool and clear tired and puffy eyes, mix 4 to 5 tablespoons of elder flower water and 1 tablespoon of witch hazel in a bowl. Well soak a couple of pads of cotton wool in the lotion, and place them on closed eyes for 10 minutes.

For elder flower tea:

Pour ½ pint (¼ litre) of boiling water onto 2 heaped teaspoons of dried flowers in a jug. Leave to infuse for 5 minutes and strain and drink, adding lemon for flavour.

This is good taken at bedtime for stuffiness, or at the first sign of a cold. It is also a good blood purifier.

To make skin soft and fair, use elder flowers in the bath. A small muslin bag filled with flowers (fresh or dried) can be submerged in the water during bathing.

Elder flowers add fragrance to wine and are reputedly good for the voice. The flower-buds can be eaten in salads and flowers were added to a 'posset' (a curdled milk drink) traditionally passed around in a large cup at christenings.

Elder flower ointment was used to heal horses of wounds in wars, and elder flower and honeysuckle were the ingredients of an ointment used to ease the discomfort of haemorrhoids.

As an alternative to aspirin, mix equal parts of lime flowers, chamomile and elder flowers, infuse them in a cup for 5 minutes and then drink. If legend be true, this mixture also helps you keep your youth.

BERRIES

The curative properties of elderberries are similar to the flowers, but weaker. They have an aperient, emetic and diuretic action, and were used considerably by our forefathers to cure rheumatism and syphilis. They are a natural laxative, for, according to Mrs Grieve's *Modern Herbal*, they 'promote all fluid secretions and natural evacuations of the body'. Alternatively, as a remedy for colic and diarrhoea, dried elderberries are made into a tea.

The berries should be picked preferably on the day of the full moon and should be dried slowly. An infusion of the fruit is good against headaches, colds, sciatica, dropsy, ravings, madness, melancholy, snake and dog bites. Green elderberries were used in an ointment for haemorrhoids by the London College of Surgeons and those with difficulties in sleeping were advised to have elderberries under their pillows so their sleep would be peaceful.

Hot elderberry wine promotes perspirations, and is good for relieving chills, influenza and asthma. From ancient days elderberry juice was simmered with sugar to form a syrupy drink called a 'Rob', which could be taken by the spoonful or diluted and drunk to ease bronchitis, 'flu, etc. Five pounds (2 kg) (20 cups) of fresh fruit were used, the juice simmered with 1 lb (450 g) (2 cups) of sugar until it had the thickness of honey. This can be bottled and stored, and if a long shelf-life is needed, the addition of a small amount of brandy before bottling will help.

ROOT

Like the bark, the elder root was also used for promoting vomiting and purging in cases of poisoning.

Warning: Only the English elder should be used, for the fresh root of the American elder is extremely poisonous. While this poison lessens with drying, it is not, especially where children are concerned, worth risking its use.

With the root of the English elder it is the second layer which is used, as with the bark.

MAGIC

IRISH/GAELIC   *Ruis*
OGHAM   ᚏ
RUNIC   ᛘ
RULING PLANET   Venus

ABILITIES	Regeneration. Cauldron of Rebirth. To do with the element of Earth.
SEASONS	Summer (early); Autumn (late)

Elder is a tree of country lanes and cottage gardens, and the Elder Mother protected such domains with her strong earth-energy. Elder is potent and there are warnings attached to its magical usage. It is always wise to ask permission of the Elder Mother before cutting or taking a piece of a tree, for she may follow and plague you, as she does those who use her with selfish intent.

In order to keep on the right side of the Elder Mother, devise a mental prayer of asking before you take what is needed. An old woodcutter's words run thus:

> *Owd Girl, give me of thy wood,*
> *An' I will give thee some of mine,*
> *When I become a tree.*

Elder was used as the wood of the pyre in cremations, and was also placed in the ground and the coffin at burials. It was anciently believed that wherever elder grew or rested was a sacred place, free from being despoiled.

In Ireland elder was used for handles in witches' broomsticks, and wreaths of elder twigs were woven as crowns and worn by witches at Samhain, to enhance their communications with the Otherworld and increase their ability to see the departed.

However, elder was also used against witches. Folkard, in *Plant Lore, Legends and Lyrics*, states that 'all the sorcerers and witches of the neighbourhood' are revealed if elder pith is sliced into flat circles, dipped in oil and lit like candles. For when floating in a dish of water they create reflections upon its surface. Similarly, in America it was said that an elder stick burned on Christmas night would reveal witches, and if a small twig of elder were cut, dipped in oil, lighted and floated on water, it would point to any witch present at a gathering.

Despite the artificially created distrust of the elder by the Church,

289

elder collected on St John's Eve (21 June) was nevertheless considered a protection on Twelfth Night (6 January), the day of the commemoration of the Massacre of the Innocents, when all male newborn babies were slaughtered on the orders of Herod.

The flowering time of elder gives it a powerful status in late spring and early summer, when its blossoms show the seductive beauty and fertility of Nature. Legend says that if we breathe deep of the blossoms' provocative perfume at midnight on Midsummer's Night, elder will 'open the portals to the faerie realms', and allow us sight of the faerie king and queen in their colourful, fleeting procession.

Elder blossoms attract and hold oil. They are used as a fixative for particular incenses which when used in meditation allow us to see clearly our goals in life in the patterns of the rising incense smoke.

The elder also helps us see dryads. When the moon is full, spend the night within a small grove of elder, 'properly prepared and with no evil in your heart', and await their appearance. Elderberry wine will also help, providing you don't overdo it!

To bless things, places or people, the leaves and berries of elder can be scattered to the four winds (east, south, west, north), preferably from the top of a high hill. Visualize and name whatever is to be blessed, then throw the leaves and berries (with as much ritual as you feel is needed) unto the directions, asking for blessing as you continue to visualize strongly. If possible, also scatter leaves and berries onto or around that which is blessed. This procedure can also be used to protect yourself from spells cast against you, by visualizing guardians or shields of protection at the four quarters (or directions) around you. In this instance elderberries especially protect against negativity and evil.

Pungent elder blossoms were traditionally used at weddings to bring good luck to the married pair. It was anciently believed that if a person was tempted to commit adultery they could carry an elder leaf to help them overcome temptation. Elder blossoms were used to bring good fortune to an unborn child, and in order to ensure a protected birth for both child and mother, pregnant women traditionally kissed an elder tree.

The elder is a feminine tree given generous qualities by its ruler Venus. It is used for protection, healing, exorcism and prosperity.

INSPIRATION

To sensitive people the elder is imbued with 'witchy' qualities and powers which deserve respect, for they are special. All growth of the elder tree was once considered sacred, for, like the Earth Mother herself, elder has been here since the beginning. It is an integral part of our flora and country magic, and, as we have seen, because of the great healing and support it has always given people, it has long been called the queen of herbs.

Ancient is elder's connection to humans. More ancient still is its connection with the earth upon which we live, which it protects and fulfils. Old and bent the elder may be, but its strength is formidable, reaching deep into the primeval and containing the stored wisdom of the ages.

The elder is most powerful when the old Celtic year ends and the new one begins at Samhain. It does not merely lead us to that point, but also conducts us through into the new year, providing many medicines and foods by which to survive the dark season of winter, until the sun again provides its warmth. This ability of the elder, to guide us through the darkness by making our days creative, may be the ancient reasoning behind the use of elder-shaped leaves in megalithic long-barrow burial mounds, to give the spirits of the departed the chance to remain creative for their new life to come, and also, because of the elder's great healing capacity, the chance to be born healthily into their new existence.

When the elder has been stripped of its fruit and its leaves begin to scatter to wintry winds, so its wizened character is displayed as its crazily-angled limbs are revealed. Then we see how aged is the species and our memories are stirred by by-gone days and the wild unkempt face of Nature, where man had little effective control. For of all our indigenous shrubs and trees, the elder most strongly retains the right to 'go its own way'.

The atmosphere around an elder seems to be 'held' by the tree, and as you move into it, it often seems as if you are entering a bubble, the surface of which can be receptive or repelling. At times you may slip through, almost as if you were awaited. At other times it feels as if a sort of password were needed to gain entrance into the elder's realm. Then, as you move around the plant, it is as though you are being examined by the tree's energy to see if you are suitable for admission. It is wise to check your intent before moving closer, for the legends of the Elder Mother cannot be ignored.

And yet because of such tangible precautions maintained by the tree, when it does accept you it bestows an honour upon you, and a responsibility, for the ancient wisdoms now await, the treasures of which will guide humanity into a better way of life. Such treasures cannot be wasted. Hence the elder's caution.

I call upon the Crone, Old Wisewoman, she who brings true vision. She is wise in the ways of all creatures and knows roots, herbs, all healing potions, whatever may be needed. She sees patterns and dreams in the glowing logs, in steam that rises from the Cauldron, and in quiet waters. She can foretell, forewarn and guide. In her, we see and understand; we bring the story to its rightful end; and we gain wisdom.

The above words of Rae Beth, taken from her book *Hedgewitch*, express the goddess of the waning moon and the waning year, when winter descends and long nights are spent around log fires. They also express the essence of the elder tree, the Wise Old Woman of the Hedgerows.

PHYSICAL USES

The elder is ancient in human history. Its hard close-grained wood was once used for fishing rods, and pith from the branches was sliced and used for floats. It was also used for shoemakers' pegs, instruments for mathematicians, combs and adult toys. Hollow elder sticks were blown through to encourage the burning of fires, and through such action elder was named *kindler* or *eller* by the Anglo-Saxons, which eventually became 'elder'. In country districts elder bellows are still known as 'pluffs'.

The *Sambucus* of elder's botanical name is supposedly derived from the 'sackbut', an ancient stringed musical instrument made from elder that accompanied the singing of psalms. Italian peasants have always used elder for musical pipes called *sampognas*. The hollow sticks of elder provide great fun for children, for they are easily adapted into whistles, pop-guns and blow-pipes. Pliny recorded that the best musical pipes were cut from the elder 'out of shot of cockcrow', i.e., away from areas of human population.

Pliny also recorded that the ancient Britons and Celts used elderberries, previously boiled in wine, as a black hair dye. As well as the berries, the bark, root and leaves of elder provide a full range of natural colours used to dye wool. The bark of elder branches and the root dye black, the leaves with alum dye green, and the berries dye blue and purple, and with alum, violet.

Elder in hedgerows or copses was believed to be a beneficial protection for livestock. Elder leaves were also valued by farmers for ridding granaries of mice and rats, for the smell of the leaves repelled such costly vermin. Bruised elder leaves also keep flies at bay and carters placed them at the back of the cart to keep flies off the horses. The drivers of hearses used elder leaves to keep the spirits of the dead at bay, as well as flies. Grown by the kitchen window elder attracts flies away from the kitchen, and elder leaves, made into an infusion, can be dabbed on the skin to keep midges and mosquitoes at bay when out in the country. A bruised leaf rubbed on the skin or worn in a hat will do likewise.

In the garden or home, any plants which suffer with mildew can be sprayed occasionally with a decoction of elder, which also protects them from aphid and insect attack. Fruit orchards were customarily sprayed with a decoction of elder leaves to cure blight in the trees.

If tender young elder shoots are picked in May (not the woody ones), the greenest can have their skins stripped off and can be pickled or boiled in salted water. They taste like spinach.

Elderberries can also be used in the making of soups, puddings, jellies, chutneys, drinks and wines. Elderberry wine, a tonic wine known as 'poor man's port', was once so popular that huge orchards of elder were maintained in Kent to obtain enough fruit for the population. Here is an old recipe for it:

Put ripe elderberries in a stone jar and place in an oven or hot water to thoroughly heat.

Squeeze and strain the berries, and to every quart (litre) of juice add 1 lb (450 g) (2 cups) of sugar.

Bring to the boil and skim the surface well, and when clear put into a cask.

To every 10 gallons (45½ litres) of wine add 1 ounce (25 g) (¼ cup) of Isinglass dissolved in cider, and 6 whole eggs. Close it up.

Let it stand for 6 months and then bottle.

A muslin bag of dried elder flowers can be added to jams and jellies when they are boiled in preparation, and this adds to their flavour. Elder flowers can also be made into delicious syrups. A health-giving tea can be made for children by plunging elder flower-heads into hot milk or water until the desired flavour is achieved.

These are just some of the many uses and recipes with regards to the generous elder.

POPLARS

BOTANICAL

Salicaceae. Deciduous.

While poplars are abundant in Europe, Britain has four main species, and of these the aspen and white poplar are said to be native. The black poplar was introduced long ago and the spire-like Lombardy poplar was brought by Lord Rochford in 1758 from its true home in the Himalayas. The grey poplar is a cross between aspen and white poplar.

Poplars are lovers of moist lowlands and valleys through which rivers run. All species of the poplar family are alike in that they never produce male and female flowers on the same tree, and they all protect their leaves from excesses of moisture.

The rapid growth of poplars begins a few days from the seed settling into the ground. In their first season black and white poplars reach a foot (30 cm) in height and in 40 years will have topped 100 feet (30 metres). The growth of aspen is not so rapid and of all the poplars it remains the daintiest, as shown in the illustration. The larger, quicker growing trees are planted where quick screening is required for sight or wind breaks and their distinctively tall spires can be seen lining old avenues on many a rise.

The roots of poplars have the same mantle of fungus as the beech, and the trees gain the same advantages.

ASPEN
Populus tremula. Deciduous.

Aspens are rarely still, for their leaves tremble at the slightest movement of air. They are intolerant of the shade of other trees and are often found growing in open fields, at the edges of damp woods, or on heaths, moors and mountains. Aspens reach heights of 60–70 feet (18–21 metres) and are common in the north of Scotland.

Cattle, deer and goats love to eat aspen leaves and will often almost strip a young tree. Older trees attract rabbits and small animals by providing food from the suckers which grow through the grass at their base. In autumn aspen leaves turn from green to red and then to beautiful golden yellows. The trees shimmer with colourful radiance.

Aspen is not long-lived, for its heart-wood starts decaying after some 50 to 60 years.

BARK
Aspens have thin grey bark, with smooth branches and twigs. In time their lower trunks may go dark and somewhat ridged, but the upper tree always remains light.

FLOWERS

In order that the tree's leaves do not stop pollination of its flowers by the wind, aspens flower before they leaf. Their catkin-flowers look like big furry caterpillars. The male catkins contain bunches of tiny stamens with purply-red heads, which are surrounded by a mass of grey fluffy down. They are on an axis, and are wound around with many layers of fringed scales and anther-bearing bracts. As the stamens push forward the catkins look red and when the anthers open they release clouds of pollen which is taken on the wind to female flowers.

The female catkins look similar to the males but contain no stamens. The seed vessels inside the down are like small peas, giving the catkins a distinctly green look. Fertilization occurs by May, when the ovaries become dry capsules and split in two lengthwise. These halves of the capsule then roll back to reveal silvery hairs to which are attached tiny black seeds. These hairs become masses of white fluff and are taken away by degrees on the wind, scattering the tree's seed in the process.

LEAVES

When aspen leaves appear from their brown sticky buds, the trees come alive with movement and sound. Aspen leaves are heart-shaped and dainty. Their very long stalks are unable to hold the leaves upright, for they are flattened in a direction at right angles to the blade of the leaf. This causes the incessant

The leaves of the aspen (left), the black poplar (top) and the white poplar (right)

movement of the leaves. The leaves which grow on shoots at the base of aspens have shorter stalks and longer blades than those of the branches above.

Aspen leaves are waterproof. At the bottom of each blade there are two minute cups lined with resin which catch and absorb moisture. As the resin protects the epidermis, aspens can safely obtain moisture from the atmosphere. Correct water balance is important to the tree, and a biological explanation of its leaf-movement shows that this may be its way of evaporating off excess moisture. It also ensures the tree takes in vast amounts of light. The only time a leafing aspen is truly still is at the brooding of a storm, when the light is cut and rain is in the air.

THE WHITE POPLAR
Populus alba. Deciduous.

The white poplar is not a common tree. It is found mainly in southern Britain, where it attains good heights. It is a tall tree with a light grey trunk.

Its green leaves have distinct silvery-white hairs underneath, which keep out the damp. When moved by the wind it is a visual delight, for when the upper and under leaves are presented, their shift in colour from green to silver appears from a distance as rippling waves. White poplar leaves are deeply toothed and can be almost five-lobed. The catkins are furry and tinged with red.

THE BLACK POPLAR
Populus nigra. Deciduous.

The black poplar is tall, with deeply furrowed almost black bark and branches which bend somewhat downwards. Its leaves are green on both sides and are of a definitive ace of spades shape. When the tree sheds its leaves it also sheds pieces of twig still attached to their base. Black poplar leaf-buds are pointed and very sticky, for they are heavily coated with a scented balsam which waterproofs the leaves. This balsam also attracts bees, especially when the tree is flowering with its brilliant red catkins.

CUSTOM & LEGEND

ASPEN

Aspen, the smallest member of the poplar family, is also known as the 'trembling', 'shaking' or 'quivering tree', for its leaves and branches move continuously upon the slightest of breezes. Because of its rustling leaves it is also called the 'whispering tree'. In ancient days the wind was regarded as a messenger of the gods and anything closely attuned to it, like the aspen, was considered sacred.

Golden crowns of aspen leaves were found in burial mounds in Mesopotamia, dating from circa 3,000 BC. In legend crowns of poplar leaves were not only worn by heroes, but also allowed heroes to visit the Underworld and return. This may explain why aspen crowns were placed in burial mounds, to enable the spirits of the dead to be safely reborn.

Church propaganda stated that aspen trembled because it still shuddered at the memory of when its wood was used in the crucifixion. However the tree is potently pagan, offering communication and entrance into the faerie realms for mortals. The traditional explanation of its trembling is that aspen has the acutest hearing of all trees, and that it moves continuously because of what it hears from afar.

WHITE POPLAR

According to legend white poplar gained its special leaf colouring from Hercules, for he made himself a crown from poplar leaves after killing the evil giant Cacus. Hercules then wore this crown into the Underworld, where the tops of the leaves were scorched with heat and the undersides were silvered by the hero's radiance.

In the *Odyssey* the white poplar was one of the Three Trees of Resurrection, the other two being alder and cypress. The white poplar and the aspen are sacred to Persephone, the goddess of regeneration, who was reputed to have a grove of poplars in the land of the sunset in the West.

According to Greek legend Persephone was abducted by Pluto, lord

299

of the dead, who took her to his region of the Underworld. Persephone's mother Demeter mourned her daughter and searched the earth for her. On finding where she was, Demeter vowed that no seed would grow until the god returned her daughter to her.

Because the earth now lay bare and barren Zeus commanded Pluto to return Persephone to the upperworld, and decreed that she should live with Demeter for two thirds of each year and return for one third to Pluto in the Underworld. From this the seasons of agricultural growth were formed, and seeds and plants flourished until each season of winter, when the goddess returned to the Underworld and the earth became dormant.

BLACK POPLAR

The black poplar is sacred to the death-goddess Hecate. In country tradition a lamb's tail was buried under every newly planted poplar tree at lamb-docking time, as a sacrifice to the goddess of death.

The black poplar almost 'weeps' with sticky balsam, a resinous oily substance, the origins of which are explained in the following Greek legend. Phaethon was a son of Helios, god of the sun. With his sisters, the seven Heliades, he pestered his father to let him drive the chariot of the sun across the heavens for one day. Helios was very reluctant but eventually agreed. However Phaethon very quickly realized it was not such an easy task, and soon the strength of the horses which pulled the chariot far outweighed his own and they went careering off course, taking the sun so close to the earth that it almost caught on fire.

Zeus was enraged at such stupidity, and he killed Phaethon with a flash of lightning and hurled him into the river Eridanus. Phaethon's sisters, who had helped him convince Helios and had harnessed the horses to the chariot for the fateful ride, watched their brother die as a result. So bitter was their weeping upon the banks of the river that the gods found compassion for them, changing them into poplar trees and their tears to amber. When looking at poplars today, the strong impression of 'amber tears' (formed by oozing balsam as it collects on the bark in teardrop shapes), lends conviction to this ancient legend.

HEALING

The Bach Flower Remedies recommend aspen for the healing of fears: fear of darkness, of death, of the religious, of secrets and unknown causes, and of fear itself. It also alleviates apprehension through fear, dealing also with brain storms, delusions, nightmares, mental fears and vague, unreasoning fears.

Contact with an aspen tree gives us a special sense of endurance, which allows us to face harsh realities in life with the ability to endure and conquer. Anciently aspen was called a shield tree, not only for the fact that shields were made from it, but also because it shields a person on spiritual levels from the all-consuming darkness associated with fear. Meditation with the aspen allows us to focus on the light and move ever closer to it.

An ointment made from black poplar-buds and their sticky balsam is good for treating bruises, inflammations and gout. White poplar was used to cure leprosy.

On a deeper healing level, because white and black poplars are ruled by Saturn, we can use them constructively to help us through a stage of life known astrologically as the 'Saturn return'. This is the time when Saturn is once more in the same position as in our natal charts, having taken 30 years to complete its orbit around the sun. Then, with its full power once more concentrated upon us, Saturn questions our very foundation, and in doing so can cause deep psychological disturbances.

So let us look at Saturn and the ways in which we feel its effects. The concrete, practical, everyday facts of life are under the influence of this large planet. Its action is slow, thorough and inevitable, extracting a strict justice that demands full payment for all it bestows. It is known as a planet of limitation, for in its negative sense, its qualities of concentration, solidity and reliability are felt as burdens of heavy responsibility. Thus if we are not careful or strong, an atmosphere of despondency begins to affect everything, causing psychological disturbances which force us to question our own beings in comparison to what we have created so far in this lifetime.

301

If we view our bodies as deep wells of emotion and memory, and Saturn as the deepest primordial foundation of that well, it is inevitable that the slightest shift or renewed intensity of that foundation will cause movement in what is contained within the well. This not only causes ripples on the surface, but also stirs up sediment which has settled to the bottom. This sediment is made up of many things: that which was set there at birth (which may contain past-life memories, our primeval genealogies and our ongoing karmic debts); and that which we have set there since birth (our subconscious desires, our primeval memories, our unhandled emotions, our pains, fears, the things we'd rather forget, etc.). Thus as the well reacts and its waters move and stir and swirl, the subconscious sediment rising to the surface puts into question our conscious worlds, our positions in life, our life-styles, material values, relationships, etc.

Understanding of such an inevitable process helps us cope with it, allowing us to see how within it we can re-evaluate and act sensibly, rather than being impelled into courses of senseless reactions which increase negative effects. Through contact with poplar trees (as explained in Magic, see p.304) it is possible to come to terms with the reasons and effects of the Saturn return, for through the aspen and the white and black poplar we can contact our young, middle-aged and old selves, out-stripping the limits of time.

The trees also absorb our fears and this can be utilized during meditation or healing work. When our fears have dissipated, the trees then fill us with new vitalizing energy. You have simply to ask a tree for help, accepting fully that on its own levels it can see, hear, understand and perform, no matter how crazy that seems. The idea is to suspend your disbelief; not necessarily 'believing', but rather accepting that it is possible. For then it can become so.

MAGIC

IRISH/GAELIC	*Eadha*
OGHAM	≢
RUNIC	√
RULING PLANETS	Mercury (aspen); Saturn (white and black poplars)
ABILITIES	(Poplars) Cycles of time. Incenses. To do with the element of Water. (Aspen) Eloquence. Psychic gifts from the winds. Aid to rebirth. Prevention of illness. To do with the element of Air.
SEASONS	Autumn; Winter

All the poplars possess three attributes: the ability to shield and resist; an association with speech and language; and an affinity with the wind. Their most powerful time is in the autumn, because of their strong visual associations with the moon and water (white and black poplars), and the beauty of their autumn foliage (especially shown by the aspen). For their divinatory qualities they are used in incenses, especially the balsam collected from their trunks, buds and leaves. They were anciently used in this way at Samhain, when it was thought essential to cast off old fears and outworn things in order to move correctly into the new year.

According to traditional recipes, poplar leaves and buds were added to 'flying ointments' which help induce the correct atmosphere for the practice of astral projection. The five-pointed leaf of the white poplar was especially venerated by French witches during the Middle Ages for this. We are led to believe they smeared the ointment over their bodies before flying through the night sky on broomsticks. A less messy way of obtaining similar results is to use leaves or balsam freshly taken from the trees and to place or smear them on specific parts of the body prior to ritual or meditation.

Poplar leaves and buds were also used in money spells, for poplars were always believed to bring good luck in the monetary sense.

The goddesses associated with poplars are also goddesses of the moon. In this lunar connection poplars symbolize and illustrate three phases of the moon. The small and dainty aspen epitomizes the young virginal goddess, the new moon, light and airy with a radiant sparkle full of promise. The luxuriantly foliaged white poplar reflects the fertile woman, the light of the full moon shown in the silvery colour of its ever-moving underleaves. The black poplar, oozing resin, almost visually draws in the light surrounding it. Its dark appearance epitomizes the dark time of the moon, the old crone drawing all unto her.

Any lunar magic worked with these aspects of the trees is very strong, especially as the trees themselves are so visually exacting, and as the larger poplars are ruled over by Saturn, a heavy stamp of authority prevails. If such magic is worked, especially in the dark of the moon, it is advised that true intent is fully realized before any ritual, for such is the power evoked that if your spell should by chance return unto you, you could receive many times what you sent out, and if your intention was to harm others from jealousy, hate, anger, etc., you could deliver yourself a bad time. If we sow thistles, we cannot expect to reap roses.

The aspen is ruled by Mercury. Its special qualities are associated with the element of air upon which it never ceases moving. As it is a tree which prefers to grow apart from other trees, it is ideal for walking or dancing around, or for sitting under for meditational purposes. Aspen's lonely situation has done much over the years to facilitate legends of people disappearing from under it into the land of faerie, as has also its 'whispering' leaves which lull you into a trance-like state. Placing an aspen leaf under the tongue reputedly bestows eloquence, a gift usually given by the faerie queen.

The aspen tree was used extensively by the Celts to make protective shields. On magical levels it protects against theft, shielding not only you but also your possessions from the attentions of others. For such reasons people were advised to plant aspens near their homes and no doubt throughout the centuries many a treasure-trove would have been marked and protected by the planting of an aspen tree. Any spell of protection is enhanced by the use of aspen. Pieces of its wood, or a branch, twig or leaf can be strategically placed over treasures, or carried to protect projects, ideas, creations, etc.

On a romantic level aspen as a shield tree was deemed sacred to heroes. And while it grows apart from other trees and most often from humans, it does encourage the company of animals, providing browsing material with its many suckers which grow at ground level. These points make it an excellent tree to be near when contemplating the shamanic arts, for the movement and spirit of animals and plants are integral to the shaman's understanding of the world.

Through contact with the aspen and other poplars we receive great visions which we can use to enrich our lives in a spiritual sense. The movement of the trees' leaves induces a mesmeric effect upon the senses which subtly dismisses the outside world from our attention. Through this we can bring our minds into focus on different levels, where perhaps the solid forms of things fade, and we begin to see things as energy or spirit, sparkling and pulsing with life. Such an atmosphere is seen at dawn or dusk, the magical times of day when we are subtly bound by Nature into her enchantment. At these times we heal, cocooned in her misty veil which washes us clean of worldly stress.

INSPIRATION

Poplar trees have always captured the imaginations of artists, their tall graceful lines and ever-moving leaves enticing the senses to creativity. Renoir, Pissarro and Monet spent much of their lives in the poplar forests of France, capturing the mesmeric beauty of the trees upon canvas, using the portals to inspirational realms.

It is recorded that in ancient days the flashing effects of moving poplar leaves conveyed the passage of time to people, for the alternation of light and dark was seen to resemble the interchanges of day and night, summer and winter.

In ancient Greece the god of time was Cronos. He is pictured as an old man carrying a scythe – Old Father Time or the Grim Reaper. Cronos was the youngest of the Titans, a son of Uranus and Ge (heaven and earth). He was the father of Hestia, Demeter, Hera, Hades, Poseidon and Zeus, by the great goddess Rhea. Cronos eventually dethroned his father Uranus and took over the government of the world, as his son Zeus was to dethrone him in his turn. He was named Saturnus by the Romans and the planet Saturn, as already discussed, is associated with large cycles of time and with poplar trees. Powerful moon magic is also associated with poplars, and as this works within smaller time cycles (moons or months), it can be an excellent aid to our deeper understanding of larger time cycles (years and aeons). The flashing scythe of the Reaper cuts away all that is outworn, making room for new growth. So he shows us that from death comes life in a continual cycle.

Cronos was also a raven god and his myths were paralleled in Britain by those of Bran (see p.250). These two fatherly gods were considered great rulers of Golden Ages on earth, when an earthly paradise was achieved by the acknowledgement of the unity of life as a Whole. However the Golden Ages crumbled as divisionary religions and politics arose, for through intellectual aggression mankind came to see itself as master of time, dominating the earth. This has reaped nothing but ecological disaster and a severe loneliness within us, far removed from earthly paradise.

So how do we get back what has been lost? How do we regain paradise? Many religions and beliefs take us close, yet it is only through acknowledging ourselves as part of Nature that we discover life's blueprint into which we fit as part of the Whole. Then we are supported by the universe, for we move in time to its rhythm. We are part of it, not superior. Nothing is superior. It just is. This does not mean we are no longer individuals, quite the reverse. For by stopping the fight to force our pattern upon things we are released from that stress, and we free energy within us with which to find our true identities and our individual ways of expressing the life-force, our talents, love-making, creations, communications, work and play, etc.

Communication with the natural world opens up our memory. We realize the things we have forgotten and become strong through recognition of our ancient selves. It has been stated many times throughout this book that different species of tree allow us to touch different aspects of ourselves, through communication with the corresponding aspect in the natural world. One way the poplar trees do this is by the movement of their leaves, for as we look at their shifting, do we not remember ancient times, of tides and cosmic cycles filled with urgent whisperings? And as the aspen weaves its spell, its sparkling energy lends us faerie eyes, and we see the veils we've erected between ourselves and other realms through our lack of understanding. These realms are within us as well as within the world, and as we acknowledge them by using their doorways in Nature, the veils fall away and we step through, reinstating ourselves as an integral part of the Whole.

PHYSICAL USES

Poplar timber is of little value for it is a light wood. Aspen's wood, very soft and beautifully white, is ideal, however, for carving and sculpting. Crossing aspen with white poplar produced the grey poplar, which gives much stronger wood, which was used for a range of objects from silk rollers to sturdy barn-doors.

As white poplar wood does not splinter or catch fire easily, it was often used for floorboards in houses.

On water poplar wood is very buoyant, and for this reason it was made into oars and paddles. *Ebadh*, the Irish for 'aspen', translates as 'most buoyant of wood'.

The Greek for aspen is *aspis*, which means 'shield'. As already mentioned, poplar wood was used for shields, and to the Celts the art of shield-making was very important and sacred, for a shield was imbued by the will or intent of the maker in order to protect the user from injury and death.

In many European countries a poplar tree was planted at the birth of a daughter to provide a dowry for her when she came of age to marry.

As a symbol of hope the aspen was used by ancient Irish coffin-makers, being made into a *fe*, the measuring-rod used on corpses.

In times of scarcity cattle were fed on hand-gathered aspen leaves.

CONCLUSION

The greatest evolution is by example.

WALLY HOPE, STONEHENGE VISIONARY, 1946–75

In ancient times Britain was known as a place of initiation and learning, where the qualities of the natural world not only sustained the people, but gave them a foundation upon which the structure of daily life was formed according to season. By acknowledging themselves as part of Nature they found inspiration, fulfilment and a sense of security, for they were attuned to the earth and its rhythms.

Today such a relationship is almost forgotten, for communication between people seems hard enough, let alone communing with Nature. We are all too busy in a world which has substituted roads for woodland and supermarkets for gardens. Instead of growing food we must find money to buy food, and then a house or room to eat the food in, a car to drive to the shops, etc., so we are caught in a chain of events (or a web of our making) which takes us even further from source. And while it is impossible to return fully to what once was in a world so different from yesteryear, it is to be hoped that visions of the future are founded on wisdoms of the past, lest our roots shrivel and our isolation becomes complete. There is still time to make wise choices and this is what this book is about, revealing the old ways through the memories of trees in order to sustain the future.

The memories of trees are ancient. They show what was and what can be, giving us ecologically sound advice. When compiling this book I've many times been drawn to wild natural places to experience things as of old, testing in a way the truth of revelation. In these places we become attuned to Spirit and the strength of the land's soul, for within them our ancestors gave reverence to the natural world through deification of the vitality of life, forming a bond which gave meaning to existence. Thus they are essential places, holding the essence of our relationship with Nature.

They are, however, now severely at risk, open to desecration in the so-called name of progress, their unique properties ignored as man and machine determine to control and alter the precious balance of the land. Yet we need them to survive, for by holding the memories of what we were and the seed of what we will be, they form our identity as individuals and a race. Hence the conclusion to this book is dedicated to saving what remains of our trees and countryside, for as the land is covered in tarmac and concrete its essence dies, and so little by little do we.

The greatest adversary in these matters is politics, its ideals sacrificing our individuality by crushing Spirit and laying waste anything that will not settle into conformity, be it people, trees, hillsides, woodland or whatever. While society has been blinded by miasmas of words and rules, heritage has been packaged for tourist admission, and the future of the natural world is judged only on its money-making merits. Anyone who questions this is scapegoated, their protestations ridiculed with a surface image of law and order overcoming chaos. Very few people are told the real facts.

Research into the ages of mankind has verified that the hunter-gatherers gave greatest respect to the land, for they were aware of how the earth sustained them. And while modern living bears little resemblance to those early times, a resurgence of that initial awareness is moving people to defend the earth.

Biological considerations are fundamental to our evolution as a species and many people are now willing to live on the bare earth in order to protect it. In the following quote from Ru, a young ecological protester who lived in a holly tree to prevent it being cut down for the sake of a bypass, we are shown the dichotomy of the present situation:

> Living in a holly tree for three months in the spring of 1994 gave me time to actually see the importance of this symbiotic

relationship with Nature on a personal level. Direct action involving 'criminal' damage and active protestation are important to any ecological campaign at present, yet this aspect clashes with the needs of the trees to be protected. The political times that we live in dictate this divergence of forms of protest and thus can be seen to be slowing down mankind's evolution.

The holly tree taught me, simply through extended proximities, how this form of internal divide and rule could be bypassed (begging your pardons) by simply being in a relationship with her until the time came for the men with chainsaws to cut her down. She did not suffer the behavioural disorders that the proposed M11 link road obviously endorsed, by its being basically a human argument. So rather than working tree magic, I became the tree's magic, until the final 'mistake' in the second week of June, when the paid sun heroes arrived to evict. A week later the holly king arrived to take the year, like a child, into winter.

Many questions arise from our present situation, for who has the right to declare that Spirit is only touched by the rich, or that the earth is sacrificed to man's greed? What type of politics beats women with children who try to meet friends at traditional celebratory places, or those who question the necessity of roads and supermarket villages in a society where the unheeded majority live just above starvation level and old people die of hyperthermia for fear of high heating bills? What Christian values determine that this should be so?

The terms 'heaven' and 'hell' do not refer to places we may ultimately go to after life. If they have any relevance it must surely be that we will create these conditions *in* life, while still on earth. Heaven was given us in the form of the natural world. We have only to respect it as so and it will continue. Hell is created from lack of respect, from division and destruction, from man thinking he is conqueror of the earth rather than partner to it. It comes from the death of species upon species of life until our isolation is complete, and is the result of the lack of compassion in the world of today.

This book was created to move us away from isolation, for it reveals our earth 'family', where all living things are related to us and interaction is the most natural thing in the world. It shows us not to be afraid, for the way to true evolution is through communication and understanding. It comes through respect and is based in reality, casting out fear and superstition. As Wally Hope says, 'The greatest evolution is by example.' It is by our waking up to understand that the earth comes first, for it is our home and provider of life. It is by accepting that we are but one species of a vast array of life-forms and that we do not rule. It is by acknowledging that we are utterly dependent upon the other forms that dwell beside us and the communication that we open up with them. Closest to us are the animals, then come the trees. They await communication and are willing to share their magic, for it is the key to our identity and the future of the earth.

Good Luck and Blessed Be.
Glastonbury 1995

ARBOREAL

This short appendix illustrates trees as life-forms and explains how they function.

TREE RINGS

The history of a tree is recorded in its annual 'rings' of growth, formed inside the trunk by the growing wood of the tree. Growth comes from a series of movements, for no plant is still as it constantly seeks water, food and support. In this search plants actually show intent. All the outside influences a tree experiences is recorded in its rings. They can be seen quite clearly when a tree has been felled and the wood is cross-sectioned, for they radiate outwards in concentric circles from the centre of the trunk. The central part of the tree is the original sapling around which the trunk has grown. Last year's ring is on the outer edge of the trunk, just below the bark.

The art of interpreting tree rings is called 'dendrochronology'. This informs us of many things: the age of the tree; the sun-rain ratio of certain years of its life; the times when trees were crowded and had to fight for space; the years of heavy forest fires; the interference of man or other pests, etc. In this way very old trees preserved in peat bogs reveal a wealth of information about conditions of the past and have helped us understand the full history of the land.

To find the approximate age of a living tree, rather than cutting it down to count its rings, measure its girth at about 5 feet (1½ metres) from the ground, and allow 1 year for each inch (2½ cm) of girth. Thus a tree measuring 10 feet (3 metres) round will be approximately 120 years old (for there are 120 inches in 10 feet); and a tree of 12 inches (30 cm) girth would be approximately 12 years old, etc. Measuring at such a height gives a truer indication of the tree's annual growth, for some trees grow extra width at the base for support in directional winds, to lessen the great strain put on the tree by the pull of its top branches. When doing this, broadleaf trees tend to gain extra base on the windward side and conifers on the side which is sheltered. The lower branches are also built up for wind-bracing strength: the broadleaved trees on the upper side of the branch and the conifers on the under.

In construction the fibres of wood are wrapped in spirals. This gives wood great strength and resistance to tearing. As a tree grows upwards it also thickens to support its extra weight. It does this by forming a ring of growth just under the bark on the outer part of the tree. Sap and water channels, which enable the tree to feed, are also just under the surface of the bark.

The middle of the tree, the original sapling, is considered dead. It is the oldest part of the tree, constantly surrounded by a thickening layer of newer wood. Having died, the middle-wood grows very hard. It provides the tree with a 'backbone' which is virtually incorruptible, so long as the newer wood remains strong and healthy and keeps it sealed from the air. Once exposed, the middle-wood rots away and hollow trees form. Yew trees provide great examples of this, for their flaky unprotective barks allow air to enter the trees and the middle-wood to deteriorate. In the case of oak, whose bark is very strong, the precious middle-wood is penetrated by wood-burrowing insects. However hollow trees can remain strong and upright, providing shelter for many forms of life. They have always been a favourite for children to play in.

TREE BARK

If you scratch the bark of a living tree you'll reveal a thin layer of green which is called the 'cambium layer'. The cambium layer is vital, for all the new wood of the tree is made by it and through it the tree feeds. If a damaging ring is cut around a tree it will not be able to feed and will die. This is why foresters are the enemies of animals which feed off tree's bark, for they 'ring' the trees at their head's height and below, thereby killing them.

The cambium layer is very complex, for it does a lot of things at once. It creates new wood cells on its inner side, which thickens the trunk of the tree, and in doing this has to grow itself, in order to encompass the increase taking place inside it. At the same time, it must also add to the inner bark of the tree so that does not split.

The cambium layer also contains all the functions of the tree's circulatory system (its sap and water systems), for the sap goes up the new wood and comes down inside the tree's inner bark. The cellular structure of a tree makes it possible for its roots to push water up it, rather like a water-pump, and for its leaves to aid this process by also drawing water up. As this happens in the new wood being made in that year, it is vital that nothing stops the flow or poisons it, as happens with certain fungi and pesticides.

TREE ROOTS

The first and main root of a tree or plant is put out from the germinating seed. This is called the tap-root and through it the plant 'plugs into' food supplies in the earth. Once the tap-root is established the tree then concentrates on the topsoil, which is richest in organic matter, by forming feeding roots, which can be found within 6 inches (15 cm) from the surface of the earth. Trees such as beech, poplars and spruces rarely root deeply, but firs, oaks and pines extend their tap-roots for several years.

Unfortunately this makes them harder to transplant, for the tap-root must be complete and undamaged if a tree is to grow healthily.

The roots of trees have a relationship with the soil which is chemical as well as physical. The active function of the constantly growing roots is to collect supplies for the tree. To do this they exude chemicals which dissolve the required elements in the soil into a gelatinous substance. Water is the solvent which carries these elements from the tree's roots to its leaves. The water then evaporates and falls back to earth, to take part once more in the chain of life. When the ground is dry, a tree's roots continually search the earth for water. On a hot day a single birch tree will absorb about 400 quarts (400 litres) of water, which it returns to the air as cooling moisture through its leaves. As the cells of the searching roots are worn out by contact with rough objects like stones in the earth, they are replaced with new ones, and when they reach nourishment a transformation occurs, for the burrowing cells of the roots are replaced by cells designed to dissolve mineral salts, which enables them to be passed as substance from cell to cell up the tree.

The roots of certain trees have aid from specific types of fungi, through which they increase their capacity to absorb more water and minerals from the soil. As if in payment for this increased efficiency, the fungi feed on the tree's sugars and carbohydrates, which in turn allows them greater capacity to aid the tree. These allies of the tree live in close association with it and are often seen to be characteristic of certain trees. For example, truffles grow with oaks, and fly agaric flourish in birch and beech woods. The main enemy of partnerships between fungi and trees is alkaline soil, which is fatal. However, the forest floor provides a continuous life-giving process, as dead plant and animal matter go back into the soil. Leaf mould also gives life to the soil through decay, returning what the tree took for nourishment. Thus from the death and decay of organic matter comes abundant life in the form of enriching bacteria and mould.

Tree roots are opportunists, going where feeding is best. They forage for elements and water whilst anchoring the tree to the ground. Roots can drown in too much water, so trees also keep tapped into drier soil to maintain their oxygen intake. Root growth is constant and stops only in severe freezing weather. The shape of a tree's root system is more reliant on the type of soil in which it lives than on the type of tree it is. As the crown of the tree spreads, so do the roots beneath it and their spread can become much wider than the crown.

Most of the roots' activity is seen where the shape of the tree allows water to fall to earth. This is called the 'drip-line'. It provides continuity to the water-cycle, for roots draw water up from the earth into the tree, from where it falls as moisture, through its leaves, to earth again. This cycle is shown to great effect in the rain-forests of the world, and is the necessity of life, for water is the cleanser and replenisher.

REPRODUCTION

Some 500 years before Christ, Herodotus reported that the Babylonians distinguished two sorts of palm tree and that they sprinkled pollen from one flower onto another to secure the production of fruit. Yet for many reasons, it wasn't until the seventeenth century that it became open knowledge that plants were sexual creatures with reproductive organs and a sex life, for this raised views which questioned orthodox religious dogma by acknowledging that the plant world was not merely mechanical matter and that plants did live some sort of 'realized' life, a point well recognized in pre-Christian days.

In ancient times it was observed that like women and female animals, the female flowers of trees exude a powerful and seductive odour when they are ready for 'mating', which attracts insect and bird life to them in order to help pollination. Likewise, the pollen of male flowers has an odour similar to the semen of men and male animals, and it acts in the same way, entering the folds of the female flower's 'vulva' and travelling the length of its 'vagina' until it enters the ovary and makes contact with the ovule. Once the male pollen has been transferred to the female flower by the wind or insects, most of this action is guided by the female ovary, for it is quite often surrounded by sweetened secretions which in some way attract fertilizing pollen to it.

PHOTOSYNTHESIS

This is the building up of complex compounds by the chlorophyll appa-ratus of plants by means of the energy of light. Plants synthesize their bulky weight from air and soil and sunlight, and they are quite inventive in tracking down their needs. For instance, plants that couldn't obtain nitrogen out of the earth in which they lived (i.e., swamp plants) evolved as a species and became meat eaters, capturing small mammals or insects and obtaining nitrogen from digesting them. A good example of this is the fly-trap species.

Trees create breathable air for human and animal life, for on the under-surface of every leaf there are pores which take in carbon-dioxide from the atmosphere and expel oxygen. They've also developed many protective devices, such as hard barks, thorns, bitter tastes, gummy secretions and tannins. Tannins especially are able to be released in high proportions by the trees when insects breed and lay eggs. Sadly the trees have not created protection to put off humans!

Scientific recordings show that plant and tree cycles correspond to influences of the sun and moon, and it's known that trees, like all living things, contain electro-magnetic energy. Kirlian photography shows a tree's electrical field as an aura surrounding the tree. This aura looks like millions of tiny points of light or rays of energy, which especially emanate out of the leaves at the ends of the branches. Monitoring of this shows a daily peaking time at midday. Then it is at its largest and strongest. It is at its smallest during the night. From this daily rhythm the plant grows.

It has also been confirmed, by the study of the rings of fir trees, that their pointed shapes and the sharpness of their needles act as lightning conductors, and that annual growth patterns correlate with periods of sun-spot and high aurora activity. This may explain the ancient tradition of hanging bright pieces of metal onto fruit trees in order to facilitate growth and good harvest.

Broadleaf trees now dominate the earth. They stem back to when the earth was tropical in its climate and are the original flower bearers.

All our herbaceous plants had tree ancestors in the ancient tropical forests. Conifers were the original dominant species, but broadleaves overtook them because the structure of their wood allows a freer and stronger flow of sap for circulation. They also have leaves instead of needles, which enables them to evaporate more water and photosynthesize quicker, getting more value from the sun. To survive the changing climate when the tropical gave way to colder weather, broadleaf trees became deciduous, and because they flowered, their pollination was aided by insects, rather than relying on the wind. Insect pollination gives a tree good advantage, in that the trees of a species need not live closely together. This allows for a greater spread of the species on the land.

Now that we understand the trees a little better, let's walk across the fields to our woodlands, taking in along the way the wealth of life contained in the hedgerows.

HEDGEROWS

As guardians of fields and meadows, hedgerows hold history within their bounds. In Celtic times long strips of land were cleared for agricultural purposes and over the centuries these became the square or rectangular fields of today, now sadly diminished in number as roads, supermarkets and housing estates claim the land. Yet in rural areas many remaining hedgerows are hundreds of years old and they are rich havens of Nature which have flourished with the aid of man.

In Britain the birth of countless hedgerows came as the peasantry was pushed from the land when the eighteenth-century enclosures took place. To create the miles of hedgerow needed to fence the fields, millions of seeds were taken from hawthorn trees, the favourite tree of the country people. From these seeds saplings were quickly raised, which were planted to form mile upon mile of hawthorn hedging. Hawthorn, by its very growth and prickliness, is excellent at enforcing boundaries and its ability to survive continual cutting back meant that thick protective hedges were quickly established.

Ecologically hedgerows are very important, for they give food and shelter to a myriad forms of life, as birds, insects, plants and mammals live around and within them. A well-formed hedge consists of closely planted bushes or small trees and is usually on a bank so that excess water can run into a ditch or stream at its foot. Hedgerow banks are good for burrowing animals and the not-too-wet state of the underhedge is ideal for snakes, small mammals, hedgehogs, hares and rabbits, providing them with shelter, food and a place to breed and hibernate.

A hedgerow matures with age and becomes rich in its variety of flora and fauna. To roughly date a hedgerow, estimate the number of woody plant species contained in about 20 paces, and for each established species present count 100 years. The most prolific woody plants and indigenous trees of the hedgerows are: hawthorn, honeysuckle, wild clematis, blackthorn, elder, crab-apple, bramble, spindleberry, elm, willow, hazel, ash, oak, old man's beard, ivy, holly, field maple, box and privet. Different areas of countryside establish their own predominants. Plants of the hedgerows are: grasses, ferns, meadowsweet, nettles, 'lords and ladies', nightshade, primrose, violet, snowdrop, various form of dandelion, comfrey and a mass of other herbs.

WOODLAND

Now we've reached our woodland. To understand how much it meant to our ancestors, here is an excellent quote on the value of trees and their 'characteristic English country beauty' from H. J. Massingham, in his book entitled *The English Countryman*. This was published in 1943, when the land was being stripped for 'agrinomics', a system which viewed groves, copses and hedgerow timber as nuisances. The quoted words are those of Lord Lymington, who pointed out that English woodlands are widely distributed, and are indissolubly related to arable and pasture land, and are not therefore amenable to 'specialised silviculture', for the part they play:

...as shelter-belts, as fertilisers to the fields from their deciduous habit, as conservers of moisture on the watersheds, as guardians against erosion on slopes, as harbourage for birdlife, as lime-producers for the soil, as drainage regulators, as a supplementary food-supply for swine and a variant for cattle, as manufacturers of humus, as depots for certain essential minerals for the soil, as raisers of soil temperature, and last but by no means least, as sources of employment for a host of local woodsmen, hurdlers, bodgers, broom-squires, coopers, carpenters, cabinet-makers, tool makers, thatchers and the like – they contribute to the balance and inter-dependence of right husbandry so richly and vitally that their importance cannot be exaggerated.

DECIDUOUS WOODLAND

'Deciduous' comes from the Latin term meaning 'to fall down' and is applied to trees whose leaves fall during cold parts of the year. Deciduous trees prefer a temperate climate where it is neither very hot nor very cold, and in such areas they form great forests and woodlands. The face of deciduous woodland is always changing, for it moves with the seasons throughout the year, leafing in spring, flowering by summer and fruiting in autumn before losing leaves in a blaze of colour to reveal bare branches during winter. The British Isles were once densely covered in deciduous forest and woodland, and there were three main gigantic stretches in Europe. However by the nineteenth century Britain had only 5 per cent of its woodland left. Just a few places such as the New Forest held the remnants of the primeval forests of gigantic oaks and beeches.

A forest is a climate-maker, for it breathes out moisture and oxygen, cleansing the atmosphere and creating rainfall. The air is warm inside thick woodland, and the trees are home and larder to the life-forms they shelter. The whole character of a wood is formed by the species of tree it houses, their shape and size, canopy and root systems. On the forest floor the fallen leaves of autumn create a blanket of leaf-litter. This protects the soil from severe weather, and becomes a rich addition to the woodland soil through decomposition and the work of insects and threads of fungi, bacteria and microbes.

In deciduous woodland there are three main levels of growth. The highest level is the canopy, where mature trees rise high above all, with branch, leaf, twig, flower and fruit. Below that is the shrub level, where taller woody plants and bushes reign. Below this is the field level of ferns, mosses, flora and herb. The floor of the wood is called the litter level, and there vegetable and animal matter fall at death to decompose. This then becomes the foundation of the woodland, fertile soil into which trees root deeply.

Man has slowly changed the face of the forest through coppicing, pollarding, planting and clearing. He has especially changed it through fire. In Britain and Europe oak is still the dominant species. In North America we find beech and maple. In the southern states poplars dominate, though the deep south thrives with oak, magnolia and hickory.

Deciduous trees shed leaves in autumn to stop evaporation of water through them. Their roots can't take up much water from the cold ground of winter and leaf loss aids their water retention, ensuring life. Those leaves that become yellow do so because the carotenoid pigments show through the now inactive chlorophyll pigment in the cells of the dying leaf. Those that colour red and russet do so because of the presence of anthocyanin pigments in the leaf, formed by the interaction of sunlight with sugars trapped in the leaves during cold spells.

Most fungi appear in the autumn when rain is added to the still warm climate. Fungi not only push their way through the moist earth, but also appear on tree trunks and dead branches on the forest floor. Their colours are vivid, like the bright orange patches called 'witches' butter'.

As autumn moves into winter, life in the deciduous forest or wood becomes dormant. All the trees are bare of leaves, except perhaps for the odd holly bush or yew, or the insistent ivy which slowly creeps along trunks and branches.

CONIFEROUS WOODLAND

When the Ice Age glaciers receded around 10,000 years ago, cone-bearing trees, which shed little water through their needle-like waxy leaves, showed a preference for the colder regions and great coniferous forests flourished.

Cone-bearers do not shed leaves in autumn and their permanent canopy allows little light to reach the forest floor. In naturally formed woodland, glades become havens of light for wildlife, but in man-made plantations all too often everything is regimentally straight, allowing little light to enhance the situation. In such gloomy atmospheres the misery of the trees is extremely apparent. However, if a stream runs through coniferous woodland, willows, aspens, alders and silver birches may grow upon its banks. These trees bring lush greens to the scene, encouraging wildlife and a magical atmosphere. Heather, juniper and larches also add variety, and because of the dim light of the forest floor it is ideal for the growth of mushrooms. It is also home for many creatures, such as insects and mites.

Conifers shed their needle-leaves continually throughout the year and always keep a good proportion of them on the tree. Over the years their leaf losses collect on the forest floor, where they become a carpet of dried needles, liberally scattered with cones in differing stages of maturity. Birds such as grouse feed on pine-needles and the cross-bill is adept, with its purposefully designed beak, at removing the seeds of conifers from deep within their cones. Other birds of coniferous woodlands are the owl and sparrowhawk. However the most often sighted tenant is the grey squirrel, whose quicksilver dashes bring gasps of astonishment from onlookers. The red squirrel native to Great Britain declines, for it can only thrive in natural pine woodland, of which little remains. Grey squirrels were introduced in the nineteenth century and while they survive man-made plantations of pine they also strip natural areas of food, leaving little or nothing for the sensitive red squirrel, which is by far the more beautiful and has none of the outright aggression of the grey.

The forests of Britain once contained wolves, bears and other large animals, as in European and American forests. Today we find only weasels, foxes, stoats, pine-martens (which are now extremely rare), deer, rabbits and badgers. Of all the large cats which once stalked our woodland, only the small wild-cat remains, and that in small numbers.

Where there is a river or stream in woodland, many other forms of life dwell in or around it – otters, fish, birds, frogs, toads, newts, dragonflies and insects, to name but a few. All these creatures are utterly dependent upon the continuity and health of our woodlands, forests and hedgerows. So also are we, for they provide our air and water, and aid psychic and spiritual health.

THE EFFECT OF HUMAN ACTIVITY UPON WOODLAND

Today many trees are dying from pollution and becoming weakened and open to attack by insects or fungi. In Britain the main trees at risk are the elm, yew, oak, sycamore, beech and chestnut.

For example, a few years ago someone brought a sprig of oak to me, asking what the crazy growths were on top of each acorn. The growths resembled hats, but were nevertheless so strongly attached to the acorns that they were obviously taking all the sustenance that would have given life to saplings if the acorns had germinated in the earth. These growths could be some new kind of gall created by insects, to which the oak would develop a natural defence, but most likely they are the results of the tree's defence system being broken down by pesticides or other forms of pollution, which leaves it open to growth mutations before its inevitable death. The fruit of the blackthorn is being affected in similar ways, giving rise to fears that whole species will disappear for lack of healthy seed.

In verification of the ravages of pollution, on 22 August 1993 the *Observer* printed an article about the state of Britain's midsummer trees. It stated that early 'autumn' colouring, sparsely foliated tree-tops or bare trees were now a common sight in Britain and that up to 90 per cent of trees were affected. It also observed that while forestry officials blamed drought for such conditions, the real culprit is acid rain, made up from excessive amounts of sulphur dioxide, nitrogen dioxide and ozone, being released into the atmosphere as waste products from chemical companies and factories. Britain produces this in vast quantities, which severely affects Europe, bringing death to many of its forests.

Yet the decline of the natural world is not only due to pollution but also to bad management by humans. This also illustrates a further loss – that of our country craftspeople, who grew and harvested in season according to Nature's law, keeping woodlands healthy. If we look back many hundreds of years, we see that woods were crucial to the economy of the country people, for they provided shelter for game, timber for the craftsman, and wood for cooking and heating.

Over many centuries ancient Britain was transformed from a land covered in natural forestation in which clearances were made to a 'land of clearance' with only isolated patches of forest. However, the average person still had the security of working the land. This changed drastically as the peasants were thrown off the land by the institution of the General Enclosures Act of 1845 and while Britain became dangerously deforested by the demands of industrialization, there was a rise in the amount of new species of trees planted as wealthy landowners landscaped their gardens and estates. On the one hand the rough grazing land of the peasants was taken from them, enclosed and cleared of growth for the plough, while on the other, having cleared so much land, landowners had to literally remake copses in order to house the game they kept for sport.

When timber became the long-term crop of private woodlands, new species of trees were introduced and established. These were mainly fir, larch and spruce, and they were planted alongside our fastest growing softwood, the Scot's pine. During the twentieth century, great conifer plantations arose as a result of the need for quickly produced timber, especially during the times of world wars, after which they became purely commercial producers.

The Forestry Commission was founded in 1919, and it advised private landowners to acquire and plant trees on any land unsuitable for agriculture. While the Forestry Commission has been guilty of planting acres of sombre, uniform conifers, it has in fact also been successful in arresting the decline of many of our remaining deciduous forests, specifically the seven National Forest Parks. It is heartening to realize that a new generation of foresters (or woodmen) are now concentrating upon replacing areas of hardwood trees, for deciduous woodland shows the seasonal beauty of Nature in its fullest glory. New forests are being born out of sympathy with Nature rather than for monetary gain, and the skills and wisdoms of old are once more taking hold.

THE COPPICE

It was discovered long ago that many species of broadleaved trees which were cut at ground level did not die, but regenerated by producing a mass of shoots which grew straight and long, and which increased annually in thickness and height. These stems could be harvested regularly according to the size of wood required and the regularity of the harvest meant that mass felling of trees could lessen. So the art of 'coppicing' allowed man to be sparing with the trees.

The word 'coppice' is a variant of 'copse', which comes from the French word *couper*, meaning 'to cut'. Copse has now come to mean a small patch of woodland.

When coppiced, the parent tree which produces the shoots is called the 'stool' or 'crown'. It may produce new shoots for up to 40 years. The main trees coppiced were willow, birch, ash, hazel, alder and hornbeam. Coppiced wood was anciently used to make brooms, staffs, staves, spears, coracles, baskets, hurdles, fishing rods, lobster-pots, etc. Shepherd's crooks, thatching spars, hay-rakes, walking sticks and numerous other uses followed on with man's development. Many, many were the peasant country crafts born from the coppice.

A similar cropping method was produced by coppicing a tree high up its trunk, some 6 or 7 feet (2 metres) from the ground. This produces a crop of thin branches and the art itself is called 'pollarding'. The pollarding method was used in woods where deer and animals roamed, for it was essential to keep the new shoots from being eaten.

Willows are our best example of pollarding and they produce a great amount of 'withies', the slender supple branches used in basket-making. The trunks of pollarded trees become very knobbly, and pollarded willows can look startlingly human and hobbled if silhouetted by the moon on a misty night. The Burnham Beeches in Buckinghamshire are ancient pollarded trees, and they have grown great characteristic 'embodied' trunks. The New Forest in Hampshire also contains old pollarded trees which are visually stimulating.

Pollarding and coppicing affects the burning quality of a tree's wood, intensifying it. It is said that famous London pastry cooks classed the pollarded wood from the Burnham Beeches as the best wood to heat their ovens, for it produced the right intensity of great heat. So emphatic were the cooks about this that coaches were sent daily to fetch the wood.

THE CRAFTSMAN

The arts of the woodman have all but disappeared, as have those of the hedger. Yet thankfully our search for an ecologically sound life-style has turned our attention back to the virtue of such skills and once more they are being employed to preserve the face of Nature. Let us now view the world of the craftsman, through which the produce of the trees becomes beautiful items for our home or tools for our work. We do this again through the words of H. J. Massingham:

> The Craftsman – He is absorbed in the worth of the work, contemplating the habits and constitution of the woods, reading the ways of Nature like a sage poring over an old folio...
>
> Every process from felling the tree to turning the object he is making, he executes himself, so that he is personally responsible for the entire chain of transformations, from woodland tree to domestic furniture. But in serving man he does not rob Nature, because his fellings are made with a view to conserving the best timber and regenerating the woodland as a whole...

But not only does the craftsman work in the same way as Nature without hurry or against the grain of things, and obtains similar results, but he is in a special relation to Nature from which he never deviates. This relation is a symbiotic one, which simply means that he uses without misusing his natural material to the mutual benefit both of Nature and himself. His attitude to Nature is never predatory as that of commerce almost invariably is, and so is by inference, though not consciously, ethical. He necessarily subdues his craft to the qualities of natural materials, the grain of the wood, the texture of the stone, the run of the straw, the consistency of the clay, and considers their characters, simply because his object is to make the most of them. He therefore does not impose his will upon Nature as science directs him to do in the phrase 'the conquest of Nature', but works in partnership with Nature, leaving her different but never worse than he found her... In a sense the craftsman is essentially a believer in the universe because his attitude to Nature, being creative, divines that force of generative workmanship which is akin to his own... His very touch upon the works of Nature expresses a life-service towards a creative universal of which he is intuitively aware.

On the other hand, the words of T. S. Eliot sum up our mistakes, stating that:

A wrong attitude towards Nature implies, somewhere, a wrong attitude towards God, and the consequence is an inevitable doom.

DIVINATION

In order to understand how people have related to trees and other natural life-forms, we can now regard their methods of divination.

According to *Chambers Twentieth Century Dictionary*, 'divining' pertains to 'seeking to know the future, or hidden things, by magical means'. This supposes a direct message from the Spirit (or the Most High) to the diviner, by which they obtain knowledge of the unknown or the future by means of omens or signs. These surround us today, but we have forgotten where and what to look for, and how to see or translate them. However, if we regard the methods used throughout the ancient world, we can glean from those ways and renew their practice to aid us now.

Many things of the natural world provide a means of divination, from scrying into a moonlit pool to the casting of twigs or the scattering of runes, from the flights of birds to the casting of knucklebones. In ancient Peru diviners predicted by means of tobacco leaves, possibly regarding the course of the veins in the leaf, or its shape, or by watching the curl of the smoke as it was burned. The shape of grains of maize also gave predictions, as did the route taken by spiders, or the direction fruit rolled when it fell off a parent plant or tree.

The use of trees for divination is as old as man himself, and such was the contact between people and trees that they were regarded as co-workers in the divinatory process.

It is recorded that ancient Brazilian priests used a young tree, or a good-sized branch about the height of a man, as a means of divination. This 'tree-stem', as it was called, still retained its leaves and branches. The diviner bored holes in specific places through its trunk beneath the foliage, and by speaking or intoning words into the holes,

331

set up a vibration which made the leaves tremble. The resulting sounds of the trembling foliage were interpreted as messages from the gods.

Many similar methods of divining from the effects of sound upon trees were practised world-wide on living, uncut trees, rather than on tree-stems as just described. Instead of making holes in the tree, diviners would knock it with a wand or staff in specific places. The sounds created in the wood or foliage were then interpreted, as were the sounds and movements of any disturbed birds, insects or animals on the tree. If we think back to ancient days when the animal and insect worlds were prolific and trees accommodated many forms of life, we can well imagine the cacophony caused by such precise disturbance – the startled awakening and scurrying of small animals, the buzzing of bee or hornet nests, the screech and flight of roosting or nesting birds, etc. All such signs were considered messages from the gods. We may also consider the 'silent' effects of trees, for Buddha was enlightened under a bodhi tree at Bodh Gaya.

Divining rods were cut from specific trees so their 'spirit' could be utilized over distance, away from the tree. Divination by means of a rod or by little pieces of twig was called 'rhabdomancy', and was written about by Cicero and Tacitus with regard to the practices of the Celts. Divining rods were of many shapes and sizes, and in Germany they were called 'wishing rods'. Nowadays we tend to think of them as forked, but in ancient days they were just as likely to be like a wand, able to 'move' the diviner as he waved it through the air, or touched things, or traced maps and designs in the soil of the earth.

The dictionary says a divining rod is 'a forked rod or a branch of a tree, which, by means of spasmodic movements of various intensities to the diviner, would indicate the presence of water and minerals underground'. Yet ancient diviners worked their art on many levels as intermediaries between the physical world and the highest inspirational and spiritual realms. Rods and wands were the vehicle by which they interpreted subtle energies pertaining to specific questions or needs, the results of which were visibly apparent through the movements of the rods and the effect upon the diviners.

The behaviour of the divining rod was seen as being under the laws of sympathy, for it was anciently believed that all life-forms had certain subtle relationships with each other. This is certainly evidenced by the way trees grow over mineral lodes, for they tend to droop their branches, and in some cases their trunks, as though strongly attracted downwards, magnetically pulled by the earth. Specific trees were felt to be in sympathy with specific elements. Hazel was (and still is) the favourite tree for dowsing the whereabouts of underground water, but traditionally all kinds of nut and fruit trees were used, hawthorn and blackthorn especially. Trees attracted to metals include hazel and rowan, as is evidenced by Cornish legend (see Hazel, p.68).

There are many modern books on the art of dowsing, by such notable writers as Guy Underwood and Tom Graves. It is an art we can all practise to varying degrees, for even if there is little need to find water or minerals in our present day, the actual process undertaken when dowsing, that of 'tuning in' to the natural world, quietening our inner selves so we may feel the intangible world about us, is a powerful thing which strengthens and guides us in the right direction. We then begin to see ourselves as an integral part of an intensely rich and varied life, where there need not be boredom, anger or greed, but rather a respectful understanding and a gladness to be part of it all.

But back to divination and other methods. Birds are intimately associated with trees, and they have always been watched and hearkened to. In the minds of the ancients, birds were divided into classes of good or ominous omen, and their songs and utterances, their flight paths and the way they ate, the direction their discarded feathers pointed when they landed on earth, etc., all gave knowledge to the diviner. To the Native Americans birds appear as spirits, all too probably under the spell of some enchanter, to be broken only by the medicine man. Certain Brazilian tribes think the souls of departed Indians enter the bodies of birds, as the Celts believed their souls entered birds, as well as trees and rocks and streams of the land.

Omens have always been read from the sky, for it was anciently regarded as the abode of the gods and goddesses. Cloud formations, lightning flashes, flights of birds, colours, rainbows, rain, thunder, snow, hail, wind, planets and stars, all were thought to contain knowledge and to show messages from heavenly beings.

Other ancient forms of divination include watching the flight paths of swarming bees or heeding unexpected meetings with ominous animals. Routes taken by animals or insects were also carefully noted, from the largest animal to the smallest insect. Reflections on water, the movement of water, moon or crystal-gazing, shell-hearing; the pattern of flames, the pictures in embers, the reflection of the sun; swirls of wind or mighty gales, the movement or stance of rocks, the patterns of a landscape, the falling of a branch, the cast of a twig; the openings of caves and wells, the very soil of the earth itself; all were used, and more, in order to divine.

THE OGHAM ALPHABET

Oghams were originally sacred glyphs. They evolved during the age of wood and stone and had become ritual alphabets by Celtic times. The sentience of trees was essential to the foundation of the alphabets and their use, for the systems referred to all aspects of life on all levels. As we look at the myths and information surrounding oghams we see the depth and extent of humanity's relationship with the natural world and with trees in particular.

In druidic lore we are told that 16 letters were formed 'out of the knowledge of the vocalization of language and speech', and that they were received from three principle letters: OIU. The Welsh traditions state that Hu the Mighty invented the ogham script, for he 'first applied vocal song to strengthen memory and record'. Lewis Spence in *The Mysteries of Britain*, states that 'Certain bardic traditions accept that specific letters of the ogham alphabet were invented by Einiged the Giant (son of Alser) for the purpose of recording praiseworthy actions.' The wooden blocks upon which these letters were inscribed were known as *coelbran*, and they formed 'part of a tradition which at least a dozen passages in bardic poems (written between 1160 and 1600) allude to'.

Ogham lettering is mainly associated with Ireland. The Irish/Gaelic ogham alphabet (Beith–Luis–Nuin) is believed derived from an ancient finger-language used by the forerunners of the druids. It was a form of encoded wisdom, its secrets passed on only through strict initiation. Oghams in general were formulated around the energies inherent in the natural world, and in the Beith–Luis–Nuin especially we move closer to that world, intensifying the associations between species of trees, and the sounds, symbols and letters of their names and all they represented.

On magical levels this alphabet was powerful, as a system of communication it aided healing, science, divination and initiatory learning, for
it contained a potent wisdom based on the seasonal energies associated
with trees, plant and animal growth. It also exuded great spiritual
power.

In Celtic myth oghams were devised by Ogma (Ogmius in Gaul). As
an archetypal sun-god, Ogma was so radiant he was called 'Sun Face'. He
was a god of literature, destined to give his name to the ogham system.
This is verified in the fourteenth-century Irish *Book of Ballymote*. In
another myth the hero Cu Chulainn 'went into a wood and cut an oak
sapling with one stroke, standing on one leg, and using one eye. He
twisted it into a ring and carved an ogham inscription on it, thus giving
its power to the people.' We also hear of the hero Lug Mac Ethlenn, who
made seven ß marks upon a piece of birch wood to prevent his wife from
being taken into the land of faerie. Thus he linked the birch tree with
'Beith' and the letter 'B'.

All sources indicate that oghams are based on sound. If we think
about it we realize that sound is multi-layered, made up of many things
at many volumes, the majority of which we don't even hear. The ancients
used this knowledge when founding the alphabets, building layer upon
layer into their fabric, and in order for us to understand the reach of such
systems we can examine the sounds of the natural world upon which
they were based. The earth itself makes sound, for it has rhythm and
movement, as have the waters of earth as they ebb and flow into tidal
patterns. Air has sound as the wind rushes through it, as does birdsong
which choruses the heavenly choirs. Animal and plant life also make
sound as they seek to feed and reproduce, for action creates sound.
Sound is life, and within the ogham systems all the above qualities of life
were recorded as signs, just as music is recorded when written upon
staves.

Upon this foundation was laid the multi-layered world of humanity,
its thoughts and actions adding to the complexity of the system. The
resonance of the spoken word and song added other layers, for the
Celts used a rich exacting language full of descriptive qualities, which
made it well able to express the concepts of psychological states and

extraordinary states of consciousness or perception. On subtle levels the ogham tradition construed a science of language through which it was possible to experience a meaningful communication with the natural world and, like a dictionary, oghams provided a complete set of symbols which reflected the order of Nature and life. They also contained the philosophy, cosmology and ideology of the age, which gave stability to the nation, family, tribe or clan, and on practical levels showed the day to day and seasonal qualities of the natural world and how man could work with them. It allowed him to relate to his past, present and future, for it contained knowledge of his tribe, its events and history kept alive within the structure. To druids it was powerful protection for the nation, for, like the trees, it was rooted into the earth itself.

It is well known that ancient bards or poets communed with their environment, forming poetic stanzas from a 'metalanguage' conveyed by Nature. This was encoded via ogham symbols into a system of classification which was ideal for diviners, seers, magicians, Nature religionists and healers, as well as for bards. This takes us into deeper levels of ogham and closer to the mystery and magic held within the whole system, for the trees themselves were the storehouses (and possible initiators) of the symbolic letters which contained multitudes of images. The ogham alphabet was an excellent mnemonic device and on a real level was a complex index of how things are organized in the universe.

In the alphabetic system trees were regarded on levels of importance. Evidence of the ancient groupings of trees is shown in the Irish Brehon Law, which in the seventh century AD used ancient wisdom to formulate guidelines of correct cultural values, in order to regain ecological balance within the land. In that the Irish Laws are notably more pagan and less influenced by Christianity than the Welsh, it is evident that the Brehon Law most closely embodies ancient lore.

Trees were categorized into four main groups: chieftain, peasant, shrub and bramble. Respect was due each tree according to its station within the system.

The most important trees were the chieftains: oak, the Godhead tree with its acorns and phallic symbology; hazel, with its branches which form magicians' wands from mercurial energies; holly, with its red berries symbolizing the food of the gods, and its protective prickly leaves; yew, with its associations with defence, death and rebirth; ash, with its ruler the sun denoting health and life-continuous; pine, with its phallically shaped cones and primeval energies; and apple, with its life-sustaining fruit which provided the 'drink of the gods', and its ability to most frequently host the mistletoe. Mistletoe was considered a 'hidden' tree.

The peasant trees were: alder, sacred to the god Bran; willow, sacred to the goddess Cerridwen; hawthorn, sacred to the spring fertility rites; rowan, with its red berries (food of the gods) and its associations with Brigid; birch, symbolic of entry into the light seasons of the year, the birth and purification of spring; elm, with its associations with elves and the passage of life through death; and beech, with the spirituality of its groves and its ability to feed humans and livestock. (A possible inclusion here could be silver fir.)

The shrub trees were: blackthorn, which heralds spring and guards the autumn; elder, which provides bounty and health; aspen and the other poplars, with their associations with the wind; juniper, which offers the best purification; box, with its ability to form dense cover; and possibly reed, considered a 'tree-power' because of its numerous uses to mankind. (Field maples may be included here.)

The bramble trees were: the dog-rose; bramble; broom; heather; ivy; vine; and possibly honeysuckle, fern, 'traveller's joy', the spindle tree, etc.

The Irish/Gaelic names for these trees are shown in the illustration opposite, as are the letters they represented; and while it is their alphabetical order, it is not their seasonal order. The attributes and myths associated with each tree are discussed within the individual tree chapters, as is the healing they provide.

The characters of the ogham alphabet are of primitive form, consisting of five groups of five letters, shown as marks or strokes made either side of, or across, a central line as shown in the illustration.

For the vowels: 'A' is a single stroke crossing the line at right angles; 'O' consists of two similar strokes; 'U' of three; 'E' of four; and 'I' of five.

The dental/aspirant letters are headed by 'H', which is one stroke to the left of the line; and 'D','T','C' and 'Q' are represented by from two to five strokes of the same kind.

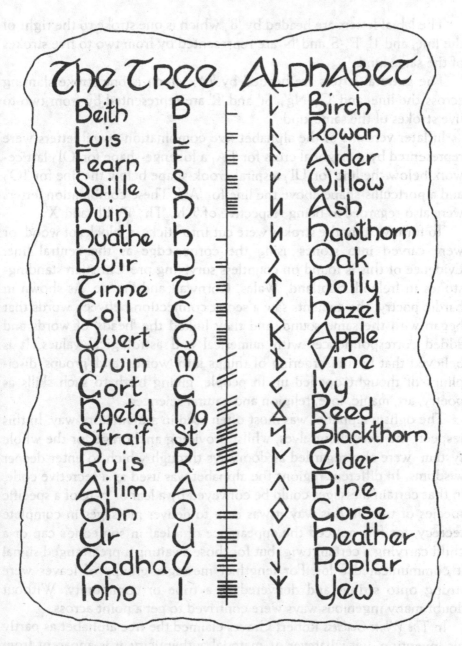

The Tree Alphabet

Beith	B	Birch
Luis	L	Rowan
Fearn	F	Alder
Saille	S	Willow
Nuin	N	Ash
huathe	h	hawthorn
Duir	D	Oak
Tinne	T	holly
Coll	C	hazel
Quert	Q	Apple
Muin	M	Vine
Gort	G	Ivy
Ngetal	Ng	Reed
Straif	St	Blackthorn
Ruis	R	Alder
Ailim	A	Pine
Ohn	O	Gorse
Ur	U	heather
Eadha	E	Poplar
Ioho	I	Yew

The tree alphabet showing the Irish/Gaelic tree names,
the letters they represent, their oghams and associated runic symbols

The labial letters are headed by 'B', which is one stroke to the right of the line; and 'L', 'F', 'S' and 'N' are represented by from two to five strokes of the same kind.

The guttural letters are headed by 'M', which is one stroke slanting across the line; and 'G', 'Ng', 'St' and 'R' are represented by from two to five strokes of the same kind.

In later versions of the alphabet five combination vowel letters were represented by a diagonal cross for 'EA'; a lozenge-shape for 'OI'; lattice-work below the line for 'UI'; a spiral crook-shape below the line for 'IO'; and a portcullis-shape above the line for 'AE'. These combination letters were also regarded as being respective of 'Kh', 'Th', 'P', 'Ph' and 'X'.

To form writing the strokes were cut into sticks or blocks of wood, or were carved into stones using the corner-edge as the central line. Evidence of this is found on countless surviving pre-Christian standing-stones in Ireland, Scotland, Wales, Cornwall and France. As shown in bardic poetry, the ancients saw a secret connection between words that began with the same sound, and they linked the 'heads' of words and added correspondences with numerical and astrological values. It is believed that by the ordering of things into 'worlds' and 'groups' disciplines of thought opened up in people, giving birth to such skills as poetry, art, magic, lore, religion and natural sciences.

The ogham alphabet was most often used in a divinatory way. In this respect, the trees themselves, whilst providing anchorage for the whole system, were also regarded as doorways through which to enter deeper wisdoms. In different regions the alphabet was used as a secretive code, in that certain messages could be conveyed by a leaf or twig of a specific species of tree. In this way it was easy to deliver messages in complete secrecy, for few noticed the appearance of a leaf in someone's cap or a child carrying a certain twig, but for those awaiting a prearranged signal it communicated a lot. For lengthier messages groups of leaves were strung onto strings and delivered to a tribe or community. Without doubt many ingenious ways were contrived to get a point across.

In *The White Goddess* Robert Graves claimed the tree alphabet as partly his invention, yet whatever its material authenticity, it is apparent from the wealth of images and the power experienced when the alphabet is tuned into that tree oghams existed in a very strong form on certain levels. That the system was distinct and separate from others, such as the runes, is also apparent, for its meanings are relevant to our relationship with the natural world rather than our actions upon it, and, as stated before, it was a cosmological map in which Nature was the teacher rather than the gods.

Oghams were also conveyed by sign-language. These included finger oghams and foot, nose, thigh and shin oghams. In these the five fingers of the hand formed the basis of the code and, when placed in different positions on specific parts of the body, gave precise signs. For example, in shin ogham the position of the 'B' group of letters was to the right of the shin-bone, the 'H' group was to the left of the bone, diagonally across the bone specified the 'M' group and straight across the 'A' group. The number of fingers used indicated which letter of the group was meant, i.e., two fingers to the right of the shin-bone signified the letter 'L'.

We are also told in old scripts that certain aspects of life took on specific form in ogham symbology, and that there were ogham systems associated with the understanding and management of animals (cattle and swine), with certain species of birds, with bee-keeping, herbs and systems of agriculture. Yet while ogham systems were integral to many aspects of life, it would seem that the writing of ogham scripts was in the main reserved for inscriptions to the dead. Today, as we travel to the far reaches of Celtic lands we may come across old standing-stones still showing ogham inscriptions. And as our fingers trace their ancient power we are connected to our past, when, maybe, we stood as our ancestors at the carving of them.

GLOSSARY OF HEALING TERMS

Anodyne	Relieves pain. Herbs used may be narcotic in their effect.
Anti-spasmodic	Calms muscles, which eases spasms and cramps and stops convulsions.
Aperient	Produces a natural movement of the bowels, gentler than a laxative.
Arterial	Helps convey blood from the heart. Consult a doctor for heart conditions and discuss herbal remedies for use alongside orthodox medicines.
Astringent	Causes tissue to contract, is binding and often stops bleeding. Tones internal organs and tightens pores of the skin. Many astringent herbs contain tannic or gallic acid.
Decoction	A decoction is used where a strong dose of the plant's constituents is needed or when thick solid herbs (woody bits, roots, etc.) are used. It is different from an infusion in that the ingredients are placed in cold water and are boiled, rather than being seeped. The resulting liquid may need to be mixed with a little water when taken.
Diuretic	Stimulates the flow of urine and cleanses and promotes health of the kidneys. Allows waste and toxins to flush through the body.
Emetic	Causes the stomach to contract to induce

	vomiting in cases of food poisoning and the removal of foreign substances. Herbs used for this may be dangerous in large doses and should be used with extreme care.
Expectorant	Loosens accumulations of phlegm in lungs, sinus cavities and bronchial passages, so it is easily coughed up.
Febrifuge	Lowers the temperature of the body and eases fevers.
Infusion	An infusion is made like a strong tea, for herbs are steeped in water to draw out the properties needed for healing. The water takes these into solution and acts like a fixative. Infuse herbs for at least 15 minutes, experimenting with the amount of herb used by allowing your body to guide you in what it needs.
Laxative	Stimulates the bowel into action.
Poultice	Used for applying herbs externally. Pour a little boiling water over the herbs to moisten them and, using a strainer to remove excess liquid, place the wet herbs between layers of gauze material. Apply this pad to the afflicted areas while it is warm.
Purgative	Causes drastic evacuation of the bowels. Strongest of laxative herbs and will often have uncomfortable side-effects.
Sedative	Relaxes nervous tension and soothes stressed muscles. Acts as a tranquillizer and may induce sleep. With some herbs avoid excessive dosage.
Stimulant	Raises pulse, respiration and nerve alertness, causing the vital signs to quicken; does not produce energy but eases its flow.
Sudorific	Induces sweating.
Tonic	Gives the body a sense of well-being and vigour.

RECOMMENDED READING

Baker, Margaret, *Folklore and Customs of Rural England*, Readers Union Ltd, 1975
Beth, Rae, *Hedgewitch*, Hale, 1990
Beyerl, Paul, *The Master Book of Herbalism*, Phoenix Publishing Co., 1984
Blake, William, *Songs of Innocence and Experience*
The Book of the Countryside, Reader's Digest
Boulton, E. H. B., *A Pocket Book of British Trees*, A & C Black, 1937
Carr-Gomm, Philip, *Elements of the Druid Tradition*, Element Books
Castaneda, Carlos, *The Eagle's Gift*, Hodder & Stoughton
—, *Journey to Ixtlan*, Simon & Schuster
—, *The Second Ring of Power*, Simon & Schuster
—, *A Separate Reality*, Simon & Schuster
—, *Tales of Power*, Hodder & Stoughton
—, *The Teachings of Don Juan*, Ballantine Books
Chancellor, Philip M., *Handbook of the Bach Flower Remedies*, Chancellor
Clucas, Philip, *Country Seasons*, Windward/W H Smith
Culpeper's Complete Herbal, Foulsham
Cunningham, Scott, *Encyclopedia of Magical Herbs*, Llewellyn, 1985
Delaney, Frank, *Legends of the Celts*, Grafton
Ellis Davidson, H. R., *Gods and Myths of Northern Europe*, Pelican, 1964
Fortune, Dion, *Esoteric Orders and their Work*
Frazer, Sir James George, *The Golden Bough*
Graham, Kenneth, *Wind in the Willows*, original publication 1908; Methuen Books 1976

Graves, Robert, *The Greek Myths*, vols I and II

–, *The White Goddess*, Faber and Faber, 1961

Grieve, Mrs M., *A Modern Herbal*, Penguin, 1931

Harding, M. Esther, *Woman's Mysteries*, Rider & Co., 1955

Hartley, Christine, *The Western Mystery Tradition*, The Aquarian Press, 1968

Hartzell, Hal, *The Yew Tree*, 1994

Hutton, Ronald, *The Pagan Religions of the Ancient British Isles*, Blackwell, 1991

Jones, Gwyn and Thomas, eds, *The Mabinogion*

Jung, C. G., *Four Archetypes*, Routledge & Kegan Paul, 1972

Keating, *History of Ireland*

Lonnrot, Elias, *Kalevala: The land of heroes*, First published 1907, reissued J. M. Dent, 1956

Massingham, H. J., *The English Countryman*, Batsford, 1943

Matthews, John and Caitlín, *The Aquarian Guide to British and Irish Mythology*, The Aquarian Press, 1988

Michell, John, *The Earth Spirit*, Thames & Hudson, 1975

Murray, Liz and Colin, *The Celtic Tree Oracle*, Rider & Co., 1988

Perkins, Benjamin, *Trees*, Century

Roney-Dougall, Dr Serena, *Where Science and Magic Meet*, Element Books, 1990

Sharkey, John, *Celtic Mysteries: The ancient religion*, Thames & Hudson

The Shell Book of Rural Britain, Keith Mossman, 1979

Smith, C. E., *Trees*, Thomas Nelson & Sons Ltd

Smith, Dr William, *A Smaller Classical Dictionary*, John Murray, 1866

Smyth, Daragh, *A Guide to Irish Mythology*, Irish Academic Press

Spence, Lewis, *Encyclopaedia of Occultism*, University Books, 1968

–, *The Magic Arts of Celtic Britain*, Rider & Co.

–, *The Mysteries of Britain*, Rider & Co.

–, *Myth and Ritual in Dance, Game and Rhyme*, Watts & Co., 1947

Swiftdeer, Harley, *Star Warrior*, Bear & Co.

Toland, John, *History of the Druids*, 1726

Tolkien, J. R. R., *The Lord of the Rings*

–, *Tree and Leaf*

Turgenev, Ivan, *Sketches from a Hunter's Album*, Pan Classics
Wallis Budge, E. A., *The Book of the Dead*, Arkana, 1985
Williamson, Henry, *Salar the Salmon*, Faber and Faber, 1935

INDEX

Entries in bold indicate main entry.

Achilles 147–8
ailim, see pine
alder 92, 158, **243–56**, 323, 327, 338
Aphrodite 108–9
Apollo 176, 250, 260–1
apple 66, 74, 80, 86, 100, **106–22**, 141, 146, 225, 227, 241, 320, 338
Apple-tree Man 116
arboreal 313–24
Ares, see Mars
Arianrhod 101, 148
Artemis 261
Arthur, King 37, 53, 111, 126–7, 180–1, 250
ash 8, 100, 112, 141, **142–71**, 184, 226, 320, 327, 338
Askr Yggdrasill, see World Tree
aspen **295–307**, 323, 338
Atlas 109–10
Avebury 221
Awen 111, 202

Bacchus 202
Bach Flower Remedies 14, 38, 55, 114, 184, 205, 218, 265, 301
Banbha 21
beech 7, 33, **212–24**, 296, 315–16, 321, 328, 338
beith, see silver birch
Beith-Luis-Nuin 335–41
Bel (Belin) 261–2
Belili 261–2
Beltaine, see festivals
Beth, Rae 292
birds 20, 31, 34, 45–6, 48, 58, 65, 74–5, 108, 176–7, 193, 200, 205, 227, 230, 235–6, 241, 248–50, 261, 278, 306, 323, 332–3
blackthorn **78–90**, 107, 124, 320, 325, 333, 338
Blodeuwedd 101, 127, 187
Boreas 48
botanical 13
    alder 243–5

apple 106–8
ash 142–5
beech 212–15
blackthorn 78–80
elder 276–9
elm 198–201
hawthorn 123–6
hazel 63–5
holly 32–4
oak 172–6
pine 47–60
poplars 295–8
rowan 225–7
silver birch 91–4
willow 257–60
yew 17–20
Bran 247–50, 252, 306
Branwen 248–9
Bridhe 180, 185
Brigantia 229–30
Brigid 180, 229–30, 252
broomsticks 100, 160, 170, 270, 289
burelles 92

caduceus 68
cambium layer 213, 315
Cardea 129
Castaneda, Carlos 129
Cerridwen 67, 111, 186
Chaucer 126–7, 151
Chiron 147
Circe 261
Clare, John 140
coll, see hazel

coniferous woodland 322–4
coppicing 76, 273–4, **327–8**
coracles 76–7, 274–5
crack willow, see willow
craftsman 328–9
Cronus 51, 176, 246, 250, 305–6
Culhwych 126–7
Culpeper 24, 102, 201, 251, 265
custom & legend 13
    alder 245–51
    apple 108–13
    ash 145–55
    beech 216–18
    blackthorn 80–2
    elder 279–83
    elm 201–5
    hawthorn 126–30
    hazel 66–9
    holly 34–8
    oak 176–82
    pine 51–4
    poplars 299–300
    rowan 228–31
    silver birch 94–7
    willow 260–5
    yew 20–4

Dadga 96
Dana/Danu 250
Darling, Mic 137–8
deciduous woodland 321–2
Deidre 21
Delphic Oracle 52
Demeter 261, 300, 305
dendrochronology 313

Diana 176, 187
Diarmid 29, 96
Dionysus/Bacchus 51–2, 118,
    177, 202
divination 26, 40, 68, 71, 117,
    135, 187, 207, 233, 282,
    331–4
divining rod 332–3
Dodona 176–7, 189
Domesday Book 17, 181, 196
dragons 74, 109–10, 154, 179,
    217, 220–1, 229, 233, 237–8
druids 22, 26–30, 34–5, 40–1, 53,
    57, 66–7, 69, 71, 72–4, 86,
    107, 111–12, 115–18, 157–9,
    177, 179, 182, 189–91, 209,
    232–4, 237–9, 253, 269, 272,
    335, 337
dryads 7–8, 11, 154, 176, 192,
    290
duir, see oak

eadha, see aspen; poplars
earth-goddess 36–7, 42–3, 116,
    154, 176, 191, 237, 271
Easter 22, 31, 104
Egypt 51, 54, 75, 81, 104, 149,
    176, 216, 230
elder 8, 158, 175, 247, 276–94,
    320, 338
Elder Mother 279, 283, 289, 292
elements (earth, air, fire, water) 1,
    5, 8, 25, 39, 41, 55, 68, 70,
    84, 99, 101, 115, 132, 157,
    160, 165, 185, 206, 232, 239,

    247, 252–4, 266–7, 272,
    289–90, 303
Eliot, T. S. 329
elm 158, 198–211, 273, 320, 338
elves 34, 202–3, 206–8, 338
Equinoxes, see festivals
Erigone 52–3
Eros 108
Esus 177, 179
Evelyn, John 284

faeries 3, 20, 23, 28–9, 34–5, 68,
    70, 77, 94, 97, 104, 119,
    133–4, 139, 158, 246–7, 261,
    283, 290, 304, 307, 336
fearn, see alder
festivals:
    Autumn Equinox 44, 88, 186,
        207, 231, 253
    Beltaine/Mayday 37, 77, 80,
        85, 94, 96, 101, 104, 115,
        126–7, 132, 182, 185, 240,
        250, 262, 269, 286
    Imbolc/Candlemas 34, 70,
        83–5, 103, 158, 180, 185,
        235, 252, 268, 271
    Lughnasadh/Lammas 27, 37,
        116, 185–6, 235
    Samhain/Hallowe'en 27, 68,
        83–5, 99, 116, 185, 235–6,
        253, 266, 271, 291, 303
    Spring Equinox 44, 101, 103,
        185, 207, 231, 252
    Summer Solstice/Midsummer
        36–7, 42, 71, 115, 148, 158,

168, 185–6, 190–1, 231,
234–5, 240, 280, 285, 290
Winter Solstice/Midwinter/Yule
16, 27–8, 35–40, 42–4, 53,
56, 80, 113, 122, 159, 190–1,
228, 231
Finn 29
Fionn 67
Flora 128
Forestry Commission 326–7
Fortune, Dion 1, 100
Freya 101, 250
Frigga 94, 101
fungi 48, 54, 58, 92, 174, 215,
229, 285, 296, 316, 322–3

Gaia 109
Gerard 24, 187
Glastonbury Thorn 80, 128, 135
glossary of healing terms 343–4
goat willow, see willow
Gog & Magog 193
Gogmagog 40
Graham, Kenneth 273
Grainne 29, 96
Graves, Robert 247, 261, 340
Green George 263–4
Gwen 112
Gwion 67
Gwydion 101, 148

Hallowe'en, see festivals
hare 104
Hartzell, Hal 24
hawthorn 8, 28, 78, 80, 84–5, 88,

107, 123–41, 158, 225,
319–20, 333, 338
hazel 44, 57, 63–77, 100, 243,
320, 327, 333, 337
healing 10, 14–15, 74, 89, 162–9,
267–8
alder 251–4
apple 113–14
ash 155–7
beech 218
blackthorn 82–4
elder 283–8
elm 205–6
hawthorn 131–2
hazel 69
holly 38–9
oak 182–5
pine 54–5
poplars 301–2
rowan 231–2
silver birch 97–9
willow 265–6
yew 24–5
Hebe 228
Hecate 22, 261–2, 300
hedgerows 107, 123, 126, 136,
139–41, 158, 189, 199, 292,
319–20
Helen of Troy 109, 146
Helice 261
Hera 109–10, 129, 176, 228, 261,
305
Heracles (Hercules) 109–10, 299
Hermes 67–8, 216
Herne the Hunter 181

Herodotus 176
Herrick 35
Hesperides 109–10, 116
holly 32–46, 191, 320, 322, 337–8
holly-god 36–7
holly king 35–7, 40–1
Homer 147
Hood, Robin 23, 181, 256
Hope, Wally 308, 311
horses 45, 77, 82, 137–8, 146–7, 170, 224, 282, 287, 293
huathe, see hawthorn

Icarius 52–3
Ice Age 53, 61
Imbolc, *see* festivals
inspiration 15–16
    alder 254–5
    apple 117–20
    ash 161–9
    beech 220–2
    blackthorn 87–9
    elder 291–2
    elm 208–10
    hawthorn 136–40
    hazel 72–6
    holly 42–5
    oak 189–93
    pine 57–61
    poplars 305–7
    rowan 237–40
    silver birch 102–4
    willow 270–3
    yew 28–30

ioho, see yew
Iseult 21
Ishtar 108
Isis 51
ivy 34, 44, 174, 320, 322, 338

Jack in the Green 36, 127, 182, 263
Jason of the Argonauts 177, 216
Jonson, Ben 26
Jupiter 177, 185, 188

Kalevala 95–6
Kipling, Rudyard 130, 207

Ladon 110
Lammas, *see* festivals
Lammas shoots 175
Leda 146
lemh, see elm
Llew Llaw Gyffes 101, 127, 148
Lugh 27, 97, 250
Lughnasadh, *see* festivals
luis, see rowan

Mabinogion 126, 248
Mac Coll 66
Macha 250
Maenads 177–8
magic 2, 15, 43, 48, 55–6, 58–9, 61, 67–8, 74, 77, 86, 120, 149, 152, 155, 163, 272, 310–11
    alder 252–4
    apple 115–17

ash 157–61
beech 219
blackthorn 84–7
elder 288–90
elm 206–8
hawthorn 132–6
hazel 70–2
holly 39–42
oak 185–8
pine 55–7
poplars 303–5
rowan 232–7
silver birch 99–101
willow 266–70
yew 25–8
Mars 39, 41, 55–6, 84, 86, 129, 132, 135
Massingham, H. J. 320–1, 328–9
Mayday, see festivals
May-pole 85, 158, 161, 168–9
Mercury 67–8, 70–2, 74, 181, 304
Merlin 21, 118–20, 180
mistletoe 34, 80, 107, 111, 115, 141, 174, 179, 190–1, 338
moon 22, 44, 72, 83, 101, 165–8, 228–9, 261–2, 266, 269–71, 290, 303–4, 306, 334
moon-goddess 100–1, 269, 303–4
moon magic 261–2, 272
moon-tree 228
Morrigan 250
Morrigu 152
Moses 128
mummers 37, 191

Naoise 21
Neith 230
Neptune, see Poseidon
Nereids 148
Norns 150
nuin, see ash

oak 1–2, 7–8, 12, 28, 32, 42, 59, 66, 74, 101, 141, 149, 153, 158, 172–97, 314–16, 320–1, 325, 337
oak-king 36–7
Odin 53, 94, 147, 149–52, 216, 250
oghams 25–7, 31, 39, 41, 55, 57, 70, 84, 97, 99, 115, 132, 157, 185, 206, 217–32, 246, 252, 266, 288, 303, 335–41
Ogma 216, 330
Olwen 126–7
Orpheus 201, 250, 260–1
Osiris 51, 149, 230

Pan 181
Paris 109
Peake, Mervyn 191
Peleus 147–8
Persephone 261, 299–300
phagos, see beech
photosynthesis 318
physical uses 16
    alder 255–6
    apple 120–2
    ash 169–71
    beech 223–4

blackthorn 89–90
elder 292–4
elm 210–11
hawthorn 140–1
hazel 76–7
holly 45–6
oak 194–7
pine 61–2
poplars 307
rowan 240–2
silver birch 104–5
willow 273–5
yew 31
pine, Scot's 44, 47–62, 105,
    315, 338
Pliny 38, 106, 293
Pluto 299–300
pollarding 155, 257–8, 264,
    273–4, 326–7
poplars 295–307, 315, 338
Poseidon 146–7

quert, see apple

Rackman, Arthur 270
rebirth 22–6, 30, 37, 42–3, 73,
    155, 201, 203, 291, 299
recipes 70, 90, 105, 121–2, 141,
    196, 223, 241–2, 253, 266–7,
    286–8, 294
reincarnation, see rebirth
reproduction 317
resurrection, see rebirth
Rhea 51–2, 305
Rollright Stones 247, 279–81

rowan 28, 53, 111, 143, 225–42,
    246, 333, 338
ruis, see elder
runes 25, 39, 55, 70, 84, 99, 115,
    132, 149, 157, 185, 206, 216,
    218, 232, 236, 252, 266, 288,
    303

saille, see willow
salmon (of knowledge) 66–9,
    72–4
Saturn 25, 28, 84, 86, 206, 219,
    301–2, 304–5
serpents, see dragons
Shakespeare, William 22, 58, 70
silver birch 8, 48, 86, 91–105,
    157–8, 316, 323, 327, 332,
    336
Silver Bough 112
sky-god 8, 27, 37, 148, 154, 178
Smith, C. E. 9
spells 86–7, 117, 160
Spence, Lewis 13–14, 28, 112
St Briget 180, 185
St Catherine 222
Stonehenge 234, 308
straif, see blackthorn
sun 27, 32, 36, 43–4, 53, 58–9,
    70–1, 74, 83, 85, 97, 99,
    103–4, 109, 111, 116, 133,
    154, 157–9, 160, 164–5, 185,
    190, 203, 220, 229, 232, 247,
    252–3, 270, 300, 334
sun-god 42, 44–5, 85, 104, 127,
    159, 186, 188, 191, 262, 271

Swinburne, Walter 126, 138

Taranis 42, 178
Theseus 53
Thetis 147–8
Thomas the Rhymer 23, 119
Thor 42, 152–3, 178–9, 228
Thoth 216
Thunor 179
tinne, see holly
Tintagel 21
Tolkien, J. R. R. 202
Tolstoy, Leo 178
tree bark 315
Tree of Knowledge 66, 111
Tree of Life 111, 228–9
Tree of Resurrection 22, 30
tree rings 313
tree roots 315–17
Tristan 21
Tuatha de Danaan 21, 66, 216, 230
Turgenev, Ivan 10–11

Underworld 27, 43, 85, 111, 116, 186, 250, 260–2, 266, 270, 283, 299–300

Valkyries 151, 250
Venus 99, 108–9, 115–16, 154, 250–3, 288, 290
Vikings 54, 151–2, 170, 179, 195
vines 51–3, 57, 202, 211, 338

walking sticks 46, 76, 89, 170–1, 236, 240
wands 11–12, 28–31, 69–70, 74, 77, 81, 161, 180, 186, 236, 269, 272, 332, 337
wassailing 112–13, 115–16, 118, 122
Wicca 56, 116
Wildman 35–7, 40–1
Williamson, Henry 73
willow 8, 66, 77, 100, 158, 245–6, 257–75, 320, 323, 327, 338
  crack 257, 259, 273
  goat 257, 259–60, 272
Winter Solstice, *see* festivals
witches 46, 81–2, 87, 92, 100, 104, 112, 160, 170, 231, 236, 253, 261–2, 265, 270, 272, 275, 270–82, 289, 303
Wodan 151
woodland 7–8, 325–7
Wordsworth, William 57–8
World Tree 148–50, 158–9, 161–2, 168–9

yew 17–31, 43, 47, 57, 153, 231, 236, 314, 322, 338
Yggdrasill 149–50
Yspaddaden 126–7
Yule, *see* festivals

Zeus 52, 108–9, 146, 176–7, 228, 261–2, 300, 305–6